A CASE FOR THE DIVINITY OF JESUS

A CASE FOR THE DIVINITY OF JESUS

EXAMINING THE EARLIEST EVIDENCE

Dean L. Overman

ROWMAN & LITTLEFIELD PUBLISHERS, INC.
Lanham • Boulder • New York • Toronto • Plymouth, UK

Published by Rowman & Littlefield Publishers, Inc.
A wholly owned subsidary of
The Rowman & Littlefield Publishing Group, Inc.
4501 Forbes Boulevard, Suite 200, Lanham, Maryland 20706
http://www.rowmanlittlefield.com

Estover Road, Plymouth PL6 7PY, United Kingdom

British Library Cataloguing in Publication Information Available

Library of Congress Cataloging-in-Publication Data

Overman, Dean L.
  A case for the divinity of Jesus : examining the earliest evidence / Dean L.
Overman.
    p. cm.
  Includes bibliographical references and index.
  ISBN 978-1-4422-0322-8 (cloth : alk. paper) — ISBN 978-1-4422-0110-1
(electronic)
  1. Jesus Christ—Divinity. I. Title.
BT216.3.O94 2010
232'.8—dc22   2009015660

∞™ The paper used in this publication meets the minimum requirements of
American National Standard for Information Sciences—Permanence of Paper
for Printed Library Materials, ANSI/NISO Z39.48-1992.

Printed in the United States of America

This book is dedicated to my Family and Friends with particular gratitude to Linda and Sharon.

ABRIDGED CONTENTS

CONTENTS

CONTENTS

PREFACE

This book began with my study at Princeton in 1965 under German New Testament scholar Joachim Jeremias, widely regarded as the leading twentieth-century specialist on the Aramaic language of the Jesus tradition. Jeremias was a brilliant and humble man with a classical education that spanned several disciplines. He and Rudolf Bultmann were two of the giants in New Testament scholarship in the last century, but they took opposing views on the authenticity of the traditional, orthodox position. I studied Bultmann, but, after learning the forensic methods required to study, practice, and teach law, I was convinced that Bultmann had made some untenable philosophical assumptions and that Jeremias had the stronger argument through his scrupulous investigation of first-century Judaism and the earliest Aramaic linguistic traditions concerning Jesus of Nazareth.

In this book I hope to convey the significance of Jeremias's work and to update some of his work by reference to some solid, recent European scholarship that supports and expands upon his arguments. In addition to Jeremias's scholarship, I explain the recent fine work of British, Scandinavian, and German scholars on the oral tradition that preceded the New Testament. The evidence discloses that the Jewish educational system in the first century was a reliable method of transmitting historical facts and sayings. I explain how we can identify this method in the transmission of the liturgical formulae of the earliest church and in our earliest Christian documents.

I begin with a detailed discussion of the creeds, confessions, hymns, and liturgical worship patterns of the earliest church. These liturgical formulae preexisted our earliest Christian writings but were incorporated into these writings in an identifiable manner. They take us back to a time almost contemporaneous with the events they describe. I set forth the criteria by which they can be identified, discussing the work of the leading scholars in the history of the earliest liturgical formulae. Although known to many New Testament scholars, the powerful, extremely early evidence corroborating an orthodox view is not widely known among the general public or even among the clergy.

I examine the evidence concerning the reliability of the canonical gospels and conclude that they have early dates of composition within the lifetime of eyewitnesses to the events they describe. I address Bart Ehrman's recent writings on textual criticism by exploring the work of his Princeton mentor, Bruce Metzger, and other leading specialists.

A coherent unity exists among the earliest creeds, confessions, hymns, and other liturgical formulae that are hidden (but identifiable) in our very earliest Christian documents. This coherent unity gives early and compelling corroborative evidence and support for the traditional position of the canonical gospels. I discuss this often overlooked evidence found in the earliest Christian letters. These liturgical formulae preexist any available writings concerning Jesus of Nazareth, date to the first decades after the crucifixion, and support the traditional, orthodox Christian belief found in the canonical gospels.

Throughout the book I focus on the very earliest evidence concerning Jesus because of his unique claim to be God Incarnate. I examine the evidence for the alleged miracle of his physical resurrection. In Oxford philosopher Richard Swinburne's terms, if true, this extraordinary event would place God's "signature" upon Jesus' life, teaching, and claims, including his claim to be divine. In this regard I examine the evidence concerning first-century Judaism and the primitive church's concept of resurrection as a physical, bodily transformation and, from a lawyer's perspective, discuss why Jesus' resurrection is plausible.

I also explain why gnostic alternative "Christian" beliefs are not in keeping with the Christian faith founded by the earliest Jewish

Christians (the disciples or apostles of Jesus) who began the mother congregation in Jerusalem at a time almost simultaneous with Jesus' crucifixion. I explain what we can know about the worship patterns of the earliest Jewish Christians and describe the strong evidence that the Gospel of Thomas and other noncanonical gospels were late second-century compositions without any independent, historical information about Jesus of Nazareth.

Finally, I discuss how to address persons of other faiths in a manner consistent with grace and truth. Although I would like to conclude that all religions lead to the same reality, that position is not logically possible. In our contemporary global community, we should engage persons of other faiths in a truthful, honest atmosphere of mutual respect and love. Authentic, trustworthy relationships among persons of different faiths will not proceed from a listless resignation to a reductionist faith consisting only of the lowest common denominator. We must be honest about the tenets of our faith and allow those who differ from us to be honest about their beliefs. A more rigorous genuineness, coupled with compassion and esteem, is required to build a solid foundation for goodwill and peaceful understanding.

ACKNOWLEDGMENTS

This book depended on the assistance and thoughtfulness of many persons. I cannot name all of the people who influenced the content of this book; there are too many over the years to acknowledge their significant effect on my thinking. The following individuals represent a portion of the many remarkable friends and colleagues who contributed to this writing: Hurd Baruch, Nathan, Elisabeth, Leif, Hayden, Henrik Bauman, James Cannon, Lana Couchenour, Craig A. Evans, Birger Gerhardsson, Craig P. Hill, James M. Houston, Richard N. Longenecker, Elaine McGarraugh, Wes Granberg-Michaelson, George and Connie Olsen, Christiana Hart Overman, John Polkinghorne, George and Judy Smith, Sarah Stanton, and Willoughby Walling II.

My family patiently encouraged me in this effort, making substantial contributions in multidisciplined areas. Most of all I want to express gratitude to the One who is the subject of this book for His unlimited, steadfast love, truth, and sacrifice.

INTRODUCTION

I Will Examine Evidence Concerning Jesus of Nazareth Because of the Uniqueness of the Claims Associated with His Life and Death

1.1 THE ASSERTION OF THE INCARNATION IS A UNIQUE AND REMARKABLE CONCEPT, AS IS THE CLAIM OF THE RESURRECTION.[1]

This is the third book in a series concerned with meaning and existence. In a companion volume to this book, *A Case for the Existence of God*, I argued that the existence of God is a plausible, rational belief. In this book I turn to an analysis of the person of Jesus of Nazareth. I am concentrating on Jesus of Nazareth because of the unique claims associated with his life and death. The classic Christian faith claims that Jesus was in his very nature God, that he was God in human form living as a man in first-century Palestine. This is an astounding claim.

Consider the size and vastness of the universe. Our home galaxy, the Milky Way, is a spiral of two or three billion stars like our sun (estimates of this number vary among experts). You and I are spinning at an immense rate of speed in this universe, with the distance across our galaxy being approximately one hundred thousand light-years. Our known universe is approximately twelve to fifteen billion light-years to its edges, and it is continually getting larger at a tremendous rate of speed.

A light-year is the distance light travels moving at the rate of 186,000 miles per second for one year. At this speed light would circle Earth at the equator (about 25,000 miles) seven times in one second. Astronomically speaking, our own galaxy is very small indeed. The largest galaxy discovered to date is found in a cluster of galaxies known as Abell 2029. In that cluster, there is one galaxy that is sixty times the size of our own. Possessing more than one hundred trillion stars, it is about one billion light-years from us. Beyond Abell 2029 there are billions of additional galaxies and stars in all directions. The most recent evidence gathered from observations with the Hubble Space Telescope indicates that there are about fifty billion galaxies in the universe, perhaps more, and each of them contain on average two to four billion stars.[2] In an effort to aid our imagination we estimate that there are about ten thousand grains in a handful of sand; there are more stars in the universe than grains of sand found on all the beaches of Earth.

When Christians claim that Jesus of Nazareth was God in human form, they are claiming that he is the incarnation of the Supreme Being behind the vast beauty and expansion of space and all that it contains. This is a remarkable concept, and, if substantiated, requires a significant expansion of our perspective concerning this man from Nazareth. The idea of the Supreme Being becoming man in order to redeem an imperfect world is truly incomprehensible. Yet, in the words of theologian Wolfhart Pannenberg, for those who knew him, he was considered to be *God and man.*

I will examine evidence for the early origin of this claim from the best and most ancient sources available, but for now my point is that our reason for centering on the Christian claim is that Jesus is sui generis in referring to God in such a close connection with his own person. According to Christian tradition, Jesus, among other indications of divine status, is alleged to have used a form of expression identifying himself as the transcendent God of the Hebrews (*egō eimi* or "I am"). Although there is some controversy in contemporary debate concerning this phrase, I will examine the very earliest available evidence that indicates that the use of this phrase placed Jesus in a role that previously was only reserved to the monotheistic God of Israel.

In the sections that follow I will look at the earliest patterns of Christian worship. In these patterns one can see that the earliest church

claimed a close association between Jesus and God. The Christian assertion of the incarnation is an unparalleled claim among the world
religions; no other religious figure in a world religion is alleged to
have claimed to be God in human form. There is simply no parallel in
any other religion. Confucius and Buddha made no such claim; they
promoted ethical systems of behavior. Mohammed would have been
appalled at any reference to himself as divine; Islam's principle creed is
that Allah is one. Judaism views such a claim as blasphemous.

My study also turns to an inquiry into the alleged resurrection of
Jesus. The Christian position is also unique in claiming that one man
died for the misdeeds of all humankind and is the only religion where
the founder is alleged to have risen from the dead. Buddha's bones
are sectioned, revered, and enshrined in several geographical areas.
Mohammed's bones are enshrined in Medina. There is no place where
the bones of Jesus of Nazareth are revered because his alleged resurrection was a *bodily* resurrection. Belief in this resurrection began the
entire Christian movement.[3] A relevant question follows a review of
this belief: Was it true?

1.2 I WILL BEGIN WITH AN EMPHASIS ON CREEDAL LITURGICAL FORMULAE THAT PREEXISTED ANY CHRISTIAN LITERARY SOURCES AND WERE LATER INCORPORATED INTO OUR EARLIEST CHRISTIAN WRITINGS.

In examining the evidence concerning the truth or falsehood of this belief in the resurrection of Jesus, I will begin by delineating what followers
of Jesus, the persons closest to him, believed in the first decades following his crucifixion. Jesus' crucifixion is attested by non-Christian sources
so I will not examine the question of how he died. My purpose will be
to examine some of the central worship patterns reflecting the beliefs of
the very earliest followers of Jesus of Nazareth during the first decades
following his death. My study will focus on the earliest literary sources
in our possession that we know for certain were written within decades
of Jesus' death. These documents contain devotional creeds, hymns, and
liturgical formulae that preexisted these literary sources and were then
incorporated into them. They present compelling evidence of a pattern
of worship of Jesus of Nazareth as a resurrected, divine being, dating
from a time almost contemporaneous with the events they describe.

Although many scholars have addressed the question of the historical Jesus, not all have addressed the well-documented confession and
worship patterns of his first disciples. These devotional patterns preexist the Christology of Paul and became part of his earliest letters. His
letters begin in about 48 CE (CE means "Common Era"; AD means "In
the year of our Lord"; they mean the same year). None of his letters
are later than the 50s so Paul is writing within approximately fifteen
to twenty years of the crucifixion of Jesus (30 or 33 CE). This is an extraordinarily brief historical period of time. This means that we have
solid, historical evidence that persons who were alive and presumably
eyewitnesses to Jesus' life worshipped him as divine within an astonishingly short time frame of the crucifixion.

In incorporating preexisting and well-known creeds, hymns, and
liturgical formulae into his letters, Paul and other authors of our earliest writings preserved the evidence of the liturgical worship patterns
of the initial congregations of the Christian faith. In certain instances,
the incorporated liturgical formulae from early Christian worship take
us back into the 30s, the decade of the crucifixion. By examining these
creeds and hymns we can uncover the original testimony proclaimed
in these worship formulae as early as two to five years after the events
they describe.

Christology concerns the theological interpretation of the person
known as Jesus of Nazareth. Paul maintains the same high (Jesus as
divine) Christology through all of his letters from the earliest to the
last. Paul's Christology did not develop over time but was remarkably
consistent from the very beginning. This consistency is evidence that
his Christology was formed before his writings and is compatible with
the creeds and hymns he incorporates. When one examines the preexisting confessions, creeds, and liturgical formulae developed by other
followers of Jesus, but incorporated later by Paul into his letters, one
sees a consistent, high Christology, reflecting the worship patterns of
the earliest followers of Jesus. As Paul Barnett writes: "Chronological
inquiry detects the existence of 'high' Christology in the immediate
aftermath of Jesus. . . . When we come to consider Paul's letters, we encounter little development in the last letter as compared with the first.
Our reasonable assumption is that Christology changed little from the
first Easter to the end of Paul's letters."[4]

The best-selling book *The Da Vinci Code* presents a flawed perspective that gnostic "Christianity" regarded Jesus as merely human. Dan

Brown, the author of the book, admits that it is only a novel, not a historical writing. I will not discuss the multiple historical errors contained in the book, but I will discuss the scholarly work that gave birth to this fiction. According to his book, his thesis depends primarily on the validity of the supposedly suppressed gnostic gospels. I will discuss the gnostic gospels, their dating, and their contents more thoroughly in chapter 7, but for present purposes, I merely wish to note Dan Brown incorrectly interprets the gnostic gospels as describing a form of psilanthropism (a belief that Jesus was only human). A reading of most of the gnostic gospels discloses that the gnostics considered *Jesus to be so divine that he could not be truly human*. In other words, the gnostic gospels, as the vast majority of New Testament scholars agree, proclaim a gnosticism that emphasizes that Jesus was too divine to be human, not that he was only a human and not divine.

A code of sorts does exist in the New Testament documents. If Brown had done his homework, he could have written a much more accurate book about a code or a series of formulae that preexisted the New Testament documents. The documents of the New Testament, on balance, are more than a hundred years older than the gnostic texts, but they contain primitive formulae hidden throughout their pages. Most of these formulae did not originate with the authors of the New Testament, but preceded them and find their origin in the primitive liturgical worship confessions, statements, creeds, and hymns that constituted the earliest form of worship in the very first churches.

Recently, Richard Longenecker, Professor Emeritus of New Testament, Wycliffe College, University of Toronto, noted how the various liturgical formulae may fall under different rubrics but can be generally referred to as "confessions": "Discussion of these early Christian confessional materials has frequently been carried on under rubrics as 'hymns,' 'prayers,' 'formulas of faith,' 'catechetical teachings,' 'liturgical formulations,' 'ecclesial traditions,' and/or 'narrative stories'—with the transliterated Greek terms *kerygma* ('proclamation'), *paradosis* ('tradition'), *didache* ('teaching'), and *homologia* ('confession') often used as descriptive titles."[5] Many confessions were like hymns and many hymns were like creeds.[6]

By reviewing the evidence contained in these liturgical formulae, we can determine the beliefs and testimony of the very early participants in the Christian faith, participants who proclaimed the resurrection of Jesus within an extremely short period of time after his death. At the very beginning of the Christian church we find these hymns and creedal statements playing a principal role in the life and worship of the earliest communities. An examination of these informative formulae discloses that the writers of our earliest Christian documents appear to be at pains to state the formulae precisely as they had received it in an "official version."[7]

These creeds present statements of the beliefs of Christian communities in existence during the apostolic period (the time when Jesus' disciples were alive and proclaiming the gospel). The earliest Christian writings in our possession are the letters or epistles found in the New Testament. The creeds incorporated into these writings come from a time when the eyewitnesses to Jesus' life, death, and resurrection were available to dispute any inaccuracies. They constitute our best evidence of the early worship practices of the first congregations. When one is attempting to determine what actually happened in the third decade of the first century (the decade of the crucifixion of Jesus and the birth of the church), one must examine the evidence available from the 30s and 40s of that century, not evidence from the second century.

The speculation of certain New Testament scholars attempting to import second-century gnosticism back into the first century is not rigorous. As I shall show, the contemporary hypothesis of a chaos of diverse early Christian beliefs in "alternative Christianities" is not supported by any first-century document. Persons who attempt to describe evidence of diversity in the early Christian movement inevitably refer to documents composed *no earlier than the mid-second century*. There was a gnostic distortion of the traditional first-century Christian belief in the second century; just as there were subsequent distortions in later centuries. However, I want to emphasize that no *first*-century document in our possession gives valid evidence of a chaos of diversity surrounding the core orthodox beliefs of the first decades of the church.

The language of these creeds and hymns is not typical of the language used by Paul or other New Testament authors. Frequently the words used in these creeds and hymns are not employed by these authors in the remainder of their writings. They appear unique to the creedal passage. For example, very early creeds and hymns incorporated into the New Testament often translate readily back into the Aramaic language, the language of Jesus and his disciples. They also have rhythmic patterns and lyrical styles with unusual vocabulary not normally used by the New Testament author and are frequently preceded by introductory phrases. The widely held opinion is that these creeds and hymns date back to the first two decades after Jesus' crucifixion, and some are even earlier. As noted, they precede the letters of Paul, which precede the writing of the gospels (which in turn precede the gnostic texts by about one hundred years), and bring us back as close in time as possible to the language and teachings of those who were eyewitnesses of the life, death, and resurrection of Jesus.[8]

One concept I wish to emphasize concerning the hymns, creeds, confessions, poetry, and liturgical formulae of the primitive church is that their content consistently supports the understanding of the history, life, death, and resurrection of Jesus as the God-man from Nazareth found in traditional, orthodox Christianity. This is vitally important to understand, for these early formulae constitute the best and earliest evidence available concerning the thoughts, beliefs, and worship patterns of the persons who were closest to Jesus. Given the compelling evidence of an orthodox Christianity contained in these preliterary liturgical formulae, those who assert a nontraditional perspective must bear the burden of producing comparable evidence from the first century that supports their positions. The evidence from these embedded, primitive liturgical gems shifts the burden of proof to those claiming and promoting a gospel at variance with the traditional classical Christian faith.

New Testament scholars and the general public tend to focus on the dates of the writing of the gospel accounts. During all of the searching for the historical Jesus, many scholars and most Christians have not emphasized the amazing creeds and formulae that are right in front of our eyes, incorporated into our oldest documents. Although they preexisted the earliest literary sources concerning the life of Jesus, the information they contain concerning his life, death, and resurrection is consistent with the canonical gospel accounts. They offer corroborative evidence of the description of Jesus consistent with the substance of writings we know as Mark, Luke, Matthew, and John. Moreover, these preexisting and very early liturgical formulae do not offer any evidence that contradicts the traditional canonical gospel accounts.

The gnostic gospels, including the gospel of Thomas, do not contain creedal formulae. I shall provide evidence that the gnostic gospels are a second-, not a first-, century phenomenon, and only give us information about a second-century distortion of a traditional faith that preceded them by more than one hundred years. The speculative claims surrounding the gospel of Thomas, the gospel of Judas, and other gnostic texts are exaggerations. As discussed in chapter 7, these texts are clearly mid- to late second-century documents, with no hard evidence of any "trajectories" from the first century and no evidence of earlier creedal gnostic liturgical formulae. In other words, those who speculate about an early first-century gnostic "Christianity" have no early evidence comparable to the orthodox liturgical formulae incorporated into our oldest documents (the New Testament letters and gospels).

As I have indicated, Paul was not the only writer to incorporate preexisting creeds and hymns. Other authors of New Testament documents also incorporated liturgical formulae into their writings concerning Jesus. Because these creeds manifest the thoughts and words of persons who knew Jesus, we need to pause and realize the significance of the historical information that can be derived from these formulae. As I shall demonstrate, they indicate a high, exalted status attributed to him, consistent with his veneration as someone more than a mere human being.[9]

These dogmatic formulae from the theological tradition of primitive Christianity are inserted into the letters of the New Testament like crystals in the theological expositions contained in these first-century documents. I want to emphasize that these gems have not received all of the attention they deserve. Although much has been written about many of them, such as the beautiful incarnational hymn in the first chapter of Colossians, the significance and wealth of information contained within these crystallized formulae have not received the light of significant public attention.

Where did these creeds come from? Why were they later embedded and incorporated into the earliest Christian literary sources in our possession? By what means can we recognize them in these writings? To begin to answer those questions one has to understand that the needs and customs of early Christian worship required the development of these creeds and formulae. For example, we know that at a remarkably early time in the history of Christian worship, liturgical formulae developed and were passed on in a precise manner in the services of baptism and the Lord's supper.

More than forty years ago, the famous Dutch New Testament scholar Vernon Neufeld wrote that it was "indeed surprising that thus far no thorough investigation has been devoted exclusively to the primitive Christian *homologia* (confession)."[10] In his book *The Earliest Christian Confessions*, Neufeld made an outstanding contribution to the description of the origin and nature of the primitive Christian confessions and delineated their importance and function in the life of the early church. Neufeld began a relatively small movement into the study of our most ancient evidence concerning the perspective of Jesus displayed in the worship patterns of the persons who were closest to him. In the twentieth century other scholars joined in this work that is only now becoming one of the most exciting and fascinating explorations of significant evidence of first-century history. The work resulting from the studies completed so far does much to dispel the bizarre and frequently strange fantasies promoted in the popular, but fringe areas of New Testament scholarship, especially in the pro-gnostic literature. Some of the New Testament scholars who gave special attention to the primitive liturgical formulae include Eduard Norden, A. Seeberg, C. H. Dodd, Ernst Lohmeyer, Oscar Cullmann, A. M. Hunter, Ethelbert Stauffer, Richard Longenecker, Martin Hengel, Ralph Martin, Joachim Jeremias, Richard Bauckham, and Larry Hurtado. I will draw on the work of these scholars and many others as I examine the best available evidence.[11]

Neufeld noted that almost immediately after the crucifixion of Jesus, his followers developed statements of faith that were formulae of great significance in the life of the very early church. These formulae were used as faith and preaching formulae (*Predigt-und Glaubens formel*). According to Neufeld, the words in these formulae or confessions (*homologia*) "represented the agreement or consensus in which the Christian community was united, that core of essential conviction and belief which Christians subscribed and openly testified. The *homologia* was the admission and acknowledgment of the individual's loyalty to Jesus Christ, and as such a personal testimony of his faith."[12]

Neufeld emphasized that the earliest *homologia* or confessions all concerned Jesus. The word *homologia* signifies "agreement." Neufeld noted that in the Platonic dialogues this Greek term was used to describe the *premises agreed upon for purposes of discussion.* (This interpretation is also supported by the confession in Judaism known as the *Shema*, which served a similar purpose in the Jewish community.)[13] Lawyers can understand this term quite readily because it forms the basis of a contract or an argument or proposition about to be set forth by the writer. In other words, the confessions of the earliest church were the statements upon which the participants in the early church agreed concerning the basis for their faith. They are extremely important because they represent the foundation upon which the mustard seed of the church took root and grew. They formed the agreement, the admission, and the promise for the persons who were closest to Jesus, the one who is the subject of all of the early confessions of the primitive church. These confessions were not only formulae for the purpose of verbal assent, but the basis upon which the members of the early church devoted their activities in daily Christian living.[14]

According to Neufeld, the basic pattern of the earliest Christian confessions contained two elements: (1) the naming of Jesus and (2) the ascription to him of the title of Lord and Son of God.[16] The consistency of the patterns found in these confessions allowed Neufeld to draw the conclusion that these confessions represented the essential core of the faith of the primitive church. These confessions provide us with powerful evidence of the unity of the earliest Christian faith and the substance underlying that unity. Ultimately, this substance can be traced back to the disciples' contact with Jesus himself. As Neufeld notes:

> The several parts of the New Testament provide evidence that the *homologia* embodied the essence of the Christian faith regarding the person of Jesus. The place of importance which the *homologia* had in the life of the church further demonstrates that these expressions of faith were significant both in the inner life of the church and in its contact with the outside world. . . . The formula expressed the heart of Christian belief. As a distinct form of tradition the *homologia* had its place primarily in the life of the early apostolic church; the gospels, however, disclose that its antecedents are to be sought in the ministry of Jesus. Rather than being a formal declaration of doctrine or belief, the *homologia* in its origin was simply the conviction and belief which the disciples gained from their contact with Jesus.[17]

As I shall show, these *homologia* or confessions, including creeds and hymns, consistently portray a high and exalted form of Christology with Jesus represented as unique and divine: the God-man who died and rose again. They were in widespread use prior to the time of the writing of the New Testament and were communicated orally both to persons participating in the church and to those outside of the church. Paul inherited this teaching and tradition from those persons who were contemporaries of Jesus.[18]

I will emphasize that these Christological hymns, creeds, confessions, and liturgical formulae provide a transparent window to the beliefs and practices of those who knew Jesus and carefully passed on the statements of their beliefs. I shall also spend some time discussing how we can recognize these formulae in the New Testament documents. I shall discuss some of these hymns and formulae in greater depth as they relate to the worship practices of the early church and to the perspective of the early church concerning the divinity, death, and resurrection of Jesus of Nazareth. New Testament scholar Ethelbert Stauffer summarized the contents of these formulae as consistent with Jesus' own interpretation of his person and work: "So far as their definitive contents are concerned, we can see the Christological affirmations and formulae of the early Church in a state of proclamation in the interpretation of himself offered by Jesus Christ."[19]

Stauffer also debunked the idea that the history of primitive Christianity had an "epigenetical process" whereby the man Jesus of Nazareth came to be seen as divine over a long period of time. To understand the consistent high Christological content and essential core beliefs of the early church, any serious student needs to examine the creeds and hymns incorporated into the first-century New Testament documents, not second-century documents that have no hard evidence relating back to the first century.

Richard Longenecker observed how Paul incorporated early confessional formulae in his letters as the foundation for his arguments and how the authors of the canonical gospels supported and remained consistent with these very early confessional materials. In 1993 Longenecker presented a paper at the American Theological Society entitled "In the Beginning was the Confession." This paper represented his foray into the development of a Christian theology based on the earliest confessions of the primitive church. Although Martin Dibelius, Rudolf Bultmann, and C. H. Dodd had previously attempted to identify the basic features of the Christian gospel, none of these scholars were motivated by a "primitivist" or "restorationist" concern. Longenecker, however, realized that prior to sermons (Dibelius's focus), prior to individual pericopes (Bultmann), and prior to the *kerygma* (Dodd), the earliest followers of Jesus of Nazareth memorized confessions or *homologia*. Longenecker concluded that these confessions were clearly incorporated by the authors of the New Testament in their writings, that a form-critical analysis could identify these confessions, and that such an analysis could highlight the central convictions of the followers of Jesus. He argued that the convictions set forth in these *homologia* were the normative Christian thought of the earliest Christian message. His work refutes some of the current speculations about a wide diversity of Christian thought at the beginning of the Christian community. Longenecker succinctly stated his thesis: "My thesis is not that the confessions of the NT contain all that the early Christians believed or affirmed. Rather, I argue (1) that the early Christian confessions contain the central convictions of the earliest believers in Jesus of Nazareth, (2) that these convictions provide the norms for a distinctly Christian theology and the benchmarks for authentic Christian living, and (3) that the various NT contextualizations of these confessions can yield paradigms for further contextualizations of the Christian message today."[20]

The earliest church's method of passing on confessional, liturgical, and creedal formulae was not haphazard. The sources of the liturgical formulae that we find embedded in the letters of the New Testament spring from a tradition for passing on important dogmatic formulae. The origin of the formulae in the primitive church found its roots in the Jewish tradition where, for example, Moses *received* the Torah and *delivered* it to Joshua. These italicized words are English translations of words that represent technical terms for receiving (*kibble min*) and passing on (*maser le*) traditional formulae. These are exactly the translated terms that the author of the canonical New Testament letters used to indicate that they were carefully "passing on" the teachings and descriptions concerning the life, death, and resurrection of Jesus that they had received from those who were his first followers. Ethelbert Stauffer traced the origin of these formulae and concluded that the authors of the New Testament letters did not create or invent them; they passed them on in a reliable manner.[21]

A careful examination of the contents of the New Testament will disclose an abundant treasure of these formulae, particularly as they are concerned with the nature of the person and status of Jesus of Nazareth. (See examples of passages bearing the earmarks of liturgical formulae in appendix A.) As Stauffer emphasized, "Christological formulae are so profuse in the New Testament that they far outnumber all other creedal formulae put together. But this serves to strengthen our thesis that it is not the idea of God, certainly not ecclesiology, but the coming of Christ that constitutes the central theme of primitive Christian thought. . . . The most elementary forms of the confession of Christ are the Christological titles, and their beginnings go back to the earthly life of Jesus."[22] The formation of the Christological formulae can be traced back to Peter's interpretation of Jesus and the Petrine formulae which we find in Acts, in the Pauline use of that formula, and in the pre-Pauline passion creedal formulae concerning the death, resurrection, exaltation, and intercession of Jesus found incorporated into Paul's letter to the Romans (Rom. 8:34). This formula is consistent with the very old pre-Pauline passion formula that Paul incorporates into his first letter to the church at Corinth (1 Cor. 15:3f).

How can we recognize these gems of creedal formulae that represent our very earliest window on the beliefs and practices of those closest to the man from Nazareth? The first New Testament scholar to set forth criteria for the identification and analysis of the earliest Christian prayers and hymns was Eduard Norden, who proposed four criteria for the identification of hymns and confessions: (1) parallel structure, (2) portions beginning with the use of second- or third-person pronouns, (3) the presence of relative clauses and participial predications, and (4) a celebratory style.[23]

Norden's criteria became the basis of subsequent refinements and further analysis that improved our ability to identify and analyze the early hymns and prayers of the primitive church. Longenecker notes the widespread agreement among scholars on the basis for identifying primitive Christian material. He sets forth the following criteria for primitive Christian hymnic materials and primitive poetic confessions:

1. the presence of parallel structures (*parallelismus membrorum*) that reflect either Jewish or Hellenistic poetic conventions or both,
2. the presence of words and phrases not characteristic of a particular New Testament author (i.e., *hapax legomena*)—or, if appearing elsewhere in that author's writings, not with the meaning or in the manner found elsewhere in his other writings—suggesting that the material in question was probably composed by someone else,
3. a preference for participles over finite verbs, suggesting an original oral provenance for the material rather than the literary setting in which it now appears,
4. frequent use of the relative pronoun *hos* ("who") to begin passages,
5. contextual dislocations, which may be either poetic material breaking into a prose section or doctrinal material breaking into an ethical section or both,

6. continuance of a portion after its content has ceased to be relevant to its immediate context, and
7. affirmation of a basic Christian conviction, which usually has to do with the work or person of Jesus Christ.

Several of these criteria also apply to the identification of confessions that are not poetic in nature. The following nine criteria indicate the presence of confessional liturgical formulae:

1. the presence of parallel structures (*parallelismus membrorum*), even though the material is not poetry,
2. the presence of an expression that does not appear elsewhere in an author's writings (*hapax legomena*) or words or phrases not used in the author's manner elsewhere,
3. a preference for participles over finite verbs, and
4. an affirmative regarding the work or person of Jesus Christ.

Added to this list have been linguistic indicators such as:

5. use of the noun "confession" (*homologia*) to signal the content of such early Christian material, either expressed or implied.
6. use of the verb "confess" (*homologeō*) with a double accusative or an infinitive to introduce a direct or an indirect quotation.
7. use of *hoti* (the so-called *hoti recitativum*) to introduce a direct or indirect quotation.
8. use of verbs having to do with preaching (*euaggelizō*, *kērussō*, or *katag-gellō*), teaching (*didaskō*), or witnessing (*martureō* or *marturomai*) to introduce confessional material, and
9. use of a participial construction or a relative clause to introduce the material in question.[24]

Longenecker agrees with Martin Hengel and dates the early primitive confessions to the first decade and to the period between AD 30 and 50. He confirms that they are earlier than Paul's major missionary letters and constitute the most ancient evidence available to New Testament and Christian research.

Hengel concludes that in the most primitive Christian communities hymns to Christ in a worship context referred to Christ as the Son through whom God acted to grant salvation. He emphasized that these hymns had their source in the very beginning of the church: "The hymn to Christ grew out of the early services of the community after

Easter, i.e., it is as old as the community itself. The starting point was formed by the 'messianic psalms' which were discovered in a new way after Easter and to which new compositions were added."[25] Hengel is struck by the fact that the early primitive church sang "new songs" that were no longer songs of lamentation, but songs of praise, thanksgiving, and celebration of victory. The cries of *marana tha* and *hosanna* were acclamations of praise and joy.[26]

Like many communities with joyful vitality, the early primitive church was a singing church so that "the flow of new life and the surging of great spiritual energy in the church naturally was felt again in song, hymn and praise . . . the services of the early church were one continual jubilation, one great concord of worship and praise."[27]

2

WORSHIP PATTERNS IN THE VERY EARLIEST CHURCH INDICATE AN IMMEDIATE VENERATION OF JESUS AS DIVINE FOLLOWING HIS CRUCIFIXION

2.1 THE LINGUISTIC EVIDENCE OF THE VERY EARLIEST WORSHIP PATTERNS OF THE CHURCH INDICATES THAT JESUS WAS WORSHIPPED AS DIVINE AT THE VERY BEGINNING OF THE CHRISTIAN MOVEMENT.

In the mid-1960s I studied at Princeton Theological Seminary under Joachim Jeremias, a remarkable German scholar widely considered to be the leading twentieth-century specialist on the Aramaic language of the Jesus tradition. Jeremias was uniquely qualified in his field, because as the son of a German pastor he had lived in Jerusalem with his father, who was the Dean (*Probst*) of the Church of the Redeemer in that ancient city. From ages ten to fifteen he had the opportunity to learn the ancient Aramaic language spoken by Jesus and his disciples. Jeremias was also the nephew of the Semitist and Near Eastern scholar Dr. Alfred Jeremias, and Joachim's mentor at the University of Leipzig was the renowned Gustaf Dalman, also a brilliant scholar of ancient Palestinian culture.

At Princeton, Jeremias presented us with a remarkable series of lectures on Jesus and the message of the New Testament that set forth his thinking over the previous sixty-five years. Parts of his lectures were later published in 1965 as his highly regarded book *The Central Message of the New Testament*. Although a course on law and society in Princeton University's political science department persuaded me to begin the study of law, Jeremias so influenced me that I continued to study theological and Christological texts over the past forty years of my professional life.

A lawyer's life requires the constant examination of evidence, allegations, and theories. What follows represents my conclusions from reviewing the evidence from the most ancient sources available. In studying the available literature, I am convinced that there are many unexamined presuppositions underlying some of the contemporary analysis of the person of Jesus of Nazareth. My reading of the evidence available leads me ineluctably to the position that the worship of Jesus as divine did not develop over time, but erupted powerfully and contemporaneously with the resurrection appearances claimed by his disciples and followers. In this regard, I concur with the assessment made by Cambridge New Testament scholar C. F. D. Moule: "What I am saying is that the evidence, as I read it, suggests that Jesus was *from the beginning*, such a one as appropriately to be described in the ways in which, sooner or later, he did come to be described in the New Testament period—for instance, as 'Lord' and even, in some sense as 'God.'"[1]

Reference to Jesus as "Lord" is clearly more based in the earliest Palestinian church than allowed by some contemporary analysis. The evidence simply does not support the allegations of some persons that devotion to Jesus gradually developed because of outside influences from pagan religions. The *very earliest* documents in our possession and the hymns and creeds embedded in those documents resonate with an experience of Jesus as the Messiah, the Christ, who is experienced and described in a manner that any thoughtful person would only attribute to God. And these experiences and descriptions are not limited to Paul, but in the oral tradition are earlier than Paul's writings and are also clearly set forth in the writings of other authors in first-century documents, such as the letter to the Hebrews, the first letter of Peter, and the Acts of the Apostles.

Moreover, there appears to be continuity between the self-understanding of Jesus and the very primitive church's interpretation of his role as Messiah. *In other words, the earliest church saw Jesus as the Messiah as a result of Jesus himself believing that he was the person to fulfill that role for Israel.*

The evidence presents a strong, cumulative case that the earliest confession of the Church in Palestine, namely "Jesus is Lord" (*kyrios Iēsous*), was not an innovation that came from sources outside the very earliest Christian community. The New Testament, as I shall note, contains many references to Jesus that equate him with *Yahweh*, the God of the Old Testament. Jesus is clearly presented as more exalted than a human being, not only in Paul's writings, but also in the writings of other authors of the New Testament. This would be true even if one were only to call to the witness stand the author of Acts, the authors of the non-Pauline epistles, and the author of Revelation.

For all of these witnesses, the exalted Lord is the same man who walked the paths of Galilee and was crucified in Jerusalem. It is this Jesus that these writers acclaim, not his mere memory or teachings. At no point in all of the literature of the New Testament is there any consistent indication that the earliest Christian experience was only a reflection on the teaching or example of a dead man of the past who had now enabled his followers to approach God with a new understanding. On the contrary, this same Jesus was considered alive and available to his followers in a new transcendental relationship. The earliest creeds and hymns proclaim a physically resurrected Jesus.

It was not his example or mere memory that launched the Christian movement; there is no evidence that Jesus was considered only as a wonder worker, and given our best evidence of the creeds and hymns dating to the very earliest worship practices of the primitive church, the burden of proof rests on those who claim he was interpreted by his closest followers as only human. The very earliest liturgical formulae indicate that his disciples saw him as a resurrected divine ruler and as one whom they could continue to experience in a dimension transcending the human and temporal.[2] As I shall discuss in detail, the earliest liturgical prayer that was used by the very primitive church in Palestine was the Aramaic formula, *marana tha*. Jesus and his disciples spoke Aramaic, and this prayer was not a polite form of address to an esteemed teacher. The Aramaic word *mar* could mean "sir" or "divine ruler," but the prayer makes no sense unless it is addressed to a teacher with divine attributes. As C. D. Moule emphasized:

> You do not call upon a dead Rabbi to "come" (*marana tha*); and since it is demonstrably possible for *mar* to signify also a divine or transcendent being, it appears that in this context it must have done so. Conversely, *kyrios*, too, could be applied to men . . . but it carried transcendental associations in the Greek speaking Jewish Christianity from which Gentile circles must have received their earliest instruction; it was closely associated with God himself.[3]

The devotional practices of the primitive church, for which there is substantial evidence, clearly demonstrate that Jesus was worshipped as divine right from the beginning of the Christian movement. This is nothing short of astounding, considering that this worship practice erupted in the context of an exclusivist monotheistic Judaism and that the early disciples did not see this worship as inconsistent with Judaism, but as the fulfillment of Jewish prophecy.

This remarkable phenomenon is well documented in Larry Hurtado's recent masterpiece *Lord Jesus Christ*, a book that precisely demonstrates that devotion to Jesus as one with God emerged in the context of a Jewish-Christian monotheism. In examining the questions how, when, and why did the worship of Jesus as divine emerge in the very primitive church, Hurtado presents a meticulous and deep scholarly analysis of the centrality of Jesus of Nazareth in earliest Christian devotion. I will draw on his thorough analysis frequently as I investigate evidence concerning the devotional patterns of worship of Jesus in the initial decade of the Christian movement in Jerusalem. This evidence convincingly points to a reverence for Jesus as divine shortly after his crucifixion. The disciples who lived with Jesus became devoted to him in ways that were previously only associated with the God of the Hebrews.[4]

As indicated, this was accomplished in the early church in a manner considered by the participants in the primitive Christian movement to be consistent with an exclusivist monotheism. The worship of Jesus began extremely early and became a routine pattern of worship well before the writing of Paul's letters. These letters begin within twenty years of the crucifixion, which means that the origins of the veneration of Jesus can be traced back to the very beginning of the Christian faith.[5] The incorporation of preexisting creeds into the letters that venerate Jesus as divine means that the origin of the worship of Jesus may be pushed back to a time almost contemporaneous with the events they describe: the life, crucifixion, and resurrection of Jesus. The evidence for this is powerful and substantial. I want to emphasize that despite speculative claims to the contrary, there is no compelling evidence of an earlier tradition that is antithetical to this unique ancient evidence demonstrating the veneration of Jesus. The evidence is such that the burden of showing reliable first-century evidence to the contrary now rests on those who would maintain that the earliest church did not venerate Jesus as divine.

This veneration was unique in history; there is no other example in the Roman era of such a devotion to a second divine person arising within the context of Jewish exclusivist monotheism. An examination of the Greek, Aramaic, and Hebrew words used to describe Jesus and God in the Old and New Testament, together with the *Didache*, the earliest liturgical manual of the church, confirms that Jesus was revered as divine at the very beginning of the Christian church. Despite imaginative speculations among some New Testament scholars, documented evidence to the contrary has not been produced. Indeed, unlike these primitive liturgical formulae contained in our earliest Christian writings, no document presenting an alternative view can be dated reliably to the first three decades of the first century or even to any part of the first century. As a lawyer examining documentary evidence, I find the support for an alternative view of Jesus to be very fragile.

Again, I want to emphasize that this practice of describing Jesus as God did not originate with Paul. When he incorporated preexisting liturgical formulae venerating Jesus, he merely affirmed a practice that was already in widespread existence at the time of his writings. I turn now to a closer examination of the evidence from the first century presented by the use of the Greek word *kyrios* as it relates to the Hebrew word for God, *Yahweh*, in the early Christian church.

2.2 THE GREEK WORD *KYRIOS* WAS READ OUT LOUD IN THE FIRST CENTURY TO TRANSLATE THE TERM *YAHWEH*, THE HEBREW NAME OF GOD.

By the time of Jesus' birth, devout Jews avoided speaking the Hebrew name for God because the word was considered too sacred to be pronounced out loud. God's name was composed of four Hebrew letters:

YHWH (*Yahweh*), known as the Hebrew tetragrammaton. When Jewish believers referred to God, they used the Hebrew word *adonai* in speaking about or to God. Among Greek-speaking Jews, the Greek word *kyrios* was read out loud for the tetragrammaton (*Yahweh*).

The phrase "Jesus is Lord" was a confession of the earliest Christians. Although the Greek word *kyrios* was used for the term "Lord" in the first century, it had several meanings. It could mean "master" or "owner" or simply be a term of politeness, such as "monsieur" in the French language.[6] It could also mean God. Evidence that the phrase "Jesus is Lord" (*kyrios Iēsous*) identifies Jesus with the God of the Hebrews is given by the first-century Jewish historian Josephus. Josephus rarely used the word *kyrios* in his writings, but he confirms the use of *kyrios* to refer to God when he describes the refusal of first-century Jews to participate in emperor worship, a principal aspect of Rome's civil religion. These Jews would not address the emperor as *kyrios* because they believed that this term was only to be applied to the Hebrew God.

Evidence that *kyrios* referred to God is given by the Greek-speaking authors of the New Testament who use the term in reference to Old Testament passages in which the name of *Yahweh* appears in Hebrew. An examination of these passages reveals that Paul used *kyrios* to refer to God in his writings. There are many examples of the use of this Greek term to refer to the *Yahweh* of the Old Testament, but a couple of quotations should suffice to illustrate the point that *kyrios* refers to God.

For example, in direct reference to Psalm 32:1–2 of the Old Testament, Paul, writing in approximately AD 57, about fifteen years after the crucifixion, refers to God as the Lord (*kyrios*).[7]

Ps. 32:1–2
How blessed are those whose offense is forgiven, whose sin is blotted out. How blessed are those to whom *Yahweh* (God) imputes no guilt, whose spirit harbours no deceit.

Romans 4:6–8
So also David speaks of the blessedness of those to whom God reckons righteousness apart from works: "Blessed are those whose inequities are forgiven, and whose sins are covered; blessed is the one against whom the Lord (*kyrios*) will not reckon sin."

Paul clearly uses *kyrios* as the Greek word for *Yahweh*. Similarly, Paul, writing in Greek in his letter to the Romans, uses the term *kyrios* to translate the Hebrew term *Yahweh* in quoting from the first chapter of Isaiah:

Isaiah 1:9
Had Yahweh Saboath not left us a few survivors, we would be like Sodom, we should be the same as Gomorrah.

Romans 9:29
And as Isaiah predicted, if the Lord (*kyrios*) of hosts had not left survivors to us, we would have fared like Gomorrah.

Other texts that use *kyrios* to refer to *Yahweh* include Rom. 9:27–28 referring to Hos.2:1 and Isa. 10:22–23; Rom. 10:16 referring to Isa. 53:1; Rom.11:34 referring to Isa. 40:13; Rom. 15:11 referring to Ps. 116:1; First Cor. 3:20 referring to Ps. 93:11.

2.3 IN THE EARLIEST CHRISTIAN DOCUMENTS IN OUR POSSESSION, *KYRIOS* WAS APPLIED TO JESUS IN REFERENCE TO *YAHWEH*.

When the early church proclaimed that "Jesus is Lord," it was using *kyrios* in its most exalted sense. For example, the author of the first letter of Peter, writing in the early 60s, ascribes to Jesus an Old Testament passage in which the term "Lord" refers to the Hebrew *Yahweh*. In First Peter 3:15, the author writes: " . . . but in your hearts sanctify Christ as Lord (*kyrios*)." (Careful study shows that "Christ" in the New Testament always refers to Jesus.) This passage refers to Isaiah 8:13: "*Yahweh Saboath*, him you shall sanctify."

Similarly, the writer of Revelation in emphasizing the supreme sovereignty of the Lord (Jesus) alludes to a passage in Deuteronomy which refers to *Yahweh* as God of gods:

Rev. 17:14
These are united in yielding their power and authority to the heart; they will make war on the Lamb, and the Lamb will conquer them, for he is the Lord (*kyrios*) of lords and King of kings, and those with him are called and chosen and faithful.

Deut. 10:17
... for *Yahweh* your God is God of gods and Lord of lords, the great God, triumphant and terrible, free of favoritism, never to be bribed.

In Romans Paul refers to the Lord Jesus and then quotes an Old Testament passage from Joel 2:32, translating *Yahweh* as *kyrios*. The context makes it clear that Paul considers Jesus to be *Yahweh*.[8]

Rom. 10:9, 13
... if you confess with your lips that Jesus is Lord (*kyrios Iēsous*)[9] and believe in your heart that God raised him from the dead, you will be saved. .... For, "Everyone who calls on the name of the Lord (*kyrios*) shall be saved."

Joel 3:5[10]
All who call on the name of *Yahweh* will be saved.

Time and time again, Paul ascribes to *kyrios* the same meaning as *Yahweh* in reference to Jesus in Old Testament passages. Numerous examples could be given, such as First Cor. 10:22 referring to Deuteronomy 32:21; Second Corinthians 3:16 referring to Exodus 34:34; First Thessalonians 3:13 referring to Zechariah 14:5.[11] In applying these Old Testament passages to Jesus, Paul clearly refers to Jesus as the *kyrios* and equates him with *Yahweh*, the God of the Hebrews. It is not plausible that Paul, in referring to Jesus as *kyrios*, was unaware that this term functioned as a substitute for the divine name of *Yahweh*. As Richard Bauckham notes: "Paul certainly knew the Hebrew text as well as the Greek, but, in fact, even a Greek-speaking Jewish Christian who knew the Jewish Scriptures only in Greek could not have been unaware of the function of *kyrios* as representing the Tetragrammaton. In many manuscripts of the Septuagint, what appeared in the written text was not *kurios*, but the Hebrew letters of the Tetragrammaton. ... Readers substituted *kurios* in reading (out loud)."[12]

Neufeld comments on the fact that, in describing Jesus as *kyrios*, the historical events of the crucifixion and resurrection were extremely important to the primitive Christian church. As noted above, the earliest followers of Jesus would never have been satisfied to see him only as a great teacher or to understand their faith in him as relying on a worthwhile myth or metaphor. History and the efficacy of the atonement and resurrection in that history were paramount and essential cornerstones of the primitive faith. This faith is based on a belief in *historical events* related to the life, death, and alleged resurrection of Jesus of Nazareth:

> The primitive *homologia* which Paul knew and expressed in his letters was *Kyrios Iēsous*, "Jesus is Lord." By this *homologia* Christians acknowledged two important facts relevant to their faith: (1) it is *Jesus*, the person who lived and died at a specific time in history, who (2) is the *Lord* of the Christian and of the church by virtue of his resurrection from the dead. It was the belief in this dual fact and its acknowledgment in the church which was essential to the Christian faith. For those of Jewish background it meant ascribing to Jesus the name which in the Septuagint was used in most cases for the God of their fathers; for Gentile Christians it meant the designation of Jesus as the true *kyrios* among many "lords." To all Christians it meant the acknowledgment of Jesus Christ as the risen and ascended Lord, the *kyrios* of every Christian *doulos* (bondservant), the Lord of the church, the Lord of the created world, indeed, the Lord of all.[13]

2.4 IN OUR EARLIEST CHRISTIAN DOCUMENTS, *KYRIOS* WAS APPLIED TO JESUS IN REFERENCE TO THE DAY OF *YAHWEH*.

The evidence for Paul applying the use of *kyrios* to Jesus in reference to *Yahweh* is further demonstrated in Paul's writing about "the day of *Yahweh*." He uses the phrase "the day of the Lord" in unequivocal reference to "the coming of the Lord Jesus Christ (*kyrios Iēsous Christos*)."

In Second Thess. 2:12, Paul writes: "Concerning the coming of the Lord Jesus Christ and our being gathered to him, we ask you, brothers, not to become easily unsettled or alarmed by some prophecy, report or letter supposed to have come from us, saying that the day of the Lord has already come." The phrase "the day of the Lord" refers to the "Day of *Yahweh*" as mentioned in Amos 5:18: "Disaster for you who long for the Day of *Yahweh*! What will the Day of *Yahweh* mean for you?"

2.5 THE OLDEST PRAYER OF THE EARLY CHRISTIAN COMMUNITY IN OUR POSSESSION IS THE ARAMAIC PRAYER TO JESUS AS DIVINE, *MARANA THA*.

Significant evidence that Jesus was worshipped as divine in the devotional pattern of the very earliest church is given by the very early date of the Aramaic prayer *marana tha*. Jesus and his first disciples spoke Aramaic,[14] and the very earliest Palestinian churches also spoke Aramaic.[15] The Aramaic word *mar* (and derivatives such as *myrh*) has essentially the same meaning as the Greek word *kyrios*. *Mar* means "Lord" and was a typical polite address indicating respect, such as one might use for an esteemed teacher or rabbi, but it could also mean divine ruler.

The Aramaic phrase *marana tha* is the oldest liturgical formula known to New Testament scholars. This is the most ancient prayer of the primitive church in our possession and appears in Paul's letter to the *Greek-speaking* church in Corinth, written about two decades after the crucifixion of Jesus. In First Cor. 16:22 Paul incorporates this Aramaic expression at the close of this verse, writing in Aramaic, "*Marana tha!*" which means, "The (our) Lord come!" As we shall see, it is in the meaning of *mar* as divine ruler that we have very early evidence that the earliest Christian church, the church in Palestine, worshipped Jesus as God. This worship in Palestine preceded any influence from the church in Antioch or other places of Hellenistic culture. It is incorporated by Paul and is pre-Pauline, derived from the early Aramaic-speaking followers of Jesus.

Although the Aramaic words can also be read merely as a confession where they mean: "Our Lord has come," this interpretation is highly unlikely. It is much more likely that a prayer formula would be preserved in the original Aramaic form in a letter written in Greek to a Greek-speaking church. The prayer formula is more likely because *confession formulae* found in the New Testament always are translated into Greek. Paul passed on *Aramaic prayer traditions* in the original Aramaic. This is corroborated by his use of the Aramaic word *abba* in Romans 8:15 and Galatians 4:6, which refer to Jesus' own use of the word to address God and also probably refer to the beginning of the Lord's prayer taught by Jesus to his disciples.[16]

The use of the Aramaic phrase *marana tha* as a prayer formula is also consistent with the use of that phrase in the *Didache*, the earliest manual of church liturgy in our possession. This manual was discovered in the Greek Codex Hierosolymitanus (circa 1053) by the Orthodox Metropolitan Bryennios at Constantinople in 1873 and published by him in 1883. It was possibly written sometime between AD 65 and 85 and was most likely used in the first century by Greek-speaking Christians in Syria. The *Didache* or *Doctrine of the Twelve Apostles* contains guidelines for ritual and prayer.[17] These guidelines support the traditional classical Christian faith, not an alternative view. The word *marana tha* appears in the liturgy for the eucharist:

> Let grace come and let this world pass away
> Hosanna to the God of David!
> If any one is holy, let him come;
> if any one is not, let him repent.
> *Marana tha!* Amen[18]

It would not make any sense to translate *marana tha* as teacher or mister where the prayer is "Our Lord, come!" What is the purpose of calling a dead mortal teacher to come? In addition to using the term to refer to *Yahweh* in the cited Old Testament passages, Aramaic documents from the early Christian era use the term as equivalent to *Shaddai* ("the Almighty"), which was also the name of the God of the Hebrews.[19] Because the term is used as a prayer to the risen Jesus in the context of liturgical worship, one should conclude that the earliest church employed the phrase *marana tha* in its highest meaning of divine ruler.

Additional evidence of the meaning of the phrase *marana tha* is given by the use of the prayer "Come Lord Jesus!" written in Greek at the end of the book of Revelation. Revelation is known for its incorporation of many ancient, preexisting liturgical formulae. The Greek equivalent to the Aramaic *marana tha* appears in Revelation 22:20. The context clearly demonstrates that the author of Revelation meant the formula as a prayer.[20]

When we look at the context in which *marana tha* is used in First Corinthians, the *Didache*, and in the Greek translation of the formula in Revelation 22, the evidence requires a rejection of the idea that this formula only meant a polite form of address to an esteemed, dead teacher. "Teacher, come!" is not a prayer which would make any sense unless the teacher had divine attributes. The evidence strongly indicates that this most ancient phrase is a prayer to Jesus as divine.

The Greek-speaking Christians of Syria and Corinth knew and used this prayer because they had learned it from their fellow Christians in the Aramaic-speaking church; that is, the Palestinian church, most likely the mother congregation where the disciples of Jesus worshipped. Even though Paul wrote some of his letters within the first two decades after the crucifixion, the term was in use before Paul's writings.

Paul used an Aramaic formula to communicate to the Greek-speaking church because the members of the church were already familiar with its use in a liturgical setting. Paul and the Christians in Corinth and Syria were not the first to refer to Jesus as divine. We know that the prayer *marana tha* was in use at a time when disciples of Jesus who had lived with him were engaged in worship.

This conclusion becomes more obvious when we consider why Paul would incorporate an *Aramaic* prayer into his letter to a *Greek-speaking* church. This would only make sense if Paul assumed that the Corinthian Christians were familiar with the Aramaic term. The prayer must have been part of the liturgical routine in the Aramaic-speaking Palestinian church so that it carried a traditional meaning that could unite worshippers of Jesus across linguistic and cultural barriers in a common devotional practice. Paul knew that this Aramaic term was so familiar to the intended Greek-speaking readers of his letter that he saw no need to translate the Aramaic prayer into Greek or to give any explanation of its meaning.

This leads to the conclusion that the practice of acclaiming Jesus as Lord derived from the very early Palestinian church. The members of this church spoke Aramaic and passed on this formula in reference to Jesus as they communicated the gospel to persons outside of Palestine. The Greek-speaking Christians of Corinth knew and used this phrase because they had learned it from their fellow Christians in the Aramaic-speaking church. The phrase obviously preceded Paul's writings. This means that Paul and the Christians in Corinth and Syria were not the first to refer to Jesus as divine. The evidence inexorably points to the conclusion that the prayer *marana tha* was in use at an extremely early time in the life of the Christian church and was a well-established practice of devotion prior to Paul's writings.

2.6 VERY EARLY HYMNS AND CREEDS PREDATING PAUL'S LETTERS AND INCORPORATED INTO NEW TESTAMENT DOCUMENTS REFER TO JESUS AS DIVINE.

Paul's use of the Aramaic expression *marana tha* in a prayer formula and his incorporation of many preexisting hymns and creeds into his writing corroborate that Paul is not the source of the adoration of Jesus as God incarnate. In incorporating these liturgical formulae, Paul merely passed on to others what he had received from earlier Christians, probably in the Jerusalem church. These Christians were the earliest followers of Christ, including the ones who lived with Jesus of Nazareth and began the church as recorded in Acts. These were the men and women who knew him during his three-year ministry in Palestine.

2.6.1 First Cor. 15:3–8 and Rom. 4:25 are extremely early creedal formulae referring to Jesus' redemptive death and resurrection.

a. The extremely early date of First Cor. 15:3–8 and the process of receiving and delivering tradition give compelling evidence of the earliest church's belief in Jesus' death and bodily resurrection.

Paul's writings contain the earliest recorded tradition of the death and resurrection of Jesus. This tradition (*paradosis*) was first passed on in oral form among contemporaries of Jesus and then placed into writing. Paul's words are the earliest reference to this tradition in our possession. In First Cor. 15:3–8 he again incorporates a preexisting creed or formula that was passed on in a careful manner. In his first letter to the Corinthians, Paul, writing within about two decades after the crucifixion, states:

> For I handed on to you [*paradidomi*] as of first importance what I in turn had received (*paralambano*) that Christ died for our sins in accordance with the scriptures, and that he was buried, and that he was raised on the third day in accordance with the scriptures, and that he appeared to Cephas, then to the twelve. Then he appeared to more than five hundred brothers and sisters at one time, most of whom are still alive, though some have died. Then he appeared to James, then to all the apostles. Last of all, as to one untimely born, he appeared also to me.[21]

The kernel of this passage is an ancient Aramaic liturgical formula that may have consisted of only the following words: "that Christ died for our sins in accordance with the scriptures, and that he was buried, and that he was raised on the third day in accordance with the scriptures, and that he appeared to Cephas, then to the twelve." Paul may then have expanded on the Aramaic formula and referred to the other appearances.

In saying that he "handed on" to the Corinthians what he "had received," Paul is using the customary idiom that denotes receiving (*paralambano*) and handing on (*paradidomi*) a tradition. Paul affirms that the gospel message did not originate with him, but he received it from others to whom it had been committed before him. The consensus of scholarship is that Paul received this tradition from the original mother congregation in Jerusalem at the time of his visit to that city a few years after his conversion.[22] It represents a core belief of the very first Christian community. This passage contains a creed that uses a style of parallel linguistic structure. The creed was not formulated by Paul. Jeremias demonstrated that in First Cor. 15:3f the terms "handed on to you" or "to deliver" and "to receive" are for passing on traditions.

This conclusion is corroborated by Jeremias's analysis of many un-Pauline phrases used in this creed. For example, "for our sins" (v. 3); "according to the scriptures" (vv. 3–4); "he has been raised" (v. 4), the "third day" (v. 4); "he was seen" (vv. 5–8); and "the twelve" (v. 5) are all phrases Paul did not use in his other writings. The use of the Aramaic "Cephas" instead of Peter's Greek name similarly points to the church's mother congregation in Jerusalem as the place of the origin of the creed.[23]

The first century was not a period composed mainly of literary means of communication. In today's world, it is difficult to understand that most information in the first century, including history and sayings, was passed on by means of oral transmission. Memorization of important events, narratives, and sayings was the dominant method of maintaining history. The transmission of tradition is described in the Greek terms *paralambanein* and *paradidonai*. New Testament scholar Richard Bauckham notes that these terms meant that the early primitive church practiced a formal transmission of tradition:

> We shall outline the character of the transmission process of the Jesus traditions as a formal controlled tradition in which the eyewitnesses played an important part. We have unequivocal evidence, in Paul's letters, that the early Christian movement did practice the formal transmission of tradition. By "formal" here I mean that there were specific practices employed to ensure that tradition was faithfully handed on from a qualified traditioner to others. The evidence is found in Paul's use of the technical terms for handing on a tradition (*paradidōmi*, 1 Cor. 11:2, 23, corresponding to Hebrew *māsar*) and receiving a tradition (*paralambanō*, 1 Cor. 15:1, 3; Gal. 1:9; Col. 2:6; 1 Thess. 2:13; 4:1; 2 Thess. 3:6, corresponding to Hebrew *quibbēl*). These Greek words were used for formal transmission of tradition in the Hellenistic schools and so would have been familiar in this sense to Paul's Gentile readers. They also appeared in Jewish Greek usage (Josephus, *Ant.* 13.297; *C. Ap.* 1.60; Mark 7:4, 13; Acts 6:14).[24]

In describing the earliest references to Jesus as a historical person, New Testament scholar James G. Dunn notes that they come from the letters of Paul and that First Cor. 15:3 is our earliest written report on the life of Jesus and his resurrection. Its very antiquity gives us important information about the very earliest perspective on the unique and exalted status of Jesus. Dunn notes the ancient nature of this report:

> The first [written reference to Jesus] is 1 Cor. 15:3 where Paul relates the foundational belief which he himself had received and which was evidently taught to converts as the earliest Christian catechetical instruction: "that Christ died. . . ." The point is that Paul was probably converted about two years following the event confessed and probably received this foundational instruction at that time. In other words, in the early 30s, Paul was being told about a Jesus who had died two or so years earlier.[25]

In calculating the date of this creed, one arrives at the conclusion that it is almost contemporaneous with the crucifixion and certainly within five years of Jesus' death. German theologian Wolfhart Pannenberg wrote one of the most influential twentieth-century studies on the doctrine of Christ. In reference to the passage in First Cor. 15:3, Pannenberg calculated that the Pauline report originated at a time very close to the events it described. His calculation may be described as follows.

First Corinthians was written by Paul in Ephesus in 56 or 57 CE. His conversion took place in 33 or 35 CE, shortly after the crucifixion of Jesus. We know from his letter to the Galatians (Gal. 1:18) that he visited Peter, James, and other disciples of Jesus in Jerusalem three years after the date of his conversion.

Pannenberg noted that the author of First Cor. 15:3 appeals to a previously coined formulation. If Paul was with Peter, James and John, and other pillars of the Jerusalem mother congregation in 36 or 38 CE, the formulated tradition that he incorporates into First Corinthians most likely had its origin within a few years of the crucifixion. As Pannenberg argued:

> If Paul's conversion is to be dated from the information in Gal., chapter 1 in the year 33 (35?) and if Jesus' death is to be put in the year 30, then Paul would have been in Jerusalem between six to eight years after the events. From this the statements in 1 Cor., ch. 15. are very close to the events themselves. This observation is strengthened by a further finding.

Not only does the author of this text stand very close to the events, but in addition he uses formulations coined previously. Thus he does not create his statements *ad hoc* from a possibly inaccurate memory, but he appeals to a formulated tradition, for whose formation little time remains between the event and the composition of First Corinthians. For various reasons, one must even suppose that this tradition arose very early, namely, prior to Paul's visit to Jerusalem. . . . If Paul had received it soon after his conversion, it must have reached back to the first five years after Jesus' death.[26]

Larry Hurtado also emphasizes the widely held view that this creed was developed by the initial mother congregation of the church in Jerusalem. His examination of the evidence also indicates that this early tradition in First Cor. 15 predates Paul and brings us back to the original disciples of Jesus (the apostles) who lived with him, saw his death, and experienced his resurrection.[27] They are the eyewitnesses who lived in Jerusalem and testified to the exalted status of the risen Jesus. Hurtado noted that the term *christos* had no special meaning outside of Christian and Jewish circles in the first century. The creed contained in First Cor. 15 must have been formulated in a community familiar with the Old Testament Scriptures and the Jewish concept of physical resurrection.

In the second chapter of his letter to the young church in Galatia (Gal. 2:6–9) Paul identified Cephas (Aramaic name of Peter) and James as leaders in the Jerusalem mother congregation. Hurtado notes that the "twelve" is a term consistently associated with the Jerusalem congregation throughout the New Testament Gospels and Acts:

All other references to "the twelve," though from sources somewhat later than Paul's letters (the canonical Gospels and Acts), also associate them with Jerusalem. Whether Paul obtained this tradition directly from Cephas and James in his personal contacts with them (which include a fifteen-day residence with Cephas in Jerusalem mentioned in Gal. 1:18) or indirectly through others, the tradition likely stems from Jerusalem, and Paul claims that it represents beliefs about Jesus affirmed by Judean circles as well as by him.[28]

b. The very early date of the Pauline report is evidence that the mother congregation in Jerusalem regarded Jesus' death and resurrection as redemptive in nature; this perspective is consistent with other very early creeds, such as the one Paul quotes in Romans 4:25.

We see from the tradition that Paul is handing over to the Corinthians evidence that Paul regarded the good news that he proclaimed as redemptive. This good news is about Jesus' death, burial, and resurrection. Paul is passing on the tradition of redemption that he had received, not inventing a new concept of redemption. The Jewish Christians referred to in this passage, such as Cephas (the Aramaic name of Peter), James, and the twelve, all shared this view of the redemptive nature of Jesus' crucifixion, death, and resurrection.

Similarly, in Romans 4:25, Paul, writing in the early spring of 57, quotes from an earlier Christian confessional formula: "It will be reckoned to us who believe in him who raised Jesus our Lord from the dead, who was handed over to death for our trespasses and was raised for our justification."

Scholars commonly acknowledge that these words allude to Isaiah 52:13–53:12 and reflect the translation from the Greek Septuagint:

Therefore I will allot him a
portion with the great,
and he shall divide the spoil
with the strong;
because he poured out himself
to death,
and was numbered with the
transgressors;
yet he bore the sin of many,
and made intercession for the
transgressors.

Paul's readers in Rome understood the idea of the redemptive nature of Christ's death. Paul assumes that his readers in Rome are familiar with the concept and sees no reason to elaborate. Paul did not play a role in founding the church at Rome and gives a greeting to members of the church, including "Andronicus and Junia, my relatives who were in prison with me; they are prominent among the apostles, and they were in Christ before I was."[29] The simple reference to the redemptive nature of Jesus' death ("for our trespasses") and resurrection ("for our justification") without any further explanation indicates that Paul assumed that this concept was already familiar to the Christians at Rome, even though he had not instructed that church on this aspect of Christological teaching.[30] As Hurtado concludes, "So Paul's own innovation or contribution was not to coin the idea that Jesus' death and resurrection were redemptive, nor to make this idea central to early Christian beliefs. The tradition that Paul cites explicitly shows that this idea had long been a key feature of circles of believers that appear to take us back to the Jerusalem church."[31]

2.6.2 First Cor. 11:23 sets forth a creed also describing Jesus' death as redemptive; Jeremias concluded that this core of the tradition of the eucharist may be traced back to Jesus himself.

The framework for the liturgy of the Lord's Supper (*kyriakon deiponon*) probably goes back to Jesus himself. Following very precisely the events of the dinner preceding the crucifixion of Jesus, the basis of the liturgy for the eucharist was passed down word for word in a reliable manner. In his thorough study of the Lord's Supper entitled *The Eucharistic Words of Jesus*, Joachim Jeremias concluded "that the common core of the tradition of the account of the Lord's Supper—what Jesus said at the Last Supper—is preserved to us in an essentially reliable form."[32] First Cor. 11:23 reads:

> For I received [*paralambano*] from the Lord that which I also delivered [*paradidomi*] to you: that the Lord Jesus on the same night in which he was betrayed took bread; and when He had given thanks, He broke it and said, "Take, eat; this is My body which is broken for you; do this in remembrance of Me." In the same manner He also took the cup after supper saying, "This cup is the new covenant in My blood. This do, as often as you drink it in remembrance of Me." For as often as you eat this bread and drink this cup, you proclaim the Lord's death till He comes.[33]

In this passage we find a pre-Pauline creedal tradition from the very earliest church. This independent tradition describes the key event in the dinner that Jesus had with his disciples the night before he was crucified. This tradition is consistent with the New Testament gospel accounts and, in the view of Joachim Jeremias, dates back to Jesus himself.

Here Paul writes an account of his receiving an independent piece of tradition of the Lord's Supper and quotes words, such as "received" and "delivered," that, according to Jeremias, are very "un-Pauline."[34] These words are not typical in Paul's writings and clearly have a Semitic (Hebrew and Aramaic) origin.[35] In noting that Paul speaks of "receiving" and "delivering," Jeremias concludes:

> 1 Cor. 11:23 says nothing other than that the chain of tradition goes back unbroken to Jesus himself. Immediate proof of this is provided by 1 Cor. 15:1ff., where Paul similarly reminds the Corinthians of an old-established tradition, the kerygma, and in so doing uses the same terms "to deliver" and "to receive." . . . For it can be established on linguistic grounds that the kerygma here quoted . . . was not formulated by Paul.[36]

As noted above, the "handing on" of liturgical formulae was not a haphazard procedure, but was a careful process. Jeremias demonstrated on linguistic grounds that this creed "circulated in the whole of the Early Church, down to the time of the composition of the gospels, as an independent liturgical tradition. It was formulated in the very earliest period, at any rate before Paul, since the version found in Paul could be shown to be a pre-Pauline formula."[37] This conclusion by the twentieth century's foremost linguistic specialist on the Semitic language of the Jesus tradition cannot be ignored. The chain of tradition undoubtedly goes back to Jesus himself. Jeremias has presented compelling evidence so that those who would contradict this evidence must bear the burden of proving their position with equally compelling evidence.

2.6.3 First Tim. 3:16 gives a hymnic reference to Christ's preexistence; as does the hymn incorporated into Col. 1:15–20, where Jesus is referred to as the visible expression of the invisible God.

The liturgical formulae incorporated into our earliest Christian documents are often identified by a variety of factors, including the existence of formulaic phrases such as the word *hōmologoumenos*, which means "undeniably" or "without controversy," used in the introduction of the following hymn found in First Timothy 3:16:

> And *without controversy* great is the mystery of godliness:
> God was manifested in the flesh,
> Justified in the Spirit,
> Seen by angels
> Preached among the Gentiles,

Believed on in the world,
Received up in glory.[38]

These verses have a unique style of writing and a rhyming pattern that set them apart from the rest of the writing in the letter. The six verbs (*manifested, justified, seen, preached, believed,* and *received*) are in the passive voice with Christ (Jesus) clearly meant as their subject. The words are poetical and succinct in a parallel Greek form uncharacteristic of Paul's writings. Cambridge scholar C. F. D. Moule noted the hymnic character of these verses:

> First Tim. 3:16 is, at any rate, a hymn, and from an early period: the very fact that, in Greek, it starts abruptly with a relative pronoun unattached (apparently) to any antecedent suggests a quotation from something that the reader already knew and would recognize; the succession of aorist indicative passive makes a monotonous rhyme; and, like many of the greatest Christian hymns, it is essentially creedal—a great adorative confession, like the *Te Deum* after it.[39]

In reading this hymn, we are overhearing something of what the very earliest Christians used in their worship. In this hymn we have a reference to Christ's preexistence in that "he was revealed in the flesh."[40] The vast majority of scholars are convinced that several passages in Paul's letters describe and assume the preexistence of Christ, the concept that Christ existed prior to his life as a human being on Earth. Another example of first-century worship and devotion to Jesus reflecting the divine preexistence of Christ is Col. 1:15–20, a passage which many scholars consider to be originally a hymn honoring Jesus. Most scholars date composition of the letter to the Colossians to around the mid-first century. Given this early dating, the passage appears to be a hymn employed in worship within the first few decades following the crucifixion, well within the lifespans of many persons who followed Jesus during his life on earth and later worshipped in the earliest churches. The passage gives us substantial evidence of the devotional practices of Christians in the early decades following the crucifixion. In reference to Jesus the hymnlike passage reads:

> He is the image of the invisible God, the firstborn of all creation; for in him all things in heaven and on earth were created, things visible and invisible, whether thrones or dominions or rulers or powers—all things

have been created through him and for him. He himself is before all things, and in him all things hold together. He is the head of the body, the church; he is the beginning, the firstborn from the dead, so that he might come to have first place in everything. For in him all the fullness of God was pleased to dwell, and through him God was pleased to reconcile to himself all things, whether on earth or in heaven, by making peace through the blood of his cross.

The high, cosmic Christology contained in the passage represents additional compelling evidence that the earliest church considered Jesus as God incarnate. The use of these words as a hymn in the church, which preceded the writing of the letter of Colossians, demonstrates the perspective that Jesus was essentially God in human form, *the visible expression of the invisible God.*

Evidence that this is an earlier hymn incorporated into the letter to the Colossians may be seen in the cadences that are clearly perceptible in the original Greek and in its compact structure.[41] Colossians 1:15–20 begins with the introductory phrase *hos estin* which means "who is." This is an introduction often used to present a creedal or liturgical formula. A majority of New Testament scholars also consider this passage to be an early, traditional hymn because of the introductory phrase, the poetic arrangement of the language, the use of devices of rhetoric, and its distinct vocabulary. In concluding that the passage is pre-Pauline and very early, Wendy J. Porter, a Canadian expert on creeds, hymns, and the music of the early church, notes that in Col. 1:15–20: "The use of an introductory relative clause *hos estin* ('who is'), a style that suggests a strophic arrangement, the use of rhetorical devices and distinct language are all considered indications that this is a traditional hymn and the majority of New Testament scholars see this as clearly a pre-Pauline hymn."[42]

Stauffer considered this hymn to be the most forceful of the incarnational summaries.[43] This is consistent with the evidence presented by Longenecker: "Colossians 1:15–20 also seems to be one of these *homologia* portions. . . . It is replete with *hapax legomena* (i.e., words or phrases not used elsewhere in an author's writings, or not with the meanings or in the manner of his other writings)—such as the expressions 'image', 'the head', 'the beginning', and 'the fullness'. Furthermore, it evidences a carefully constructed and balanced structure, or what is called *parallelismus membrorum.*"[44]

In Paul's letters Jesus is seen as the *visible expression of the invisible God* to such an extent that the functions and honor normally allowed only to *Yahweh* in Jewish exclusivist monotheism are accorded to Christ. His letters demonstrate that this exaltation of Jesus was already well established in the earliest church by the time of his writings. There is no indication that Paul was aware of any serious disagreement with this high view of Jesus among any of the existing Christian churches. Paul certainly had disagreements over more peripheral matters of faith with other Christians and was bold to describe his differences with other Christians, such as the questions of Torah observance, the status of the Gentiles, and Paul's apostolic legitimacy; but there is no evidence in his letters that he knew of any group that opposed this exalted view of Christ. There is simply no first-century evidence that any members of the Christian circles with which he was acquainted refused to honor and worship Jesus in a manner that was normally reserved only for God. No first-century document gives even a hint of an alternative Christology existing among other groups of Christians at this very early time in the life of the church.[45] Despite the strained speculations of nonmainline scholars (see chapter 7), there is no substantive, solid evidence of a material diversity in the earliest church concerning this high view of Jesus. The only substantive controversy concerned whether Gentile converts should obey the Jewish law. When the very early church considered Jesus, there was a uniform high Christology.

With respect to the speculation that this passage is evidence of an early first-century gnosticism, Larry Hurtado gives credence to a recent study by Christian Stettler that held that this hymnlike passage in Colossians did not have a gnostic theme. Stettler demonstrated that this passage has a coherence, a unity, that implicates its origin as a hymn within a very early liturgical setting of Christian worship or that the author composed the passage as a hymn describing the supremacy of Christ. In either case, the passage was a component of the devotional life of early first-century Christians. Stettler employed a line-by-line analysis to show that the vocabulary of the passage came from Greek phrases used in Jewish communities familiar with the Old Testament:

> For example, the reference to Christ as the one in whom "all the fullness was pleased to *dwell*" adapts Old Testament/Jewish traditions of God's dwelling in, and filling, the temple of Zion. The same applies to the similar statement in 2:9, that in Christ "all the fullness of deity dwells

bodily." As for the term "fullness" (*plēroma*)—itself, in none of its several uses in Colossians or Ephesians does it carry any of the technical connotation that it acquires in later gnostic texts/groups (e.g., in Valentinianism, where it refers to a scheme of divine emanations distinguishable from the high God). Instead, we probably have here a distinctive, early Christian adaptation of a Greek term whose prior religious usage had been mainly in biblical reference to the "fullness" of the world/earth and the sea.[46]

The Colossians' hymn is evidence that the early church was already worshipping and honoring Jesus as divine prior to Paul's writing. This conclusion is corroborated by the use of the *marana tha* prayer formula and the absence of evidence of any Pauline innovation of devotion to Christ. The evidence inexorably leads to the conclusion that the reverence of Jesus as divine was prevalent in Aramaic-speaking and Greek-speaking Christian circles in the 30s, the same decade as the crucifixion.[47] Writing in the middle of the first century, Paul was carrying on the pattern of devotion that was already followed in earliest Judean Christian traditions, not inventing a new pattern or a new Christology.

2.6.4 In First Cor. 8:5–6 Paul incorporates another early confession indicating the cosmic, preexistent, creative, and divine role of Christ.

In another section of his first letter to the Corinthians, Paul also appears to refer to another primitive preexisting liturgical adoration of Jesus, closely associating him with God and an active role in the creation of the universe. This cosmic role of Jesus is seen in the early confession found in First Cor. 8:5–6. Here Paul applies the monotheism of the Jewish faith to God the Father and the Lord Jesus Christ. Neufeld argues that he does this to reflect a polemical interest in upholding the Christian mission against a polytheistic Hellenism. Corinth had a polytheistic environment, and Paul is keen to set forth a faith in Jesus as Lord as consistent with the Jewish monotheistic position: "Indeed, even though there may be so-called gods in heaven or earth—as in fact there are many gods and many lords—yet for us there is one God (*heis Theos*), the Father, from whom are all things and for whom we exist, and one Lord, Jesus Christ (*heis Kyrios Iésous Christos*), through whom are all things and through whom we exist" (1 Cor. 8:5–6).[48]

Paul does not elaborate on the meaning of this passage; he assumes that his readers are already familiar with the concepts. He simply takes for granted that these ideas are understood by his readers.[49] Paul's presumption of his readers' acquaintance with the concept of Jesus' preexistence is further evidence that the concept did not originate with Paul, but was part of the thought of very early Christian circles that predate the time of his writings. This position is buttressed by the evidence from Jewish eschatological thought. Hurtado points out that the tradition of the preexistence of Jesus is reflected in Jewish apocalyptic/eschatological traditions so that the concept of his preexistence most likely arose in the very early Jewish Christian church, which would have been familiar with Jewish eschatological tradition. This again means the idea should not be attributed to the influence of pagan or Hellenistic thought,[50] but comes from an early time in the beginnings of the Jewish Christian church, probably from the beginnings of the mother congregation in Jerusalem where the disciples met and worshipped.

2.6.5 The ancient Christ hymn incorporated into the second chapter of Philippians is evidence of very early adoration of Jesus as divine.

As noted above, "Jesus is Lord" (*kyrios Iēsous*) was a declaration of the earliest Christians. This declaration derived from the belief that the resurrected Jesus was exalted at the right hand of God and given authority and power over the cosmos and everything in it. Paul wrote the letter to the Christians at Philippi from prison, some time in the second or third decade after the crucifixion. The authenticity of Paul's letter to the church in Phillipi is not disputed by even the more skeptical New Testament scholars, and the prevalent view among scholars is that the second chapter contains a hymn that originated long before Paul incorporated it into his letter. Paul does not see any need to explain this hymn or justify its Christological significance. He communicates a devotional practice reflected in the hymn. The passage is historical evidence of the early worship of Jesus.[51]

As we have seen, the application of Old Testament *kyrios* passages to Jesus presupposes an understanding of Jesus as divine. This is also clearly the understanding in this Christological hymn incorporated by Paul in Philippians 2:6–11. Paul uses this hymn to encourage the Philippian Christians to let the same mind be in them that was in Christ Jesus. He recites the hymn referring to Jesus in the following words:

who, though he was in the form
    of God,
did not regard equality with
    God
as something to be exploited,
but emptied himself,
    taking the form of a slave,
    being born in human likeness,
And being found in human form,
    he humbled himself
    and became obedient to the
        point of death—
even death on a cross.
Therefore God also highly
    exalted him
    and gave him the name
    that is above every name
so that at the name of Jesus,
every knee should bend,
in heaven and on earth and
    under the earth,
and every tongue should confess
    that Jesus Christ is Lord
    [Kyrios Iēsous Christos],
    to the Glory of God the Father.[52]

The hymn uses language that would have a very clear meaning to Jews in the first century. The language refers to a well-known passage in Isaiah 45, where the Lord God (*Yahweh*) declares:

By myself I have sworn,
from my mouth has gone forth
    in righteousness
a word that shall not return:
"To me every knee shall bow,
    every tongue shall swear."[53]

The hymn's interpretation of this passage in Isaiah is that every knee shall bow at Jesus' name and every tongue shall confess that Jesus

Christ is Lord. By divine decree the name of Jesus is now to have the meaning of Lord in the highest sense—the same sense of the Hebrew *Yahweh*.[54]

In this early passage, the worshipping church acknowledged that God had given his own name to Jesus. Such a giving did not refer only to the name of God, but to His power and lordship. As distinguished New Testament scholar Oscar Cullmann noted:

> In Judaism, as in all ancient religions, a name represents also a power. To say that God confers upon Jesus his own name is to say that he confers upon him his whole lordship. . . . The lordship bestowed upon the *Kyrios Iēsous*, who is now equal with God, manifests itself especially in the fact that also all the invisible powers of creation are subjected to him, so that now "every knee should bow in heaven and on earth and under the earth and every tongue confess: Jesus Christ is Lord." This idea is the foundation of every New Testament passage which actually identifies Jesus with God.[55]

New Testament scholar F. F. Bruce agreed with Cullmann. In writing about this pre-Pauline hymn he concluded:

> It is deliberately affirmed that God has conferred his own name, with the unique dignity attaching to it, on Jesus. It might not be appropriate to reword "Jesus Christ is Lord" as "Jesus Christ is *Yahweh*"; but nothing less than this is involved. This usage did not originate with Paul, but repeatedly he ascribes to Jesus Old Testament texts and phrases in which the word "Lord" represents the Hebrew *Yahweh*.[56]

Ernest Lohmeyer, a German New Testament scholar at the University of Griefswald, who was executed by Stalin-dominated Soviet authorities occupying the former East Germany, produced a highly regarded study of the above-quoted Philippians verses, demonstrating that they were a hymn of Christ with a rhythmical format comprised of six strophes of three lines each. In his words, the passage is *ein Carmen Christi in strengem Sinne*.[57] Jeremias agreed with Lohmeyer and others that the hymn was originally composed in Aramaic and later translated into Greek.[58] Ralph P. Martin, who wrote what may be the definitive book concerning this hymn, *Carmen Christi: Philippians 2:5–11 in Recent Interpretation and in the Setting of Early Christian Worship*, corroborates Lohmeyer and Jeremias's view of an Aramaic origin:

The linguistic and stylistic evidence goes to show that the hymn was both pre-Pauline and a product of a Jewish-Christian community. There are features which make it likely that it was composed first in a Semitic tongue and later translated into Greek. Traits of style of which are "impossible" in Greek; phrases which appear to be simply "translation equivalents" from a Semitic language into Greek; and the use of words and expressions which are drawn directly from the Old Testament—all these facts indicate the Semitic provenance of the hymn in its putative original form; and the best description of the section . . . is that it is a Judaeo-Christian psalm.[59]

In Lohmeyer's book, *Kyrios Jesus*, which Martin refers to as a tour de force, the German scholar's careful, ground-breaking analysis concluded that *the location of the composition of the hymn was the very earliest Jewish-Christian community in Jerusalem.* This means that there is some possibility that the hymn was repeated in Aramaic in the liturgy of the mother congregation in Jerusalem where James, Peter, John, and Mary would have worshipped. Lohmeyer concluded that the hymn was actually used in the eucharistic liturgy during the celebration of the Lord's Supper.[60]

There is almost universal agreement with Lohmeyer's work concerning the poetic and hymnic form of the Philippians passage, and the linguistic evidence confirms his principal conclusion. The passage is certainly distinguishable from the other verses surrounding it and unlike any Pauline or other epistolary style.

As noted above, New Testament scholar Ethelbert Stauffer set forth twelve criteria of creedal formulae in the New Testament in his book *New Testament Theology.* Among the criteria relevant to this passage are: a distinguishing linguistic usage, stylistic pattern, and terminology, separating the passage from its surrounding context; the ceremonial nature of the passage demonstrated by an artistic structure, including rhythmical patterns, well-formed phrases, and parallelisms contrasting with the surrounding context, which has a different narrative style; and a "monumental stylistic construction" common to confessional liturgical formulae.[61]

Given its probable Aramaic origin and the likelihood that it was used in a service commemorating the Lord's Supper by the contemporaries of Jesus, one must ask the question why such men and women came to believe that, in Jesus of Nazareth, God had visited this earth in human form. What had happened that gave rise to the astounding claims made in this very early hymn of Christ and in the other liturgical and hymnic formulae we have considered?[62]

2.6.6 The earliest available evidence from creeds and liturgical formulae preexisting any Christian writings portray Jesus as the Christ and God's Son.

Approximately 530 times in the New Testament Jesus is referred to as *Christos*. This Greek term is used to translate the Hebrew term *mashiach*, which in English means the "anointed one." As noted above, in the New Testament, Christ as *Christos*, for all intents and purposes, is synonymous with Jesus. Jesus is seen as the messiah, the anointed one of God. In writing his letters, Paul often used the definite article ("the" or "*ho*") without any explanation, as if he expected the readers of his letters to know the Jewish traditions associated with the title. He would write *ho Christos*, meaning "the Christ." The term is frequently found in references to Jesus' crucifixion and resurrection.[63] The use of *ho Christos* without any explanation of the term means that Paul knew that his Greek-speaking readers were acquainted with the Jewish significance of the term. As Hurtado notes, "The prevalence of *Christos* in Paul's christological expressions can be accounted for only by positing the messianic claim as a feature of Christian proclamation for a considerable period earlier than his letters. Probably we have to take the claim back to the earliest circles, those whom Saul/Paul the Zealous Pharisee sought to gag and destroy."[64] This means that, consistent with the gospel accounts, this term was applied to Jesus at the very beginning of the Christian church. (I will discuss the concept of the Jewish messiah as it applies to Jesus more thoroughly in Section 3.6. I want to clarify at this point that I am not equating the ancient Jewish reverence for the messiah with the Jewish reverence for God.)

Paul also referred to Jesus as *the* divine Son of God, using the definite article to connote the unique status of Jesus as *the* Son as opposed to any reference to sons of God(s) in Jewish or pagan sources during the Roman era. In Paul's earliest letter, First Thessalonians, written about 50, Paul uses what most scholars consider a confessional formula from the 40s and possibly 30s (the decade of the crucifixion). Similar to the use of *ho Christos* for Christ, this reference to Jesus as a divine Son from heaven is an incorporation of a much earlier tradition in the Church:

"His Son (*ton huion*) from heaven, whom He raised from the dead, even Jesus who delivers us from the wrath to come."

The evidence points to the following unequivocal conclusion: In the first and second decade following the crucifixion, taken as a whole, from several creeds, Jesus was described in confessional formulae recited in liturgical worship settings as *the* unique and divine Son of God.[65]

2.6.7 Pre-Pauline liturgical prayers and benedictions treat Jesus as divine.

In addition to the prayer, *marana tha* ("Our Lord, come!"), which clearly referred to Jesus and began in Aramaic-speaking circles very early after the crucifixion, Paul's writing contains further significant evidence of a worship and prayer pattern closely associating God and Jesus. Writing sometime between AD 48 and 51, within only two decades of the crucifixion, in his first letter to the Christians at Thessalonica, Paul incorporates what is widely accepted as a preexisting liturgical statement. Using this earlier liturgical formula, he associates Jesus with God in the prayer practice of the early church:

> Now may our God and Father himself and our Lord Jesus direct our way to you. And may the Lord make you increase and abound in love for one another and for all, just as we abound in love for you. And may he so strengthen your hearts in holiness that you may be blameless before our God and Father at the coming of our Lord Jesus with all his saints.[66]

This passage is evidence of a worship pattern in the earliest Christian communities that emphasized the important role of Jesus in acting in a manner closely connected to God. The passage makes no sense if Jesus is not seen as endowed with power so that he can answer prayer. This is consistent with the references to Jesus so commonly contained in the benedictions of Paul as he concludes his letters (e.g., in First Corinthians he concludes his letter by incorporating another earlier, Christian liturgical formula with the following benediction: "The grace of the Lord Jesus be with you. My love be with all of you in Christ Jesus").[67]

Most scholars consider these benedictions as references to earlier liturgical statements that were already in existence at the time of Paul's writings.[68] This is consistent with the evidence presented by Luke in Acts, where Stephen, at his stoning, prays to Jesus to receive his spirit:

"While they were stoning Stephen, he prayed, 'Lord Jesus, receive my spirit.'"[69]

Praying to Jesus as one with divine attributes is clearly part of the activity of the church at its very beginning. In the first chapter of First Corinthians, Paul also provides evidence of Christians invoking the name of Jesus and calling upon his name, a clear appropriation of a biblical phrase consistent with divine reverence of Jesus:

> To the church of God that is in Corinth, to those who are sanctified in Christ Jesus, called to be saints, together with all those who in every place call on the name of our Lord Jesus Christ, both their Lord and ours: Grace to you and peace from God our Father and the Lord Jesus Christ.[70]

2.6.8 Paul's letters provide valuable historical as opposed to theological evidence of early Christian worship.

John Dominic Crossan, in his book *The Birth of Christianity*, takes a position that I think is unsupportable—that Paul should be excluded in assessing the beliefs and practices of the earliest church. His main reason for excluding Paul's letters is his allegation that Paul was influenced by Platonic dualism. However, rather than actually going back to the first two decades of the Christian movement (30s and 40s), Crossan develops his view from documents written much later than Paul's letters. Excluding Paul makes no sense because Paul's writings are the earliest writings in our possession that describe the practices and beliefs of the earliest church. His letters date from within two decades of the crucifixion, which took place most likely in 33. They are our most authentic sources describing the practices and devotion of the earliest group of Jewish Christians. As Hurtado notes, they are "the earliest form of the Christian movement to which we have direct access from undisputed firsthand sources."[71]

Paul's letters provide valuable evidence of the beliefs and practices of the pre-Pauline circles of Christians. On *historical*, as opposed to theological, grounds alone, the letters give impressive evidence of a devotional pattern already well established at the time of his writings, a time close to the crucifixion event itself. These are our earliest existing sources, and they are rich with evidence that the worship of Jesus as divine commenced at the very beginning of the Christian movement. Early on, Jesus is seen as the visible expression of the invisible God. The historical evidence supports the conclusion that the earliest Christian circles did not regard the worship of Jesus as the worship of a second god, but as an extension of the Jewish exclusivist monotheistic worship of *Yahweh*.[72]

As we have seen, Paul's letters incorporate earlier traditions, hymns, creeds, and practices so that they constitute extremely important *historical* evidence of the traditions, practices, devotion, and beliefs of the earliest Jewish Christians in the decades prior to the 50s. Any *historical* analysis of the early church that does not contain a thorough discussion of the evidence in Paul's letters is seriously flawed.[73]

Moreover, Paul knew well the beliefs and practices of the Jewish Christians of Jerusalem and in Judea/Palestine and was well acquainted with these Christians during the 30s and 40s. We know from his own writings and the documentary evidence of Acts that he met and knew the leaders of the earliest Jewish Christian community, such as Peter and James, the brother of Jesus. Thus, from his personal activity in Christian circles in the earliest years, and from his position of persecuting the church immediately after Jesus' crucifixion, he was well aware of the beliefs and practices of the very earliest Jewish Christians.[74]

As noted, Crossan and others who attempt to exclude Paul's writings rely on documents written much later than the Pauline writings. The canonical gospels were written between AD 65 and 90 or earlier. Apocrypha gospels, such as the gospel of Thomas (see discussion in chapter 7), are mid- to late second-century writings. I want to emphasize again that Paul's writings actually move us back into the 30s and 40s because Paul's conversion experience took place within a couple of years of Jesus' crucifixion and he incorporates preexisting worship, liturgical expressions, and formulae. Prior to that time he was very familiar with the beliefs and practices of the first Jewish Christians as he attempted to destroy the new faith as a zealous Pharisee.

One must bear in mind that Paul knew the theology of the Judean Christian church. In his letter to the church at Galatia he refers to the churches in Judea as saying, "The one who formerly was persecuting us is now proclaiming the faith he once tried to destroy." Thus, he considered his own faith to correspond to the faith of the Jewish Christians in Judea. And he was keen to keep good relationships with the leaders of the Jerusalem church, such as Cephas (Peter), James, and John and even extended himself to raise an impressive offering for the Jerusalem church. As stated above, Paul reasserted traditional beliefs and practices tied to early Jewish Christian circles, such as the *marana tha* prayer formula addressed to Jesus. Hurtado has convincingly demonstrated that "the original provenance of this Aramaic liturgical expression . . . is Judean Christianity, and the Jerusalem church in particular."[75] Thus, devotion to Jesus had its source in the Judean Christian circles that included Jerusalem. This is consistent with the references in Acts where we find Judean Christian circles following the practice of baptizing "in the name of Jesus"[76] and believers described as "all those who invoke your (Jesus') name."[77] Hurtado's examination of the evidence concerning the early Judean Christian community is detailed and logical:

> In summary, the Pauline evidence that points toward the devotional life of Judean Christianity constitutes the following: (1) Paul freely cites traditional formulae of belief and traditions of religious practices from Jewish Christian circles as fully appropriate for, and reflective of, the practice of his own congregations; (2) these traditions specifically affirm a broad commonality in beliefs about Jesus as Christ/Messiah, about his death and resurrection as redemptive, and about the eschatological context in which his significance is understood; and (3) these traditions include religious practices in which Jesus functions as recipient of cultic devotion, practices that seem to have been a part of the devotional life of Judean circles as well as the Pauline congregations.[78]

2.6.9 Other early authors in addition to Paul attribute divine status to Jesus.

As emphasized frequently above, Paul is only one of many authors writing in the first century who give a perspective of Jesus that is closely associated with God.[79] This is extraordinary when one considers that this perspective was seen as consistent with a monotheistic Jewish tradition during a time when eyewitnesses to Jesus' life and execution were not only available to prevent distortion, but were themselves participants in the veneration of Jesus as divine.[80]

Richard N. Longenecker in his book *The Christology of Early Jewish Christianity* notes that the attribution of the title "God" to Jesus can be seen in the letter to the Hebrews, which was not written by Paul, but by an unidentified Jewish author well versed in the Old Testament. The date of his writing probably was prior to AD 70 because it does not mention the destruction of the temple in Jerusalem and the end of the

Jewish sacrificial system, but rather uses the Greek present tense when discussing the temple.

In referring to Jesus, the author of Hebrews quotes a portion of Psalm 45 attributing to Jesus the title of God and God's creative activity:

> But of the Son he says,
> Your throne, O God, is forever
> and ever,
> and the righteous scepter is the
> scepter of your kingdom.
> You have loved righteousness and
> hated wickedness;
> therefore God, your God, has
> anointed you
> with the oil of gladness beyond
> your companions.[81]

> And,
>   In the beginning, Lord, you
>   founded the earth,
>   and the heavens are the work of
>   your hands,
>   they will perish, but you remain;
>   they will all wear out like
>   clothing;
>   like a cloak you will roll them up,
>   and like clothing they will be changed.
>   But you are the same;
>   and your years will never end."
>   But to which of the angels has he ever
> said,
>   Sit at my right hand
>   until I make your enemies a
>   footstool for your feet.?

These verses are a direct quote of Psalms 45:6–7, 102:25–27, and 110:1 and clearly indicate the Hebrews author's intention of attributing the divine nature to Jesus. As Longenecker notes: "By his employment of Ps. 102:25–27 in the following verses with reference to Jesus, there is little doubt that the writer to the Hebrews had every intention of attributing not only the title but also the creative activity of God to the Son."[82]

Likewise, the author of Second Peter, writing between AD 65 and 68, refers to Jesus as both God and Savior: "Simeon Peter, a servant and apostle of Jesus Christ, to those who have received a faith as precious as ours through the righteousness of our God and Savior Jesus Christ."[83] Longenecker concludes: "The phrase 'the righteousness of our God and Savior Jesus Christ' is very likely a similar ascription (attributing the title of God to Jesus), the use of the article evidently signaling the idea that the two titles are to be understood as referring to the one person, Jesus Christ."[84]

As support for his conclusion, Longenecker refers to a general rule in the translation of Greek literature that when the article "our" connects two nouns of the same case, the two nouns always relate to the same person. In other words, the title "Savior" refers to the title "God" and they both refer to Jesus in the quoted passage from Second Peter. Longenecker sets forth this grammatical rule to verify this connection and the conclusion that Jesus is given the title of "God" in Second Peter 1:1:

> Though often disputed it is none the less a generally reliable rule that "when the copulative *kaí* connects two nouns of the same case, if the article *ó* or any of its cases precedes the first of the said nouns or participles, and is not repeated before the second noun or participle, the latter always relates to the same person that is expressed or described by the first noun or participle; i.e., it denotes a further description of the first-named person."[85]

The author of Revelation also gives Jesus the titles reserved for God. In Revelation 1:17–18, the author relates his experience on the island of Patmos and quotes the risen Jesus: "When I saw him, I fell at his feet as though dead. But he placed his right hand on me, saying, 'Do not be afraid; I am the first and the last, and the living one. I was dead, and see, I am alive forever and ever, and I have the keys of Death and of Hades.'"[86]

The reference to the "first and the last" alludes to God as the Alpha and Omega, the beginning and end of all things. This is well described in Isaiah 4:6: "Thus, says the Lord, the King of Israel, and his Redeemer, the Lord of hosts; I am the first and I am the last; besides me there is no God."[87]

The use of the phrase "the living one" refers to Old Testament passages where God is described as "the living God" as opposed to dead pagan gods.[88]

This attribution to Jesus of the status of God by describing him as the Alpha and Omega, or the first and the last, is repeated in the last chapter of Revelation where these words are ascribed to Jesus: "See, I am coming soon; my reward is with me, to repay according to everyone's work. I am the Alpha and Omega, the first and the last, the beginning and the end."[89]

The exalted status of Jesus in the early church is also reflected by the author of Revelation where he describes Jesus receiving devotion and honor along with God. This is completely unprecedented in the Jewish tradition of the Roman era. Jesus is presented as an appropriate recipient of devotion within an exclusivist monotheistic belief and practice.[90] This very high view of Jesus is described as follows:

> Then I looked, and I heard the voice of many angels surrounding the
>   throne and the living creatures and the elders; they numbered
>   myriads of myriads, and thousands of thousands, singing with
>   full voice,
> "Worthy is the Lamb that was
>   slaughtered
>   to receive power and wealth and
>   wisdom and might
>   and honor and glory
>   and blessing!"
> Then I heard every creature in heaven and on earth and under the
>   earth and in the sea, and all that is in them, singing,
> "To the one seated on the throne
>   and to the Lamb
>   be blessing and honor and glory
>   and might
>   forever and ever!"
> And the four living creatures said "Amen!" And the elders fell down
>   and worshipped.[91]

This inclusion of Jesus as a person worthy of worship was without precedent in ancient Jewish monotheistic tradition. *Why did this happen?*

The most plausible reason for the inclusion of Jesus in the divine identity of monotheistic tradition was the effect of potent religious experiences among the participants in the earliest Christian circle. The available evidence demonstrates that the belief that Jesus died for sins, was resurrected three days after his death, and appeared to his followers was widely circulated in the very beginning of the church.[92]

I am not arguing at this point that the referenced resurrection experiences were accurate reflections of reality. For the moment, I am only making the assertion that the experiences themselves, whether true to reality or not, were the basis for the radical change in behavior among the early Jewish circles of the Christian movement. As Hurtado writes: "Whether one chooses to consider these particular experiences as hallucinatory, projections of mental processes of the recipients, or the acts of God, there is every reason to see them as the ignition points for the christological convictions linked to them."[93]

2.6.10 Ancient creeds of oral tradition from the earliest liturgical formulae corroborate the canonical gospel accounts of the life of Jesus.

I am emphasizing that the creeds and hymns incorporated into letters of the New Testament precede the writing of these letters that in turn precede the writing of the New Testament gospel accounts that, in turn, precede the dates of the Nag Hammadi gnostic manuscripts (such as the gospel of Thomas) that were composed in the second to fourth century AD and found in 1945 near Nag Hammadi, Egypt. The creeds and hymns incorporated into the New Testament letters establish a number of facts concerning the life of Jesus. The information contained in these creeds constitutes significant corroborative evidence to the accounts contained in the four canonical gospels. It is important to understand that the perspective and facts set forth in the creeds are consistent with the canonical gospel accounts. The creeds are not consistent with later counterorthodox writings of the second century or with alternative gospel accounts.

For example, the creed found in Romans 1:3–4 states, " . . . the gospel concerning his Son, who was descended from David according to the flesh and was declared to be Son of God with power according to the spirit of holiness by resurrection from the dead, Jesus Christ our Lord."[94] From this creed we know that the earliest church believed that Jesus was descended from David, born physically, declared to be Son of God, rose from the dead, and was considered to have divine attributes.

The creed in Acts 4:27 notes that Herod and Pontius Pilate acted with a crowd against Jesus in Jerusalem: "For in this city [Jerusalem], in fact, both Herod and Pontius Pilate, with the Gentiles and the peoples of Israel, gathered together against your holy servant Jesus, whom you anointed."[95] The creed in Acts 2:22 notes (1) that Jesus was from

Nazareth; (2) that he was a man showing deeds of power, wonders, and signs; and (3) that he was crucified: "You that are Israelites, listen to what I have to say: Jesus of Nazareth, a man attested to you by God with deeds of power, wonders, and signs that God did through him among you, as you yourselves know."[96]

Also in Acts another creed describes the preaching and healing actions of Jesus which began in Galilee and refers to the ministry of John the Baptist:

> You know the message he sent to the people of Israel, preaching peace by Jesus Christ—he is Lord of all. That message spread throughout Judea, beginning in Galilee after the baptism that John announced: how God anointed Jesus of Nazareth with the Holy Spirit and with power; how he went about doing good and healing all who were oppressed by the devil, for God was with him.[97]

We have already seen how an early description of the Lord's Supper, including a description that it occurred the night before Jesus' crucifixion, was set forth in the creed incorporated into the first letter to the church in Corinth (1 Cor. 11:23f). This description is rather detailed in describing what Jesus said and did. His death, burial, and resurrection are mentioned in the creed of First Cor. 15:3ff. The creed in First Tim. 3:16 quoted above, consistent with many other creeds, refers to his resurrection and ascension. The hymn in Phil. 2, also quoted above, identifies Jesus as the messiah or Christ. His testimony before Pilate is also referred to in the creed contained in First Tim. 6:13: "In the presence of God, who gives life to all things, and of Christ Jesus, who in his testimony before Pontius Pilate made the good confession. . . ." In Acts 10:42 a creed states that after the resurrection Jesus told his followers to preach that he is the one who will judge all persons: "He commanded us to preach to the people and to testify that he is the one ordained by God as judge of the living and the dead."[98]

The creed found in Romans 4:25 is also pre-Pauline and clearly shows the early church's perspective that the death and resurrection of Jesus was seen as an act of redemption that justifies persons from their sin: ". . . who (Jesus our Lord) was handed over to death for our trespasses and was raised for our justification."[99]

These are examples of creeds and hymns that, to the best of our knowledge, existed prior to *any* available writings. These ancient creeds and hymns coincide well with the accounts of the New Testament gospels concerning many aspects of the life, death, and resurrection of Jesus of Nazareth. They are the earliest sources we have concerning his person. (See appendix A for some passages that may be considered hymnic or creedal in nature.)

For the purposes of this book, I am only attempting to show that there is strong and very early evidence *for the proposition that prior to the Pauline letters (that is, within the first two decades of the church's existence), there were oral liturgical formulae that substantially corroborate the history set forth in the New Testament gospel accounts.* The evidence is consistent with the information contained in the gospels, and none of the evidence indicates that the canonical gospels contain information that is inconsistent with the material contained in these very early sources. The evidence demonstrates that these liturgical formulae were used in worship at a time when eyewitnesses to Jesus' life and execution were available to correct or criticize their content. We have no evidence whatsoever that any such correction or criticism ever existed. (For example, there is no comparable evidence for preexisting, early creeds, hymns, and liturgical formulae in the gnostic gospels, including the gospel of Thomas or the gospel of Judas. As I shall discuss in chapter 7, the overwhelming consensus of New Testament scholars is that the gnostic gospels were written in the mid- to late second century, approximately 100 years after the canonical gospels and approximately 125 or more years after the dates of the preexisting creeds and hymns contained in the canonical letters and writings. See chapter 7 for a description of substantial evidence of a late second-century date for the gospel of Thomas.)

Martin Hengel has devoted a lifetime of research to the study of the development of the Christian church in its earliest post-Easter community in Jerusalem to its broader and eventual worldwide mission. His focus has been the first thirty years of Christian history. His work is contrary to some contemporary speculative theories that carry the notion that the *very earliest* Christianity was a chaos of competing diverse core beliefs. Although he recognizes some diversity in the early church, he is amazed at the coherent unity involved in the earliest, primitive faith:

> For all the multiplicity brought about by the work of the Spirit, I would still see *earliest* Christianity as an intrinsically connected and in essentials quite amazingly coherent movement which developed out of the activity

of Jesus and the "saving event" of his crucifixion and resurrection. A link with the earthly and exalted Lord and the eschatological gift of the Spirit remained the bond which held together all the Christian groups which we find within the New Testament (cf. e.g., 1 Cor. 15.11), though in individual cases the accents may have been placed differently. Anyone who wants to reduce earliest Christianity to often quite different and indeed unconnected "lines of development" can no longer explain why the church in the second century remained a unity despite all the deviations and how the New Testament canon could come into being. In their view the church should have fallen apart into countless groups.[100]

The creeds, hymns, and other liturgical formulae in the New Testament letters date back to the first two decades following Jesus' crucifixion. They give a unified, coherent portrait of Jesus that is consistent with the gospel accounts. Although several scholars attempt to argue for the existence of alternative, equally valid forms of Christianity that date back to the mid-first century, there is no evidence of any first-century compositions that support their position. They inevitably rely on speculations concerning second-century compositions without any hard evidence of an alternative line of Christian development from the first century. This is not an issue that should be determined by what is politically correct today, but an issue that should be decided on the basis of historical method and an examination of the historical evidence. The available hard evidence is found in the earliest known liturgical formulae embedded in the first-century New Testament documents, and, as discussed in this book, those formulae present a consistent portrait of Jesus as God incarnate.

IN THE SYNOPTIC AND JOHANNINE GOSPELS JESUS USED THE TERM "I AM" (*EGŌ EIMI*), WORDS THAT FUNCTION AS THE NAME OF GOD IN THE FIRST CENTURY; HENCE HIS CONVICTION FOR BLASPHEMY IN HIS TRIAL BEFORE THE SANHEDRIN

In chapter 4 I will describe why the canonical gospels can be reliably dated to a time when there were eyewitnesses available to correct any errors. The availability of eyewitnesses and the evidence of the reliability of the oral transmission of stories and sayings of Jesus discussed in chapter 5 present a stable foundation for the trustworthiness of the gospel accounts. With this in mind, I will now discuss some of the evidence from these accounts concerning the perspective of Jesus as God incarnate. From time to time some persons raise the question why Jesus did not say directly, "I am God." Well, the evidence from the gospel accounts indicate that he actually did.[1]

3.1 "I AM" (*EGŌ EIMI*) STATEMENTS IN THE SYNOPTIC GOSPELS AND THE FIRST-CENTURY JEWISH CONCEPT OF BLASPHEMY INDICATE THAT JESUS' WORDS WERE INTERPRETED AS REFERRING TO HIMSELF AS DIVINE.

In each of the gospels the actions of Jesus are knowingly likened to the actions of God. For example, in Mark, Jesus is often presented as having authority over the world of natural forces. In one chapter, Mark gives a narrative where Jesus is asleep in the stern of a boat when a great windstorm causes the waves to threaten the boat. His disciples wake him and he orders the wind and the sea to be still. His disciples are filled with great awe and ask each other, "Who then is this, that even the wind and the sea obey him?"[2]

Similarly, Mark writes about the miracle of Jesus walking on the sea near the disciples' boat. When the disciples cry out, he immediately speaks to them and says, "Take heart, it is I; do not be afraid." The precise Greek is actually very important here because not only does Mark present Jesus as one with authority over the world of natural forces, but the words of Jesus are translated more accurately as "Have courage! *I am*; do not be afraid." Focus on the words "I am" (*egō eimi*). These are the words used in the Septuagint, the Greek translation of the Old Testament, that function as the name of God. (The Septuagint was in use at the time of Jesus and at the time of the writing of the gospel of Mark.) When Moses is in the presence of the burning bush receiving the charge from God to go to Egypt and set the Israelites free, God identifies himself as "I Am":

> But Moses said to God, "If I come to the Israelites and say to them, 'The God of your ancestors has sent me to you,' and they ask me, 'What is his name?' what shall I say to them?" God said to Moses, "I Am Who I Am." He said further, "I am has sent me to you."[3]

In the Septuagint the words "I Am" are translated into Greek as *egō eimi*. *Egō eimi* are the precise Greek words in the gospel of Mark that Jesus uses in reference to himself, given to encourage the disciples and as a reason for them not to be afraid. These are also the same Greek words contained in the gospel of Matthew's rendition of the story of Jesus walking on the sea. In Matthew, Jesus refers to himself as "I Am" (*egō eimi*).[4] Likewise, in the gospel of John's description of this miracle, Jesus refers to himself as *egō eimi* ("I am"). By using these words, Mark, Matthew, and John all provide evidence of a distinct transcendent view of Jesus as divine.

The signals of this transcendent view are also present in the last sentence of the gospel of Matthew, where Jesus gives assurance of his presence to the end of the age, which requires one to think of him as intrinsically divine.

Go therefore and make disciples of all nations, baptizing them in the name of the Father and of the Son and of the Holy Spirit, and teaching them to obey everything that I have commanded you. And remember, *I am (egō eimi)* with you always, to the end of the age.[5]

The charge of blasphemy in referring to himself as God's Son is the reason for Jesus' condemnation at his trial as recorded in the fourteenth chapter of Mark. Here Jesus also responds using *egō eimi*, a claim that infuriates the high priest, chief priests, elders, and assembled scribes:

Again the high priest asked him, "Are you the Messiah, the Son of the Blessed One?"
Jesus said, "I am [*egō eimi*]: and
'you will see the Son of Man
seated at the right hand of
the Power,'
and coming with the clouds
of heaven."
Then the high priest tore his clothes and said, "Why do we still need witnesses? You have heard his blasphemy! What is your decision?" All of them condemned him as deserving death.[6]

The reference to the high priest's tearing his clothes demonstrates that Jesus' response was taken as a statement that he was divine. In Jewish tradition the high priest was to tear his garments if he ever heard blasphemy. The author is clearly portraying Jesus as a transcendent, divine figure. Hurtado noted that the Gospel of Mark was written prior to 70 and consequently contains evidence of Jewish opposition to the Jesus devotion of Christians in a pre-70 context. In examining the Markan description of Jesus' trial before the Sanhedrin, Hurtado makes two observations: (1) the charge of blasphemy was clearly the basis for the verdict that Jesus should die; and (2) the charge of blasphemy was a direct reaction to Jesus' affirming his divine sonship and transcendent nature ("the Christ, the Son of the Blessed"). The issue of Jesus' claim to divinity is the key issue of the trial. As Hurtado wrote: "The account of the Sanhedrin 'trial' of Jesus in GMark is very much focused on this key religious issue. Either these Christological claims amount to a radical infringement upon the honor of God, or they are true."[7]

Bruce M. Metzger[8] agreed with this analysis and wrote about the similarity between the gospel of John and the earliest literary stratum of the Synoptic gospels, which gives honor to Jesus as divine. Because of his stature in New Testament research over the past seventy years, it is worth quoting Metzger's position at length:

> More than once the Jews sought to kill Jesus for blasphemy, "because he was not only breaking the sabbath, but was also calling God his own Father, thereby making himself equal to God" (John 5:18, compare 10:30–33). By means of a series of unparalleled statements, such as "I am the bread of life" (John 6:35), I am the light of the world" (8:12), and "I am the resurrection and the life" (11:25), Jesus is represented as utilizing the theophanic formula that in the Old Testament is reserved for the most exalted descriptions of Jehovah (i.e., Yahweh; see Exod. 3:14 margin). It is not surprising that this Gospel concludes with an account in which the risen Jesus not only accepts the apostle Thomas's words of adoration, "My Lord and my God!" but also pronounces a blessing on all who make a similar confession (John 20:28–29).
>
> Though the language used by the Synoptic Gospels concerning Jesus as the Son of God differs from that of the Fourth Gospel, the impression that they make on the reader is the same: Jesus both claims and receives the honor that is rendered only to the Deity. In addition to a dozen or so Synoptic passages where the title "the Son of God" is applied to him by others, with his express approval (such as Matt. 16:16; Mark 3:11, 5:7, 14:61; Luke 8:28), both Q and Mark represent Jesus as speaking of himself as "the Son" or calling God his Father in a new and unique way (see the discussion of *Abba*, pp. 171–72). Both directly (in his acknowledgment before Caiaphas, Mark 14:62) and indirectly (in the parable of the wicked tenants, Mark 12:1–9) Jesus makes claim to be not only God's son, but *the one* beloved Son of the Father, who will come with the clouds of heaven. In one of the most important christological passages in the New Testament, preserved in Q (Matt. 11:27; Luke 10:22; Q is short for *Quelle* or "source" in German and is a hypothetical text source for material— about two hundred verses—common to the gospel of Matthew and the gospel of Luke but not appearing in the gospel of Mark). Jesus speaks of his "unshared sonship": "All things have been handed over to me by my Father, and no one knows the Son except the Father, and no one knows the Father except the Son and anyone to whom the Son chooses to reveal him." Here, in the oldest literary stratum of the Synoptics, and with language that is every bit as exalted as that used in the Fourth Gospel, Jesus claims not only that he alone stands in a special relation to God,

but also that he is the only one through whom others can be brought into a similar relation.[9]

Bruce Metzger's conviction of Jesus' divine claim is palpable in his writings. Metzger was one of the foremost New Testament scholars of the twentieth century. He cast a giant light on New Testament research, chairing the most significant global New Testament committees. A humble and kind man, he remained convinced of the classical, orthodox faith until his recent death.

Before moving on to the next section, I want to clarify that Metzger's reference to "the Jews" should not be interpreted to mean the Jewish people as a whole, but rather a small number of Jewish leaders. After Jesus' trial before the Sanhedrin, he was handed over to the Roman governor Pilate who gave the order for his execution. I want to join New Testament scholar Craig A. Evans in emphasizing that Christian doctrine is that all of us sent Jesus to the cross. He died for the sins of the whole world. No one should blame the people of Israel for the death of Jesus:

> One thing needs to be made crystal clear; the Jewish people should never be blamed for the condemnation and death of Jesus. Not only is such an accusation bad theology, it is bad history. Historically speaking, Jesus was condemned by a very small number of influential Jewish men. He was not condemned by the people as a whole. Even those who cried out for his crucifixion later in the day were but a relatively small number. Theologically speaking, Jesus died for the sins of the whole human race. In that sense we all sent him to the cross. No one particular people should be blamed."[10]

3.2 WORSHIP (*PROSKYNEIN*) OF JESUS IN THE SYNOPTIC GOSPELS SIGNALS A TRANSCENDENT PERSPECTIVE OF JESUS' NATURE.

Matthew's frequent use of the Greek word *proskynein* in describing the reverence people give to Jesus also signals a transcendent view of him. The Magi tell King Herod that they are searching for Jesus so that they might worship (*proskynein*) the newborn child. This word can mean reverence, but it can also mean divine worship, as *proskynein* is also the word that Jesus used in Matthew to refer to the worship of God.[11]

It is in this sense of worship of the divine that Luke, the author of Acts, clearly gives divine status to Jesus, concluding his gospel with a description of the disciples giving Jesus full reverence as "they worshipped (*proskynēsantes*)" Jesus.[12]

Jesus' transcendent nature is also depicted in Matthew at the conclusion of the story of his walking on the water, when he is worshipped as the Son of God: "And those in the boat worshipped (*proskynein*) him, saying, 'Truly you are the Son of God.'" Matthew is consistent with all four canonical gospels in presenting Jesus as God's *unique* "Son." All of the authors of the New Testament gospels affirm Jesus as the unique, divine Son of God.[13] This is a consistent position in Matthew where Jesus is described as unique and called "*the* Son." In describing Peter's confession of Jesus as the Messiah, the author of Matthew quotes Peter as saying, "You are the Messiah (*Christos*), the Son (*ho huis*) of the Living God."[14] Similarly, Jesus refers to himself as God's unique Son, using the definite article (*the* or *ho*), and indicates his transcendent status in describing his close relationship with the Father in the eleventh chapter of Matthew: "All things have been handed over to me by my Father, and no one knows the Son (*ho huis*) except the Father and anyone to whom *the* Son (*ho huis*) chooses to reveal him."[15]

The close association of Jesus with God as the unique Son of God with divine attributes is corroborated in the last sentence of Matthew quoted above, where Jesus is presented with transcendent status and charges his disciples to baptize "in the name of the Father and of the Son and of the Holy Spirit."[16]

This is consistent with Jesus' eschatological end-time statement earlier in Mark, where he identifies himself as the unique son of the Father by using the definite article and referring to himself as *the* Son: "But about that day or hour no one knows, neither the angels in heaven, nor the Son (*ho huis*), but only the Father."[17]

Similarly, in Luke, Jesus is quoted as using the definite article three times in the same sentence where he refers to himself as *the* Son (*ho huis*), emphasizing his unique status with the Father as he is given authority over all things: "All things have been handed over to me by my Father; and no one knows who the Son (*ho huis*) is except the Father, or who the Father is except the Son (*ho huis*) and anyone to whom the Son (*ho huis*) chooses to reveal to him."[18]

CHAPTER 3

3.3 "I AM" STATEMENTS IN THE GOSPEL OF JOHN ARE IN ABSOLUTE FORM AND IN FORMS WITH MEANINGFUL PREDICATES; IN EACH CASE THE "I AM" IS ASSOCIATED WITH THE NAME OF GOD.

The use of *egō eimi* as a saying of Jesus is also frequently used in the Gospel of John. In the temple in Jerusalem, Jesus responds to the crowd and suggests his preexistence by applying the words *egō eimi* to himself: "Very truly, I tell you before Abraham was, I am [*egō eimi*]." The crowd then picks up stones to kill him, since death by stoning was the penalty for blasphemy.[19]

Sometimes Jesus' statements are in an absolute form, such as in John 13:19, where Jesus asserts that he is telling his disciples what will happen before it happens so that they "may believe that *I am* [*egō eimi*]." Some English translations of this verse end with "I am he," but the Greek more clearly makes the divine reference, ending with only *egō eimi* or I am.

The gospel of John also contains numerous statements by Jesus where *egō eimi* is followed with a predicate explaining a certain aspect or characteristic of Jesus. For example, "*I am* the light of the world" (John 8:12); *I am* the resurrection and the life" (John 11:25); "*I am* the way, the truth, and the life" (John 14:6); "*I am* the true vine, and my Father is the vine grower" (John 15:1). In each case the Greek words are *egō eimi*, representing a powerful association of Jesus with the name of God.[20]

3.4 PREEXISTENCE IN THE GOSPEL OF JOHN MATCHES THE PREEXISTING LITURGICAL FORMULAE INCORPORATED INTO PAUL'S LETTERS.

As mentioned in connection with Jesus' reference to existing as *I am* prior to the time of Abraham, the gospel of John portrays Jesus as affirming his preexistence. In the eleventh chapter the author quotes Jesus as saying, "*I am* the bread that came down from heaven."[21] As indicated in my examination of evidence from Paul's earlier writings, the concept of Jesus' preexistence was prevalent in the first two decades of the earliest church. A clear statement of preexistence begins the gospel of John:

In the beginning was the Word, and the Word was with God, and the Word was God. He was in the beginning with God. All things came into being through him, and without him not one thing came into being. . . . He was in the world, and the world came into being through him; yet the world did not know him. . . . And the Word became flesh and lived among us, and we have seen his glory, the glory as of a father's only son, full of grace and truth.[22]

The gospel of John is consistent with the evidence of the worship of Jesus as preexisting as noted in our examination of the devotional patterns and prayers of the earliest church set forth in the ancient creeds and hymns incorporated into Acts and the New Testament letters. As previously stated, these letters begin within seventeen to twenty years of the crucifixion and the hymns and creeds incorporated into these letters demonstrate the theme of preexistence of Jesus from an even earlier date in the life of the young church. Preexistence is a consistent theme in John and reflected in many passages. In one striking saying Jesus claims, "Whoever has seen me has seen the Father."[23] While maintaining the uniqueness of the Father, the gospel of John presents Jesus as one who manifests God's glory on earth and is associated with God in such a way that he is to be worshipped and glorified as the Father is worshipped and glorified.[24]

3.5 HONOR AND EFFICACY OF JESUS' NAME IN PRAYER AND WORSHIP IN THE SYNOPTIC GOSPELS INDICATE A CLOSE ASSOCIATION OF JESUS WITH GOD.

This close association with God is also manifested in the efficacy given to prayer and worship in the name of Jesus. Throughout the gospel of John, the followers of Jesus are told to pray in his name. This is consistent with the honor of Jesus' name contained in the Synoptic gospels; so in Mark we read: "Whoever welcomes one such child *in my name* welcomes me";[25] "whoever gives you a cup of water to drink because you bear *the name of Christ* will by no means lose the reward."[26] Jesus' name is seen as efficacious in healings and in exorcisms in the seventh chapter of Matthew[27] and the tenth chapter of Luke.[28] As noted above, the emphasis in the early church on the use of Jesus' name is well established from the evidence of earlier writings, such as Paul's first letter to the Corinthians, where he writes:

To the church of God that is in Corinth . . . together with all those who in every place call on the name of our Lord Jesus Christ, both their Lord and ours. . . . Now I appeal to you, brothers and sisters by the name of our Lord Jesus Christ . . .[29]

The gospel of John, the Synoptic gospels, and the letters of the New Testament consistently set forth a theme that the name of Jesus was worthy of devotion and efficacy that had previously only been reserved for God.

3.6 ONE CANNOT REGARD JESUS MERELY AS THE MESSIAH IN THE FULFILLMENT OF OLD TESTAMENT PROPHECY.

One cannot regard Jesus merely as the Messiah, and not also as the Lord. The two are different and distinct concepts. Although the early Christian community clearly regarded Jesus as the fulfillment of the ancient messianic prophecies, the ancient Jewish concept of reverence for the Messiah was not equivalent to a reverence for God. One must understand the profound distinction between the Jewish reverence for God and for other agents, messengers, or messiahs. In Jewish thought, God is distinct from other beings, even other "divine" or spiritual beings, such as angels. When one attempts to explain the very early devotional patterns of worship of Jesus in the most primitive Christian community, one cannot equate the kind of reverence given to other beings and the reverence given to Jesus. In our earliest Christian sources, we see within the first two decades of the church, a devotion to Jesus as divine. This is a unique and unprecedented movement in an exclusivist monotheistic Second Temple Judaism.

If one is to engage in serious historical analysis, one needs to account for the worship of Jesus linking him with God in an unprecedented and startling way. Hurtado advises the historian not "to blur unhelpfully the very real differences between ancient Jewish reverence for martyrs, messiahs, or other figures, and the distinctive pattern of devotion to Jesus in early Christian sources." He goes on to note that there is simply no evidence for any other figure in Second Temple Judaism receiving the kind of divine devotion accorded to Jesus that so closely associated him with God. One cannot use the reverence accorded to Jewish martyrs or even the Jewish Messiah as a sufficient historical precedent.[30]

As noted above, the earliest Christians understood Psalm 110:1 as a reflection of this linking of Jesus with God:

> The Lord says to my lord,
> 'Sit at my right hand
> until I make your enemies your
> footstool.'

In the gospel of Matthew, Jesus asks the Pharisees about this verse. First he raises the question of whose son is the messiah? They respond that the messiah is to be the son of David.[31] David wrote Psalm 110 so Jesus asks them why David called the messiah "Lord?" He then asks, "If David thus calls him Lord, how can he be his son?"

Psalm 110 is cited in reference to Jesus in Acts 2:34-35 and in Hebrews 1:13; 10:12-13. In Acts, Peter refers to Psalm 16:10 as a prophecy of Jesus's resurrection and then gives the following summation to his fellow Israelites:

> This Jesus God raised up, and of that all of us are witnesses. Being therefore exalted at the right hand of God, and having received from the Father the promise of the Holy Spirit, he has poured out this that you both see and hear. For David did not ascend into the heavens, but he himself says,
>
> The Lord said to my Lord
> 'Sit at my right hand,
>   until I make your enemies your
>   footstool.'
>
> Therefore let the entire house of Israel know with certainty that God has made him *both Lord and Messiah*, this Jesus whom you crucified.

One may argue that, after Easter, Peter remembered the words of Jesus to the Pharisees and saw a divine nature attached to the messiah. This is consistent with the very early pre-literary oral creedal language that the author of the letter to the Hebrews incorporated into Hebrews 1:3 in reference to Psalm 110:

> He is the reflection of God's glory and the exact imprint of God's very being, and he sustains all things by his powerful word. When he had

made purification for sins, *he sat down at the right hand of the Majesty on high.*[32]

The author of the Hebrews goes on to make the distinction between reverence to God the begotten Son and reverence for angels:

For to which of the angels did God ever say, 'You are
    my Son; today I have *begotten* you? ...Or again,
I will be his Father, and he will be my Son...' But of the
Son he says, "Your throne, *O God*, is forever and ever...
But to which of the angels has he ever said,
        'Sit at my right hand
            Until I make your enemies a
            footstool for your feet?'[33]

The first two lines above are a quotation of Psalm 2:7. The reverence for the Son appears to be the reverence accorded to God. This interpretation fits well with another Messianic verse from Psalm 45:

Your throne, O God, endures
        forever and ever,
    Your royal scepter is a scepter of equity:
you love righteousness and hate
        wickedness.
    Therefore God, your God, has
        anointed you
    with the oil of gladness beyond
        your companions . . .[34]

I am not arguing that the Jewish expectation was for a divine Messiah (even though I will later note some evidence to that effect from the Dead Sea Scrolls). I am saying that after Jesus's resurrection his disciples learned the meaning of the Old Testament writings and had their eyes opened to the divine status of the Messiah hidden in these scriptures. This was the experience of the persons on the road to Emmaus described in Luke 24:13-25 where the risen Jesus (see Chapter 6, *infra*) began with Moses and all the prophets and interpreted to them the things about himself in all the scriptures. In Peter's great speech on Pentecost he said that God had made Jesus *both* Lord and Messiah. The idea of Jesus being both God and man, however, was not part of the "mainstream" Jewish expectation for the Messiah.

The early church interpreted the Jewish scriptures as proof texts for Jesus as the messiah. For example, the gospel of Matthew has numerous citations to Jewish prophesies being fulfilled in Jesus of Nazareth. Proof texts arguments also pervade the gospels of Mark, Luke and John and the early Christian letters. The very early evidence is consistent with Peter's speech in Acts and the worship of Jesus as divine.

I have already described the very early Christian confession formula incorporated by Paul in Romans 4:25 (See Section 2.6.1 b., *supra*) that draws upon the dramatic description of the suffering servant from Isaiah 52:12-53:12. (If you have not read this passage recently, please take the time to read it today, if possible.) At verse 52:13, the suffering servant is prophesied to be "exalted and lifted up." In Isaiah these words always refer to God. This reference to God is also consistent with the familiar words that we sing in George F. Handel's *The Messiah* that quotes Isaiah 9:6-7: "For unto us a child is born, unto us a son is given, and the government shall be upon his shoulder, and his name shall be called: Wonderful, Counselor, the Mighty God, the everlasting Father, the Prince of Peace."

A review of the vast amount of literature debating the arguments pro and con for the fulfillment of Old Testament prophecies in the person of Jesus of Nazareth is beyond the scope of this book. An analysis of the arguments would require separate volumes. The proof from prophecy appeal pervades the understanding of the earliest Christian community and permeates the earliest Christian documents. This appeal continued in the early church through the writings of the second century church fathers and still continues in contemporary exegetical writing. Perhaps the earliest high point of this appeal was in the writing of Justin's *Dialogue with Trypho* written in approximately 160 A.D. It is important to note that Justin is passing on an earlier tradition of the first century church regarding proof text passages from the Old Testament that support the concept of Jesus fulfilling these passages. A full description of the *Dialogue* is not necessary for my purposes. I only want to draw the reader's attention to Justin's focus on Joshua's name and its relation to the name of Jesus.

The name for Jesus in Greek is *Iēsous*. This name is also the Greek name for Joshua. With respect to the Hebrew language, the name of Jesus is a derivative of the Hebrew name *Yeshua*. *Yeshua* is a shorter version of the name of Joshua (*Yehoshua*). *Yehoshua* is from a Hebrew verb (*yasha'*) that means "to deliver or save" and is a form of the name for God (*Yahweh*). So the etymology of Jesus's name stands for *"Yahweh saves."* (See Matthew 1:21: "She will bear a son, and you are to name him Jesus, for he will save his people from their sins.")[35] Justin argues that the name of Jesus is the name of God in the Old Testament. Hurtado summarizes Justin's position:

> Justin lays out the argument that *Iēsous* is actually the name of God referred to in the book of Exodus. Here the crucial text is Exodus 23:20, where God promises to send his 'angel/messenger' (*angelos*) to guard Israel and bring them into the Promised Land; God warns Israel not to disobey this figure 'for my name is in him.' Justin then contends that 'he who led your fathers into the land is called by this name "Jesus" [*Iēsous*] ('Joshua')'. Further, he points out that this name was actually given to the figure (whose previous name was Hoshea, Num. 13:16), and he contends that the statement that this figure was given 'my name' (i.e., God's name) means that the name of Jesus/Joshua is the name of God.[36]

Although I will not address the enormous number of Old Testament verses that have been listed as relating to messianic prophecies, I will address a controversial phrase in Psalm 22. This psalm of David is quoted in very early Christian documents (e.g., see Mt. 27:35, 46; Mk 15:34; Jn 19:24; Heb 2:12). It was composed hundreds of years before crucifixion became a standard form of execution, but the psalm contains a description of suffering similar to the suffering one would have during a crucifixion. For example, the psalmist describes the dislocation of all of his bones (vv. 14, 17), his thirst and severe dehydration (v. 15). His enemies cast lots for his clothes (v. 18). Most significantly, his hands and his feet are pierced.(v.16).

The text of Psalm 22:16 (v. 17 in Hebrew) is the subject of substantial debate. The words, "they have pierced" (Greek, *oruxsan*) are found in the Septuagint, the oldest translation of the Jewish text completed centuries before the birth of Jesus. Most of the Hebrew Masoretic texts give the following reading: "For dogs have encircled me; like a lion my hands and my feet." The phrases "they have pierced" (*ka' aru*) and "like a lion" (*ka' ari*) have identical Hebrew letters, except that "pierced" has the Hebrew letter *vav* at the end of the word and "lion" ends with the Hebrew letter *yod*. Because of the similarity in form a scribe could make a mistake and write one letter for the other. So which meaning is correct?

The oldest Hebrew copy of this psalm in our possession comes from the Dead Sea Scrolls and from the discovery of a fragment at Nahal

A CASE FOR THE DIVINITY OF JESUS

Hever that contained the words in question. The last letter of the key word is *vav*. The meaning in the psalm is "pierced." The evidence from the Septuagint, the oldest Hebrew manuscript or fragment in our possession, and several Masoretic manuscripts read *ka' aru* or pierced. This wording is not a later Christian interpolation.

This only makes logical sense. After all, the phrase, "like a lion my hands and feet" is not only without a verb, but is nonsensical. Moreover, the portrait of the sufferer is consistent with what we know occurs in the physical trauma of a crucifixion. Physicians from the Mayo Clinic published an article describing the physical ramifications of a crucifixion. The psalm agrees with their description. The word pierced is also consistent with other prophetic verses, such as Isaiah 53:5 where a suffering servant is "pierced through" (*mecholal*) for our transgressions, and Zechariah 12:10: "They will look on me, the one they have pierced (*dagaru*), and they will mourn him as one mourns for an only son."

I note that recent texts from Qumran indicate that the concept of a divine son was part of the messianic expectations of some sections of pre-Christian Judaism. Texts from the Dead Sea Scrolls attest that some Jews believed that the Messiah would possess divine qualities. For example, he will be "begotten of God" (1QSa); he will be called "Son of God" and "Son of the Most High" (4Q246); heaven and earth will obey him; he will heal the sick and raise the dead (4Q521); and, he will be as Melchizedek and the very things said of God should be said of him (1Q13).[37]

My partner and colleague Hurd Baruch has called my attention to a persuasive argument that neither he nor I have ever seen articulated anywhere else. Pope Benedict XVI has made a powerful case for Jesus's divinity (and Messiahship) grounded in the Torah itself.[38]

The Pope's thesis is based especially on Deuteronomy 18:15, the verse in which God makes this promise through the lips of Moses: "The Lord your God will raise up for you a prophet like me from among you . . . him you shall heed." This prophecy was applied to Jesus by some in his lifetime, but the expected Prophet was a figure distinct from the Messiah.[39] Origen had a glimmer of the promise of this passage: "some prophet was specially expected who would be similar to Moses in some respect, to mediate between God and humanity, and who would receive the covenant from God and give the new covenant to those who became his disciples."[40] The Pope explains his own, much fuller, insight as follows:

The promise of a 'prophet like me' thus implicitly contains an even greater expectation: that the last prophet, the new Moses, will be granted what was refused to the first one—a real, immediate vision of the fact of God, and thus the ability to speak entirely from seeing, not just from looking at God's back. *This naturally entails the further expectation that the new Moses will be the mediator of a greater covenant than the one that Moses was able to bring down from Sinai (cf. Heb 9:11-24). . . . What was true of Moses only in fragmentary form has now been fully realized in the person of Jesus: He lives before the face of God, not just as a friend, but as a Son; he lives in the most intimate unity with the* Father. We have to start from here if we are truly to understand the figure of Jesus as it is presented to us in the New Testament; all that we are told about his words, deeds, sufferings, and glory is anchored here. This is the central point, and if we leave it out of the account, we fail to grasp what the figure of Jesus is really all about, so that it becomes self-contradictory and in the end, unintelligible.[41]

That is the starting point, but not the end of the argument, for the Pope has to demonstrate why he puts Jesus forward as "the new Moses." His explanation is twofold—the first part being that the teachings of Jesus are so radical and profound that they could only have come from Jesus's face-to-face communion with the Father. Indeed, "Without this inner grounding, his teachings would be pure presumption"; "his Sonship in communion with the Father—is the prior condition that makes possible the irruption of a new and broad reality without betrayal or high-handedness."[42]

The second part of the Pope's explanation shows that Jesus does not derogate from the role of Israel but greatly enhances it by universalizing the salvation promised to Abraham and his descendants:

He has brought the God of Israel to the nations, so that all the nations now pray to him and recognize Israel's Scriptures as his word, the word of the living God. He has brought the gift of universality, which was the one great definitive promise to Israel and the world. *This universality, this faith in the one God of Abraham, Isaac, and Jacob—extended now in Jesus' new family to all nations over and above the bonds of descent according to the flesh—is the fruit of Jesus' work. It is what proves him to be the Messiah. It signals a new interpretation of the messianic promise that is based on Moses and the Prophets, but also opens them up in a completely new way.*

The vehicle of this universalization is the new family, whose only admission requirement is communion with Jesus, communion in God's will.

. . . It is entry into the family of those who call God Father and who can do so because they belong to a "we"—formed of those who are united with Jesus and, by listening to him, united with the will of the Father, thereby attaining to the heart of the obedience intended by the Torah.[43]

In sum, the Torah expressly indicates that God's saving revelation was *not* complete in what had already been announced. Moses prophesied the coming of a second Moses—a divine one, who would speak with God face-to-face. The proof that Jesus was the one Moses foresaw is to be found in the fulfillment through Jesus of God's promise to all mankind, that he would use Israel as the instrument for making the gentiles, too, his adopted sons and daughters, with an inheritance of eternal life.

4

RELIABILITY OF THE CANONICAL GOSPEL ACCOUNTS IS SUPPORTED BY THE HISTORICAL EVIDENCE

Some persons who may not have examined the Christian faith in depth believe that the essence of the faith is that one should be a good person, have a good heart or a benevolent disposition. In other words, they view Christianity as a moral code or ethical system. Consequently, many of the historical aspects of the faith may not be considered by them to be as important as the issue of how one follows this code or how one lives a life of integrity. Although living a good life or having a benevolent disposition is an important aspect of the Christian faith, the real essence of the faith is centered on the historical person of Jesus of Nazareth and on one's communion with him. Jesus' teaching is important, but his person, his atonement, his resurrection, and his ongoing communion with men and women are at the center of the faith.

A significant question is whether this communion has its basis in actual historical events. The Christian faith is a historical faith. What exactly happened in the life, death, and resurrection of Jesus is central to the question of the efficacy of his actions and life. In other words, if Jesus is not the person described in the New Testament documents, but only a good moral teacher, the faith is merely a moral system, and life lived in communion with him is an illusion.

The reliability and trustworthiness of the New Testament documents are important in forming one's opinion of Jesus and the significance of his life, death, and resurrection. The letters of the New Testament with which we have been concerned in our study are not widely disputed with respect to their reliability by a wide consensus of scholars. When we come to the question of the origin and reliability of the canonical gospel accounts, there is some disagreement concerning their authenticity. The evidence, however, indicates that the trustworthiness of these gospel accounts rests on a rather stable and consistent foundation.

4.1 THE ACCURACY OF OUR COPIES OF NEW TESTAMENT WRITINGS CAN BE AUTHENTICATED.

We have reasonable evidence to believe that the documents of the New Testament in our possession accurately reflect the core Christian faith described in their original composition. As many authors have noted, we have many more copies of ancient New Testament manuscripts available to us than we have of any other ancient classical documents that are accepted by historians as authentic.[1] We have complete manuscripts of the New Testament dating to no later than AD 350 and fragments dating from AD 100 to 125 and possibly earlier. In total, we have about 5,500 ancient Greek manuscripts. Because of the vast number of manuscripts and the very minor differences in their texts, we can be quite certain that we have the core of the earliest versions. The academic discipline of textual criticism has the purpose of determining the precise original wording of historical documents. Because one or two mistakes easily can happen in the process of copying documents, the greater the number of ancient manuscripts available to the textual critic, the more precisely he or she can reconstruct the exact wording of the original manuscript. In the words of F. F. Bruce: "Fortunately, if the great number of MSS (ancient manuscripts) increases the number of scribal errors, it increases proportionately the means of correcting such errors, so that the margin of doubt left in the process of recovering the exact original wording is not so large as might be feared; it is in truth remarkably small."[2] For corroboration on his conclusion, Bruce recalls the verdict of Sir Frederic Kenyon, truly one of the great scholars regarding the authenticity of ancient manuscripts:

CHAPTER 4

The interval then between the dates of original composition and the earliest extant evidence becomes so small as to be in fact negligible, and the last foundation for any doubt that the Scriptures have come down to us substantially as they were written has now been removed. Both the *authenticity* and the *general integrity* of the books of the New Testament may be regarded as finally established.[3]

4.2. BART EHRMAN'S BOOK *MISQUOTING JESUS* CARRIES A SOMEWHAT MISLEADING TITLE BECAUSE THE BOOK DOES NOT SET FORTH ANY EXAMPLES OF VARIANTS IN THE MANUSCRIPTS THAT REQUIRE AN ALTERATION IN ANY SIGNIFICANT CORE BELIEF OF THE CHRISTIAN FAITH.

Bart Ehrman's recent book, *Misquoting Jesus*, carries a somewhat misleading title because the book does not set forth any examples of variants in the texts of the New Testament gospel accounts that require an alteration of the basic structure of the Christian faith. Ehrman addresses minor variations in texts that make no changes in the core beliefs of the New Testament authors. His deductions do not follow from the evidence presented; none of the textual variants cited requires an alteration in any significant core belief of the Christian faith.

Most New Testament scholars are puzzled by Ehrman's reaction to his discovery at Princeton Seminary that the manuscripts contain some scribal errors. Craig Evans, a distinguished New Testament scholar and a member of National Geographic Society's advisory board, notes that the existence of scribal errors is something that Ehrman should have learned at Moody Bible Institute or at Wheaton College because every student in New Testament studies is introduced to this aspect of the manuscripts in introductory courses in textual criticism. Ehrman's loss of faith took place during his second semester at Princeton in a course taught by Cullen Story on the gospel of Mark. When Ehrman realized that Mark (or a scribe copying his work) may have made a mistake by referring to Abiathar rather than Abiathar's father, Ahimelech, Ehrman decided to throw away his whole Christian faith: "Once I made that admission, the floodgates opened. For if there could be one little, picayune mistake in Mark 2, maybe there could be mistakes in other places as well."[4]

Evans is perplexed because this hardly seems like a sound rationale for doubting the reliability of the whole New Testament. It is important to recognize that Ehrman's position is that if the Bible contains one mistake, the whole Bible should be disregarded. This is a non sequitur; it does not follow logically from his discovery.

The truth of the Christian message is based on the resurrection of Jesus, not on the accuracy of every minor word in the New Testament. After all, the real issue is whether Jesus was raised from the dead. If he was, I would not be concerned with whether Abiathar or Ahimelech was the priest in David's time. In other words, if one knew for certain that Jesus of Nazareth rose from the dead, would he walk away from that knowledge because Mark or a scribe wrote the wrong name of an insignificant figure? I would think that he would want to know more about the meaning of the resurrection and learn from the eyewitnesses who appear to have been around when the creeds, hymns, and liturgical formulae were developed in worship settings.[5] As Craig Evans writes:

> The truth of the Christian message hinges not on the accuracy of Scripture or on our ability to harmonize the four Gospels but on the resurrection of Jesus. And the historical reliability of the Gospels does not hinge on the inerrancy of Scripture or on proof that no mistake of any kind can be described in them. Ehrman's struggle with faith—and I feel for him—grows out of mistaken expectations of the nature and function of Scripture, mistaken expectations that he was taught as a young, impressionable fundamentalist Christian.[6]

Ehrman's reputation as a scholar is enhanced by his study with Princeton's Bruce M. Metzger, a preeminent scholar in the textual study of the New Testament and the apocryphal literature. Ehrman dedicated his book to Metzger. As I noted above, Metzger was an erudite, humble man with a deep conviction in the reliability of the New Testament documents. His reaction to his textual critical work was one of an increasing commitment to his Christian faith, exactly the opposite of Ehrman's reaction. Metzger studied and taught at Princeton from 1938 until his recent death in February 2007. He held not only an endowed emeritus chair at the seminary but was also a member of the Institute for Advanced Studies where Einstein worked. Metzger chaired the Standard Bible Committee of the National Council of Churches and oversaw the revision of the *New Revised Standard Version of the Bible* (also published as *The New Oxford Bible*).

Anyone who reads Metzger's well-written classic on the New Testament will readily see the deep and committed belief of the author. In *The New Testament: Its Background, Growth and Content* (third edition), Metzger gives a detailed analysis of the historical and theological integrity of the New Testament, holding that over 90 percent of the New Testament text is solidly established and the remaining 10 percent does not require the alteration of any Christian doctrine. In referring to the variations among the New Testament manuscripts, most of which are simple misspellings and inconsequential details, he unequivocally concluded that none of the variants affects any Christian doctrine:

> It should be mentioned that, though there are thousands of divergencies of wording among the manuscripts of the Bible (more in the New Testament than in the Old), the overwhelming majority of such variant readings involve inconsequential details, such as alternative spellings, order of words, and interchange of synonyms. In these cases, as well as in the relatively few instances involving the substance of the record, scholars apply the techniques of textual criticism in order to determine with more or less probability what the original wording was. *In any event, no doctrine of the Christian faith depends solely upon a passage that is textually uncertain.*[7]

So why did Ehrman become an agnostic from his discovery of a wrong, inconsequential name in Mark 2 when his highly regarded mentor, Metzger, taught that no doctrine of the faith was challenged? As noted above, Evans thinks that Ehrman misunderstands the nature of the Christian faith. The good news of the faith is not about the inerrancy of every adjective or name in the New Testament, without regard to its significance. The New Testament documents are not viewed like the Qur'an—which is regarded as the dictated word of God, imbued with a holiness in its very existence—but as a faithful, historical portrait of the events of God's redeeming action in Jesus of Nazareth. As Evans notes, Peter's proclamation at the beginning of the church was about the resurrection, not about the inerrancy of every word in the Scripture: "Peter didn't stand up and proclaim, 'Men of Israel, I have good news; the Bible is verbally inspired and therefore inerrant and, moreover, the Gospels can be harmonized.'"[8]

The majority of scholars hold that God inspired but did not dictate. God used human beings who made mistakes, but this does not mean that the essentials were distorted. The doctrines on which the Christian faith rests have a secure historical foundation and a reliable, rational process of transmission, oral and written.[9] As Metzger wrote:

> It is obvious that it would be unwarranted to regard any of the Gospels as a journalist's verbatim report of what happened yesterday. What the evangelists have preserved for us is not a photographic reproduction of all the words and all the deeds of Jesus, but something more like four interpretative portraits. Each of these portraits presents distinctive high-lights of Jesus' person and work and taken together, the four provide a varied and balanced account of what Jesus said and did.[10]

The Christian faith is about the validity and witness to the life, teachings, crucifixion, and resurrection of Jesus of Nazareth, with an emphasis on the latter. The historical event of the resurrection is at the core of the preaching of the earliest church. I will explore the evidence for Jesus' resurrection in chapter 6, but for now I want to note the relevance of this evidence to the case for Jesus' divinity. In his recent book, *Was Jesus God?*, Oxford philosopher Richard Swinburne sets forth a powerful, logical philosophical argument that Jesus was God incarnate. Swinburne rightly claims that to give us an adequate reason to believe that Jesus was God, the signature of God should be placed on Jesus' life by an extraordinary act that only God could perform. Jesus' bodily resurrection would constitute such an act. It would be an authenticating miracle that would establish his claim of divinity.

The resurrection of Jesus is the event that turned the disciples around from frightened, desperate men and women to persons who were willing to face torture and death for the proclamation of the good news of the resurrection. Metzger was convinced of the truth of the resurrection of Jesus. He did not mince words in his conclusion:

> The evidence for the resurrection of Jesus Christ is overwhelming. Nothing in history is more certain than that the disciples believed that after being crucified, dead, and buried, Christ rose again from the tomb on the third day, and that at intervals thereafter he met and conversed with them. The most obvious proof that they believed this is the existence of the Christian church. It is simply inconceivable that the scattered and disheartened remnant could have found a rallying point and a gospel in the memory of him who had been put to death as a criminal, had they not been convinced that God owned him and accredited his mission by

raising him from the dead. It is a commonplace that every event in history must have an adequate cause. What caused such a radical change in these men's lives? The explanation is that something unprecedented had occurred: Jesus Christ was raised from the dead! Fifty-some days after the Crucifixion the apostolic preaching of Christ's resurrection began in Jerusalem with such power and persuasion that the evidence convinced thousands. Divergencies in detail are certainly to be found in the accounts of the first Easter, but these are such as one would expect from independent and excited witnesses. If the evangelist had fabricated the resurrection narratives, they would not have left obvious difficulties and discrepancies—such as those involving the number of angels at the tomb, the order of Jesus' appearances, and similar details. That the accounts have been left unreconciled, without any attempt to produce a single stereotyped narrative, inspires confidence in the fundamental honesty of those who transmitted the evidence.[11]

When one looks at the overall context of the transmission of the Christian tradition, oral and written, and the plethora of evidence from many sources supporting the orthodox position, one cannot simply dismiss the veracity of the proclamation because of inconsequential scribal errors. One cannot rationally decide to become an agnostic on the basis of such errors without considering the multiplicity of evidence contained throughout the entire New Testament and even non-Christian sources. For example, one cannot dismiss the teaching of the divinity of Jesus if one verse teaching such a doctrine is considered to be of questionable certainty. There is no such verse, but, assuming for the sake of argument that there was such a questionable verse, the divinity of Jesus would only be in question if the vast majority of the verses proclaiming his divinity were also uncertain. In other words, the question of the veracity of the New Testament orthodox position must be answered by examining the entire context of the available evidence.

Metzger commented that throughout his lifelong work of textual criticism his personal faith grew as the result of his work. He stated that his work had increased the basis for his personal faith because he could see the firmness with which the materials have come down to us with a multiplicity of manuscripts, many of which are very ancient and reliable. He noted that he had looked into these questions all during his life, that he had dug deeply into the texts of the manuscripts; and as he studied more and more thoroughly, his confidence and trust in Jesus grew. Metzger's faith increased as he conducted his textual criticism of the manuscripts.

The fact that the Bible appears to be a human book is nothing new to any New Testament scholar. If God chose to use imperfect human beings to write accounts of his actions in the world, one can expect human errors to occur. But the key question which may escape a rigid, legalistic worldview is: What is the Christian message? Is the message that the King James version was inspired word for word? Or that any particular text was inspired precisely word for word? The Christian faith is about one who lives: Jesus of Nazareth, and what he has done through his life, crucifixion, and resurrection. The core belief is expressed in the earliest Christian creed given in First Corinthians 15 discussed in chapter 2 above. This creed was composed within a few years of the crucifixion. The real issue is whether Jesus rose from the dead or not. If he did rise from the dead, then one must examine his claims, life, and teaching and consider the totality of evidence presented throughout the entire New Testament text. I would not extrapolate too broadly from the minor question whether Abiathar or Ahimelech was high priest when David ate the bread of the Presence.

The first Christians risked their lives by boldly proclaiming that Jesus was crucified, raised, and empowered as Lord. This was the Christian message then and it is the Christian message now. It is about a person, not about every letter of a text being 100 percent accurate. The presupposition that the faith hinges on Abiathar being high priest and not Ahimelech is a false presupposition. The orthodox Christian faith has so many early creeds, confessions, hymns, and letters supporting the message of the person of Jesus that any impartial juror should consider the total context of all of the evidence.

The proclamation of the Christian message is about the demonstration of God's all-inclusive, unconditional love, demonstrated by the atonement of Jesus in the crucifixion, the power and hope brought forth in his resurrection, and his Lordship over creation. When one has a religious sentiment that centers on a rigid legalism, the magnificence of the Christian message is lost. Bruce Metzger warned against the tendency of legalism in religious thought. All of us should constantly struggle against this tendency. It is a natural human propensity in religious practices to set ritual and formalism above a dynamic relationship. We tend to fall into rote patterns of behavior. In noting this problem in the creation of a Pharisaic ethos Metzger wrote: "In most religions there is an ever-present tendency to regard outward formalism as more important than inward disposition of the heart, and in Pharisaism this natural tendency often became so strong as to give rise to the modern use of the name *Pharisee* to describe a self-righteous formalist or hypocrite."[12]

Harvard's famous psychologist of personality, Gordon Allport, determined that a faith centered only on a legal structure strangles a believer's personality. A person who holds the Christian faith to be something other than a relationship with the person of Jesus inevitably finds himself ensnared by the coils of legalism. Paul Tournier agreed with Allport and warned against a rigid, misplaced faith in a legalistic religious system:

> The fulfillment of duty, the renunciation of all pleasure, good resolutions, the daily attempt to conquer one's faults, shame at one's instincts, the fear of being found fault with, judged, misunderstood—all this is substituted for the zest of a love towards God. And on all these points one remains continually at fault, ever more hopeless, with defeat after defeat, constantly and increasingly fretted by guilt. This moralism itself multiplies defeats, because despair leads on to defeat by sapping the vital forces of the soul, and defeat leads to despair. It is precisely from this inexorable and vicious circle that God would deliver us by His unconditional forgiveness, and it is tragic to see those who believe in Him and who seek to serve Him living lives crushed by sinister coils even more than unbelievers, until they are no longer even able to love a God who seems to them so hard and cruel.[13]

If one accepts the New Testament as an instrument of God and reads it as a text that discloses the mind and Spirit of God, the text can become a means of personal transformation. The proof of the pudding may be in the tasting and in the transformation of one's personality toward a more integrated wholeness.[14]

I want to take a moment and describe an event that was called to my attention by Willoughby Walling II at Princeton in the mid-1960s. He referred to the masterful work by E. V. Rieu in translating the four canonical gospels from Greek into English. Emile Victor Rieu (1887–1972) was educated at Balliol College at Oxford University, then became the editor of the Penguin Classics and perhaps the most authoritative English-speaking Greek scholar of his time. His translations from the Greek of *The Odyssey* and *The Iliad* were held in the highest esteem. Sir Allen Lane asked him to use his remarkable understanding of the Greek language to translate the four canonical gospels. Although he was not familiar with these texts, he undertook the assignment purely as a matter of scholarly endeavor, for previously he had never read or studied the gospels.

E. V. Rieu approached these texts in the same manner he would approach any other recently discovered Greek literature. At the time, his son, who was a lay reader in the Anglican church, said: "It will be very interesting to see what Father makes of the Gospels. It'll be still more interesting to see what the Gospels make of Father."

His son's remark proved to be prescient, for after translating these four canonical gospel accounts, E. V. Rieu told J. B. Phillips, another translator of the New Testament: "It (the process of translation) changed me. My work changed me. And I came to the conclusion, as I said, I think, in my introduction, that these works bear the seal of the Son of Man and God. And they are the Magna Carta of the human spirit."[15]

It is worthwhile to pause and read exactly what E. V. Rieu wrote in his introduction. He had approached the gospels as he had approached *The Iliad*, but his work on them profoundly altered his life. We have a considerable lesson to learn from his insights. If we are open to being transformed, we may not be approaching an ordinary literary work when we approach the gospels:

> I have tried to catch a few glimpses of the Perfect Man through the eyes of his disciples, concentrating on his human attributes because it was as a man that they themselves first learnt to know and love him. Indeed they labour to portray his full humanity and make it clear that it was not till the very end, or after it, that they realized the fact, and understood the purpose, of his descent from Heaven. The significance of his self-revelations was hidden from them for a little while by Providence, to be afterwards made clear; and I have thought it right and natural to follow in the way that Providence laid down for them. For the rest, let the Gospels speak. Of what I have learnt from these documents in the course of my long task, I will say nothing now. Only this, that they bear the seal of the Son of Man and God, they are the Magna Charta of the human spirit. Were we to devote to their comprehension a little of the selfless enthusiasm that is now expended on the riddle of our physical surroundings, we should cease to say that Christianity is coming to an end—we might even feel that it had only just begun.[16]

If one reads the Bible as one would any other book and does not allow the deep significance of its words to penetrate one's heart, one remains only on the superficial surface of the Bible. There is nothing wrong in using textual criticism in the reading of this great book. But such an approach will not allow one to go beyond the shallow waters of its meaning. There is a significantly deeper method of reading the Scriptures, a method that searches and beholds the powerful, pulsating love described in its pages. Dietrich Bonhoeffer understood this distinction when he wrote:

> Naturally one can also read the Bible like any other book, as for example from the viewpoint of textual criticism, etc. There is certainly nothing to be said against this. Only that it is not the way that reveals the essence of the Bible, only its superficial surface. Just as we do not grasp the word of a person whom we love, in order to dissect it, but just as such a word is simply accepted and it then lingers with us all day long, simply as the word of this person whom we love, and just as the one who reveals himself to us as the one who has spoken to us in this word that moves us ever more deeply in our hearts like Mary, so should we treat the Word of God. Only if we dare for once to enter into relationship with the Bible as the place where the God who loves us really speaks to us and will not leave us alone with our questions will we be happy with the Bible.[17]

In my experience, the Scriptures bring insights and meaning to life, death, and all the travails and joy of human existence. If one is open to their meaning for one's personal life and for the sources of strength and peace available through the power of the words of Scripture, one can be deeply transformed by slow, thoughtful meditation on its passages. For me there is no similar writing that grasps the reality and promise of the human condition.

One thoughtful approach to the texts of Scripture is found in the tradition of *Lectio Divina* or a prayerful meditation on a passage. The traditional formulation of this type of prayerful reading was made by Guigo the Carthusian in the twelfth century (*lectio, meditatio, oratio, contemplatio* or reading, meditation, prayer, contemplation). The basic art of *Lectio Divina* consists of first reading a text in a calm, passive repetitive manner, gradually allowing the reading of the text to become a reflection into the inner center of one's awareness. One then enters into a dialogue with God, a conversation that describes the meaning of the text and what the words mean to the reader. This conversation progresses toward the contemplation of the Divine. The art of *Lectio Divina*, however, is not a rigid following of a format; the reader often reads out loud with an attitude of reverence and a willingness to encounter God. Above all, the reader maintains a willingness to be transformed by this encounter. As I mentioned, the proof of the pudding, then, derives from the tasting.

4.3 THE DATES OF COMPOSITION OF GOSPEL ACCOUNTS ARE WITHIN THE LIFETIME OF EYEWITNESSES TO THE LIFE OF JESUS OF NAZARETH.

4.3.1 Frequently accepted dates are quite early.

Even the more skeptical of contemporary New Testament scholars date Mark around AD 70, Matthew in the 80s, Luke and Acts in the 80s, and John in the 90s. Because writings in the early second century refer to these gospels, even the most skeptical scholars cannot honestly date them later. F. F. Bruce gives the following frequently accepted dates for the New Testament documents and particularly the gospels, but notes his inclination to date the Synoptic gospels somewhat earlier on the basis of the destruction of Jerusalem and the temple in AD 70:

> The New Testament was complete, or substantially complete, about AD 100, the majority of the writings being in existence twenty to forty years before this. In this country [U.K.] a majority of modern scholars fix the dates of the four gospels as follows: Matthew, *c.* 85–90; Mark, *c.* 65; Luke, *c.* 80–85; John, *c.* 90–100. I should be inclined to date the first three Gospels rather earlier: Mark around AD 64 or 65, Luke shortly before 70, and Matthew shortly after 70. One criterion which has special weight with me is the relation which these writings appear to bear to the destruction of the city and temple of Jerusalem by the Romans in AD 70. My view of the matter is that Mark and Luke were written before this event, and Matthew not long afterwards.[18]

These later dates still present good evidence, especially when they are coupled with the corroborative evidence about the life of Jesus from the early letters of the New Testament written within two to three decades after the crucifixion.

4.3.2 Even with more skeptical later dates, eyewitnesses were available to correct errors in the canonical gospels.

The evidence indicates that the Synoptic gospels were all composed well within the time period when persons who had been eyewitnesses to the events of Jesus' life were alive and available to correct any inaccuracies in the gospel accounts. Even using the more skeptical later dates of composition, the dates are sufficiently early for the authors of the canonical gospel accounts to have interviewed and learned from eyewitnesses to the life and death of Jesus. The presence of eyewitnesses available to correct any errors is sufficient whether the documents have the earlier dates or the dates given by a majority of contemporary scholars. As F. F. Bruce notes:

> But, even with the later dates, the situation is encouraging from the historian's view for the first three Gospels were written at a time when many were alive who could remember the things that Jesus said and did, and some at least would still be alive when the fourth Gospel was written. If it could be determined that the writer of the Gospels used sources of information belonging to an earlier date, then the situation would still be more encouraging.[19]

We must also not forget that this means that any hostile eyewitnesses to Jesus' life and death were also available to refute the claims of the early church. Despite the presence of hostile eyewitnesses, we have no record or evidence whatsoever that the material contained in the gospel accounts and Acts is incorrect. On the contrary, the charges made by non-Christian Jews against the claims of the early church implied their agreement with the historical events of Jesus' life and death.[20]

Although in this book I discuss an argument made by many scholars for earlier dates than those given by F. F. Bruce above, the earlier dating is not essential to the question of the reliability of the New Testament documents (especially when one couples the dates of the New Testament documents with the corroboration of the gospel accounts contained in the earliest letters of the primitive Christian community). The standard dating of the gospels gives dates within the lifetimes of persons who were eyewitnesses to Jesus, his ministry, and his crucifixion. They are adequately close to the events they describe to give these eyewitnesses an opportunity to protest any distortions. Yet there is not a shred of evidence that would indicate that anyone objected to any of their content on the ground of historical accuracy. Again, even the standard dating is adequate to assure that eyewitnesses were available to correct any distortions or inaccuracies.

Further evidence of the historical accuracy of the Synoptic gospels is contained in the fact that we do not find evidence in these gospels that would argue strongly in favor of any particular position among the theological disputes that developed early on in the Christian church. The absence of such evidence indicates that the gospel writers were attempting to give a truthful account of Jesus' words and actions. As New Testament scholar Craig Blomberg notes:

> The strongest argument against the idea that Christians felt free to invent sayings of Jesus, however, comes from what we *never* find in the Gospels. Numerous Christian controversies that surfaced after Jesus' ascension which threatened to tear the New Testament church apart could have been conveniently solved if the first Christians had simply read back into the Gospels solutions to those debates. *But this is precisely what never happens.* Not once does Jesus address many of the major topics that for the rest of the first century loomed large in the minds of Christians—whether believers needed to be circumcised, how to regulate speaking in tongues, how to keep Jew and Gentile united in one body, whether believers could divorce non-Christian spouses, what roles were open to women in ministry, and so on.[21]

4.3.3 Evidence from first-century Christian history gives a rationale for earlier dating of gospel accounts.

4.3.3.1 The dating of Acts gives a benchmark for the dates of composition of canonical gospels.

One plausible method of attempting to determine the date of the writing of the gospel narratives in the New Testament is to begin with the dating for the writing of Acts. If the evidence points to an early date for Acts, we know that the gospel of Luke would have an even earlier date because it was written by the same author prior to his writing of Acts. Luke also appears to have Mark and possibly Matthew available to him. If so, these gospel accounts would be even earlier.

The dating of Acts give us a benchmark in determining the dates of the composition of the Synoptic gospel narratives. We have corroborative evidence from non-Christian sources for the dating of events related to the narrative of Acts that indicates that Acts may have been written in the very early 60s. A brief summary of some of the evidence will be useful to frame a context for the discussion.

Acts ends rather abruptly with Paul under house arrest in Rome with no indication of the results of his appeal. This is extraordinary, given that Luke devotes the last eight chapters of Acts to Paul's arrest, imprisonment, trial, and appeal. Luke also does not mention the execution of James, the brother of Jesus, in AD 62. James was a central pillar in the early church, the leader of the church in Jerusalem, and played a much more significant role in Acts than Stephen, whose execution is well described in Acts by Luke. Nor does Luke mention the great war of the first century: the Jewish-Roman war of AD 66–70, the incredible destruction of Jerusalem, and the destruction of the Temple in AD 70. This is most remarkable when one considers the central role of Jerusalem and its Temple in Acts, and in first-century Judaism.

The most reasonable explanation for the absence of any reference to the death of James, the outcome of Paul's trial, and the destruction of Jerusalem and its Temple is that Luke wrote Acts prior to any of these events. In other words, Acts was most likely written no later than AD 62, the year of James's execution.

Because Acts was written after the gospel of Luke, the gospel account must have been written before AD 62. Luke appears to have relied on Mark. This means that the most accurate date for the composition of Mark would then be before the late 50s. We are now looking at dates of composition within the first two decades after the crucifixion of Jesus.

4.3.3.2 The failure of the author of Acts to mention the destruction of Jerusalem and its Temple is only easily understood if Acts was written prior to the fall of Jerusalem in AD 70.

I turn now to an examination of some of the evidence for these omitted events in the gospel accounts and in Acts and consider their significance for the author of Acts. The fall of Jerusalem took place in AD 70 and is an extremely important event in Jewish history and in the life of the early Christian church. The city of Jerusalem plays a major role in Acts and in the description of the events leading up to and including the founding of the early church in Jerusalem. The failure of the author, who gives every indication of being a sincere and accurate historian, to mention such a catastrophic event is only easily understood if Acts was written prior to the fall of Jerusalem. The absence of any reference to an event that included the destruction of the Temple is a resounding silence in the story if Acts is not dated prior to AD 70.

The devastation of Jerusalem and the destruction of the Temple were perhaps the most significant events in Jewish history during the first century. The magnitude of the devastation and destruction of the center of worship for the Jewish nation was on a scale unknown to the Jewish people living in the first century. To emphasize the significance of the destruction of Jerusalem and its Temple, I will review a brief history of the Jewish revolt against Rome that lasted between AD 66 and 70. This is often referred to as the Jewish war with Rome.

The revolt had its origins in a series of events beginning at the start of the first century. In the early decades of the century, various revolutionary groups rose up in a rather unorganized fashion to resist Roman rule. Members of these groups were often referred to as bandits (*lēstēs*). (The "Bandits" or thieves crucified with Jesus and referred to in Matthew 27:38 may have been members of a revolutionary group, as indicated by the use of this Greek term.)

After Agrippa's death in AD 44, the number of groups resisting Roman rule increased. One of these groups was known as the Sicarri, or "assassins" who killed Roman officials and Jewish leaders who cooperated with Rome. In many respects they employed tactics similar to modern-day terrorists.

The increase in revolutionary activities and a series of incompetent Roman governors led to a succession of incidents in AD 66, culminating in the Roman seizure of the treasury of the Temple for the purpose of paying a deficit in financial tributes to the Emperor, the halting of sacrifices for the Emperor and his family, and a massacre of Roman soldiers in August of AD 66.

To end the revolt, Nero sent Flavius Vespasian with more than three legions into Galilee, where he began his campaign by subduing the town of Jotapata. After overcoming Jotapata and then all of Galilee, Vespasian surrounded Jerusalem in the summer of AD 68. Nero, however, committed suicide that year, and Vespasian waited for orders from his successor, anticipating that he would receive a command to lay siege to Jerusalem. The succession of a Roman Emperor was chaotic: the assassination of Nero's immediate successor, a senator named Galba, the murder of Galba by Otho; Otho's suicide; and the installation of Vitellius as Emperor. In July of AD 69. Vespasian was hailed by the Alexandrian and Judean legions, and Vitellius was assassinated after his troops were defeated by the army of the Danube. Vespasian proclaimed himself Emperor and left his son Titus with four legions to lay siege to Jerusalem.

One of Titus's assistants was Josephus. Josephus was the most important ancient Jewish historian in terms of the early Christian church and the life of Jesus. He was born about AD 37 in a noble, priestly family, named Joseph ben Mattathias, and became a Pharisee. At the age of twenty-seven, he led a delegation to meet Nero and had his first impression of Rome. In AD 66, when the Jewish revolt began against Rome in earnest, he became a commander in the Jewish military in Galilee. During the revolt he surrendered to the Romans, gave up the Jewish cause, and urged his fellow Jews to surrender to the Romans because of Rome's superior forces. He became a Roman citizen, took a Roman name (Flavius Josephus), and acted as an interpreter to Titus. His principal occupation was as a writer in the service of Emperors Vespasian, Titus, and Domitan, living in an apartment in their palaces.[22] His two major works were *The Jewish War*, written between AD 75 and 80 and describing the Jewish revolt of AD 66–70, and *Jewish Antiquities*, written in the early 90s, which described the whole history of the Jewish people from creation to AD 66.[23]

Because he was an eyewitness to the siege and destruction of Jerusalem, Josephus's writings in *The Jewish War* give us a vivid account of the events of AD 70 and the remarkable devastation of Jerusalem and the Jewish Temple. The siege lasted from the spring of 70 until August of 70. The burning and destruction of the Temple occurred on August 30, the very day on which the former Temple had been destroyed by the king of Babylon. Josephus's writings are too voluminous and difficult to follow in their archaic format for our purposes. For those who want to understand the magnitude of the massacre that overwhelmed Jerusalem at the time of the burning of the Temple, I recommend reading Paul L. Maier's book *Josephus*, which carefully condenses Josephus's writings without surrendering any important passages from the works of this prolific Jewish historian. What becomes clear in reading this history is that the Jewish War was *the* great war of the first century, ending in catastrophic and tragic events and culminating in a brutal massacre with almost unending slaughter and a devastating destruction of the most important city for Jews and Christians in the first century.

Jerusalem has a central role in the book of Acts and in the events leading up to the founding and activities of the primitive church. Much of the early activity of the primitive church, and indeed the location of the mother congregation of the primitive church, was in Jerusalem. The leaders of the primitive church were Peter, James, and John in Jerusalem. Paul later joined them as a very significant apostle and, adding to the significance of Jerusalem, traveled to Jerusalem for consultation with the leaders of the young church. Paul even arranged for a large offering of money to the church in Jerusalem. Jerusalem was extremely important to the young church's activities. The absence of any reference in Luke's gospel or in Acts to the Jewish War, the devastation of Jerusalem, and the destruction of the Temple is difficult to understand, unless Acts was written prior to the events of AD 70. The absence of any reference to such a remarkable event in Jewish history and in a city so central to the action of the early church is a gaping hole in the story if Acts is not dated prior to AD 70.

The author of the gospel of Luke and Acts structures his work around the city of Jerusalem and frequently refers to the Temple. New Testament scholar Gregory A. Boyd comments on this remarkable silence in Acts and concludes that the only reasonable explanation for the omission is that the author of Luke had no knowledge of the destruction of Jerusalem. This could only have been true if he wrote Acts before the destruction occurred. In commenting on the absence of any references to the fall of Jerusalem, Boyd writes:

> For an author where narrative is centrally structured around Jerusalem (Luke 24:13; Acts 1:8) and who makes frequent mention of the temple (Acts 2:46; 3:1-2, 8, 10; 5:20-25; 21:28-30; etc.), their omission is most surprising. For an author who took the time to mention the much less significant expulsion of the Jews from Rome under Claudius (18:2), the omission is indeed astounding. And for an author who is interested in how persecution of the church helped spread the Gospel around the world (e.g., 8:4), this omission comes close to being inexplicable—except on the supposition that he had no knowledge of these events![24]

This gaping hole is not confined to Acts but to all of the literature that constitutes the New Testament documents. Despite the central role of Jerusalem in the gospel accounts and the significance of the Temple in Judaism and in Christian historical theology, none of the New Testament documents contains a reference to the destruction of the Temple and the devastation of Jerusalem. As John A. T. Robinson notes:

> One of the oldest facts about the New Testament is that what on any showing would appear to be the single most datable and climactic event of the period—the fall of Jerusalem in A.D. 70, and with it the collapse of institutional Judaism based on the temple—is never once mentioned as a past fact. It is, of course, predicted; and these predictions are, in some cases

at least, assumed to be written (or written up) after the event. But the silence is nevertheless as significant as the silence for Sherlock Holmes of the dog that did not bark.[25] . . . Explanations for this silence have of course been attempted. Yet the simplest explanation of all, that 'perhaps . . . there is extremely little in the New Testament later than A.D. 70' and that its events are not mentioned because they had not yet occurred, seems to me to demand more attention than it has received in critical circles.[26]

Jerusalem was at the center of the earliest Christian community. This city was the location of the initial mother congregation that began the global church. The letters to the young churches in our earliest Christian documents are replete with references to its Temple and the city itself. The astounding silence concerning their unparalleled devastation and destruction calls for a rational explanation.

4.3.3.3 Later dating is based not on historical facts but on a metaphysical presupposition against prophecy or against even efficacious insight.

4.3.3.3.1 One of the major reason scholars give a later date is because of Jesus' presumed prediction of the destruction of Jerusalem.

In reviewing the evidence for the dating of the New Testament documents, including the gospels and Acts, I find it remarkable that one major reason given by scholars for the standard dating of Mark (AD 70), Matthew and Luke (AD 75–85), and John (AD 95) is Jesus' presumed prediction of the destruction of Jerusalem found in Matthew 24:15–22, Mark 13:14–20, and Luke 21:20–24. The presumption among many contemporary scholars is that Mark's passage was written first and available to Matthew and Luke. The passages read as follows:

Matthew 24:15–22
So when you see the desolating sacrilege standing in the holy place, as was spoken of by the prophet Daniel (let the reader understand), then those in Judea must flee to the mountains; the one on the housetop must not go down to take what is in the house; the one in the field must not turn back to get a coat. Woe to those who are pregnant and to those who are nursing infants in those days! Pray that your flight may not be in winter or on a sabbath. For at that time there will be great suffering, such as has not been from the beginning of the world until now, no, and never

will be. And if those days had not been cut short, no one would be saved; but for the sake of the elect those days will be cut short.

Mark 13:14–20
But when you see the desolating sacrilege set up where it ought not to be (let the reader understand), then those in Judea must flee to the mountains; the one on the housetop must not go down or enter the house to take anything away; the one in the field must not turn back to get a coat. Woe to those who are pregnant and to those who are nursing infants in those days! Pray that it may not be in winter. For in those days there will be suffering, such as has not been from the beginning of the creation that God created until now, no, and never will be. And if the Lord had not cut short those days, no one would be saved, but for the sake of the elect, whom he chose, he has cut short those days.

Luke 21:20–24
When you see Jerusalem surrounded by armies, then know that its desolation has come near. Then those in Judea must flee to the mountains, and those inside the city must leave it, and those out in the country must not enter it; for these are days of vengeance, as a fulfillment of all that is written. Woe to those who are pregnant and to those who are nursing infants in those days! For there will be great distress on the earth and wrath against this people; they will fall by the edge of the sword and be taken away as captives among all nations; and Jerusalem will be trampled on by the Gentiles, until the times of the Gentiles are fulfilled.

As noted above, the predictions found in these passages constitute one of the main reasons for the standard dating of the gospels, but this reason is based on the assumptions (1) that Jesus could not have predicted the fall of Jerusalem and the destruction of the Temple and (2) that these passages refer to the events of AD 70. Those assumptions are not supported by any historical evidence but are purely metaphysical assumptions. In other words, the assumption is made that Jesus could not have actually prophesized the destruction of Jerusalem and the Temple, and consequently, the writing of such a prophecy must have occurred after the event. But this is a questionable conclusion based on a metaphysical presupposition against the possibility of prophecy, not a historical analysis.

Josephus actually records the prophecy of another Jesus, a rude peasant and son of Ananias, who, at the feast of the Tabernacle, prophesized the destruction of Jerusalem and its Temple in AD 60 when Albinus was governor of Judea.[27]

If Jesus, son of Ananias, could make such a prediction prior to AD 70, why could not also Jesus of Nazareth? The dating of the Synoptic gospels and Acts after AD 70 on the presupposition that Jesus could not have predicted the fall of Jerusalem is an extraordinarily whimsical conclusion. Anyone familiar with the strife between the Jewish people and the Roman occupiers could foresee that this event was a possibility. New Testament scholar Bo Reicke finds it an astonishing uncritical peremptoriness: "An amazing example of uncritical dogmatism in New Testament studies is the belief that the Synoptic Gospels should be dated after the Jewish War of A.D. 66–70 because they contain prophecies *ex eventu* of the destruction of Jerusalem by the Romans in the year 70."[28]

In Acts Luke is describing how the life and teaching of Jesus are fulfilled in his resurrection and in the establishment of the church. If Luke wrote after AD 70, why did he not point out how Jesus' prophecy in Luke 21 was fulfilled by the Roman destruction of Jerusalem? He attempted to show the fulfillment of the ministry of Jesus. Why did he not describe the fulfillment of his prophecy by such a devastating event as Titus's legions' complete destruction of the Temple? Boyd concludes that Luke must have written before the destruction of Jerusalem.

> But what presses this point even further is the recognition that the Jesus of Luke's first volume prophesies the destruction of this temple (21:6). Since one of the driving motifs of Acts is to show how the ministry of Jesus was continued and fulfilled in the life of the church (Luke 1:1–4; Acts 1:1–2), Luke's failure to record how this central prophecy of Jesus' was fulfilled is difficult to explain unless we suppose that he was writing *before* its fulfillment. These considerations, taken together, strongly suggest a date of composition sometime before the fall of Jerusalem, the start of the Jewish-Roman war, and even before Nero's persecution in A.D. 62.[29]

4.3.3.3.2 The "abomination of desolation" could not have referred to the Temple's destruction if Acts was written after AD 70.

J. A. T. Robinson calls our attention to the discourse in Mark 13:14–20 and notes that the initial question in the discourse is never really answered by Jesus. The only subsequent reference to the Temple is only implied later in Mark 13:14–16 where Jesus refers to the "abomination of desolation" usurping a place that is not his and that those in Judea should then take to the hills. But, as Robinson well argues, this reference to "the abomination of desolation" could not logically refer to the Temple's destruction if it was written after AD 70 because the admonition to take to the hills would be nonsensical. In AD 70 everyone would have known that the hills were in the hands of the Roman army at that time. An admonition to run into the hands of the Roman soldiers about to attack Jerusalem would make no sense. The Christians in Jerusalem actually fled to Pella, a city of the Decapolis, several years prior to AD 70. As Robinson explains:

> It is clear at least that "the abomination of desolation" cannot itself refer to the destruction of the sanctuary in August 70 or to its desecration by Titus' soldiers in sacrificing to their standards. By that time it was far too late for anyone in Judaea to take to the hills, which had been in enemy hands since the end of 67. Moreover, the only tradition we have as to what Christians actually did, or were told to do, is that preserved by Eusebius apparently on the basis of the Memoirs of Hegesippus used also by Epiphanius. This says that they had been commanded by an oracle given "before the war" to depart from the city, and that so far from taking to the mountains of Judaea, as Mark's instruction implies, they were to make for Pella, a Greek city of the Decapolis, which lay below sea level on the east side of the Jordan valley. It would appear then that this was not prophecy shaped by events and cannot be dated to the period immediately before or during the War of 66–70.[30]

4.3.3.3.3 Jesus' prediction can be seen as a keen insight.

Even if one cannot overcome his or her metaphysical presupposition against prophecy, the passages in Mark 13 do not have to be regarded as a prophecy but only as *an insight* into the Jewish abhorrence of the desecration of the Temple by any idolatrous image, such as the desecration of the sanctuary with such an image in 168–167 BC under Antiochus Epiphanes.[31] The references contained in Mark 13 are very uncertain symbols to require any retrospective dating. Robinson's conclusion is shared by G. R. Beasley in his commentary on this chapter of Mark: "It would seem a just conclusion that the traditional language of the book of Daniel, the Jewish abhorrence of the idolatrous Roman ensigns, attested in the reaction to Pilate's desecration, and Jesus' insight into the situation resulting from his people's rejection of his message, supply a sufficient background for this saying."[32]

4.3.3.3.4 The execution of James is not mentioned in Acts, but Acts records vividly the stoning of Stephen.

Luke also does not mention the death of James in 62 or the martyrdom of Peter which probably occurred in AD 64. This is also remarkable considering Luke's description of the execution of Stephen (Acts 7:57–59) and another James, known as the brother of John (Acts 12:2). Acts records vividly the stoning of Stephen, the first Christian martyr. Early church historian Roland Bainton noted that Stephen's stoning was done "in accord with the command of Deuteronomy 13 that any Israelite, who enticed his people to go after the gods of the heathen, should be 'stoned with stones that he die.'"[33] Stephen's death dispersed many disciples and was the start of the beginning of the spreading of the gospel out from Jerusalem. Although significant in the life of the early church, Stephen and James, the brother of John, did not play comparable central roles in Acts as the roles of Paul, Peter, and James, the brother of Jesus.

In the last book of *Antiquities*, book twenty (XX), chapter 9, Josephus describes the death in AD 62 of James, the brother of Jesus and leader of the early church in Jerusalem. In recounting the action of Ananus, the high priest during a hiatus in Roman gubernatorial authority, Josephus writes: "He assembled the sanhedrin of the judges, and brought before it the brother of Jesus called Christ (*Christos*), whose name was James, and some other. When he accused them as breakers of the law, he delivered them to be stoned."[34]

R. T. France was convinced this passage is authentic and not a later Christian interpolation to Josephus's original writing.[35] The same conviction is also held by Robert Van Voorst, in his excellent study on non–New Testament ancient evidence for Jesus. Van Voorst concludes that these words are authentic to Josephus's original writing and not Christian interpolations: "The overwhelming majority of scholars holds that the words 'the brother of Jesus called Christ' are authentic, as is the entire passage in which it is found. The passage fits its context well. As for its content, a Christian interpolator would have used laudatory language to describe James and especially Jesus, calling him 'the Lord' or something similar. . . . Josephus's words 'called Christ' are neutral and descriptive, intended neither to confess nor deny Jesus as the 'Christ.'"[36]

This means that Luke must have written the Acts of the Apostles prior to AD 62. Luke centers much of his discussion on martyrdom and describes the suffering of the early church. To ignore the stoning of James, who was the leader of the church in Jerusalem, would be an incredible omission by Luke. The most plausible explanation for the omission is that Luke wrote the book of Acts before the stoning of James and before the destruction of Jerusalem and the Temple.[37]

4.3.3.3.5 The absence of any reference to the outcome of Paul's trial indicates a pre–AD 70 date for the composition of Acts.

It is strange that the last eight chapters of Acts center on the work of Paul and end with Paul under house arrest in Rome waiting for his trial. Eusebius, the historian from Caesarea, wrote in his *Ecclesiastical History* (AD 325) that Paul was martyred under Nero in AD 67 or 68. Acts, however, ends abruptly with no mention of the results of his trial or of his death. First Clement 5–6, a letter to the Corinthians from Clement, Bishop of Rome (AD 88–97), contains early evidence that Peter and Paul suffered martyrdom during the Neronian persecutions of AD 64. This is consistent with the understanding of the early church fathers, including Dionysius, Bishop of Corinth (AD 180), and Tertullian (AD 200). The book of Acts is completely silent about the deaths of Peter and Paul or even the outcome of Paul's arrest and trial.

The abrupt ending to Acts is remarkable and uncharacteristic of Luke's thorough style. If Luke wrote after the outcome of Paul's trial and failed to describe that outcome, it would be in some respects similar to his gospel account ending with Jesus being delivered to Pilate without any indication of his trial, his flogging, and his suffering, or his disciples claiming that he rose again. Luke gives no indication whatsoever of the slaughter and massacre of Christians under the Neronian persecution of AD 64. John A. T. Robinson, in examining this remarkable silence, rightly concludes that the burden of proof is on those who would maintain that Acts was composed later than AD 62:

> The burden of proof would seem to be heavily upon those who would argue that it *does* come later, and there is nothing, as far as I can see, in the theology or history of the Gospel or Acts that *requires* a later date if the prophecies of the fall of Jerusalem do not. From the internal evidence of the two books we should therefore conclude (as did Eusebius)

that Acts was completed in 62 or soon after, with the Gospel of Luke some time earlier.[38]

4.3.3.3.6 Matthew's references to the levitical system and Sadducees indicate an earlier date of composition than AD 70.

Further evidence of a dating before AD 70 for each of the Synoptics is the references to the levitical system and the Sadducees. After 70 the levitical system no longer operated and the Sadducees' influence disappeared after the destruction of the Temple. Moreover, the teaching of Jesus in Matthew 17:24–27 concerning the payment of the half-shekel temple tax indicates a pre-70 environment, because after 70, Josephus informs us that the tax was to be paid to the treasury of the temple of Jupiter Capitolinus in Rome. Robinson notes that the Mishnah states that "[the laws concerning] the Shekel dues . . . apply only to such time as the Temple stands."[39]

4.3.3.3.7 Evidence from Acts' primitive Christian vocabulary indicates an early date of composition.

Another significant aspect of Acts that indicates an early dating is the author's use of theological phrases that are known to be the language of the primitive church. These phrases only were used in the first decades of the church's existence and then were no longer part of the Christian vocabulary. As Boyd notes,

> Several other pieces of internal evidence from the Book of Acts point in the same direction. First, a significant portion of Luke's theological vocabulary appears very primitive. His reference to the Jews as "the people," to the Eucharist as "breaking of bread," and to Sunday as "the first day of the week" (instead of "the Lord's day"; Rev. 1:10; Didache 14:1) is arguably evidence for the primitiveness of his sources.[40]

4.3.3.3.8 Robinson concluded that Matthew was written before AD 62 and the other Synoptic gospels were written in the 50s, within about twenty years of the crucifixion.

After examining the evidence, Robinson concluded that Matthew was composed before 62 and that the other Synoptic gospels were probably completed in the decade of the 50s: "In this case we have pushed Matthew back at any rate before 62, which is exactly the date to which we were driven for Acts, with Luke a little earlier. This would mean that the final stage of the formation of the synoptic gospels roughly coincide with the end of the 50s."

If Mark and Luke were written no later than the later 50s, these accounts were in existence within two decades of the crucifixion with many eyewitnesses, hostile and friendly, available to critique and challenge any distortions. As we have noted, we have no evidence at all of any challenges or critiques during the period in which eyewitnesses would have been alive and familiar with these accounts even if we use the more skeptical later dates. With an earlier dating within the first two decades and the presence of a multiple number of eyewitnesses, we have even stronger reason to consider the silence of any critics as remarkable as the silence for Sherlock Holmes of the dog that did not bark. The even earlier dates for the composition of the letters of the New Testament are also important because these letters corroborate the canonical gospel accounts.[41]

4.4 ALTHOUGH NOT ESSENTIAL FOR THE RELIABILITY OF THE GOSPELS, EVIDENCE FOR TRADITIONAL ATTRIBUTION OF AUTHORSHIP MAY BE PLAUSIBLE.

Although several New Testament scholars take a contrary view, many scholars present significant evidence that the first gospel appearing in most modern New Testament editions was written by Matthew, a tax collector who became a disciple of Jesus after encountering him and experiencing his love and friendship.[42] This is consistent with Papias's statement that "Matthew compiled the Logia (sayings of Jesus) in the 'Hebrew' speech (i.e., Aramaic), and every one translated them as best he could."[43]

This statement becomes very reasonable when one translates the sayings back into Aramaic. The reconstruction of the sayings into the original Aramaic reveals a "regular poetical rhythm, and even, at times, rhyme."[44] As anyone who recites poetry or sings using rhyme well knows, the regular pattern allows for more easy memorization. This was a mark of Old Testament poetry, and Jesus, who knew the Old Testament well, appears to have used poetry to enable his disciples to memorize his sayings more easily and accurately.

These scholars also hold the plausible traditional position that Mark, a close friend of Peter and Paul; Luke, a physician who worked and traveled with Paul; and John, who probably was the apostle John or John the Elder, wrote the other three canonical gospels.[45]

This traditional position does not have any other competition in the early church. None of the early church fathers set forth any claims that authors other than the traditional authors were behind the four canonical gospels. Unlike the more suspect apocryphal gospels, such as the gospel of Peter or the gospel of James, the authors of the canonical gospels were relative minor characters in the development of the early church. Accordingly, many scholars ask why the early church would ascribe authorship to relative unknowns. After all, if one wanted to give authority to a gospel account, why not name a more important figure from among Jesus' apostles, such as Peter or James, the brother of Jesus? Yet the early church leaders were unanimous in holding that Matthew, John, Mark, and Luke were the authors.

Papias (ca. 140), for example, quotes an earlier source that states that Mark was a close associate of the apostle Peter and that he had written down what he had heard Peter preach about Jesus. This is corroborated by the evidence of Peter's sermon in Acts 10:37 where Peter's sermon follows the same outline as the gospel of Mark by beginning with the baptism of Jesus by John the Baptist, his anointing with the Holy Spirit, his good deeds and healing activities in Judea and in Jerusalem, his crucifixion, and his resurrection. If Mark was writing down then what he had heard from Peter, he appears to have written in a manner consistent with Peter's sermons as recorded throughout Acts.[46]

Ancient evidence from the first century concerning the composition of Mark is given by Clement, who was Bishop of Rome (AD 88–99). He describes Mark writing his gospel when Peter was preaching in Rome:

> Mark, the follower of Peter, while Peter was preaching publicly the gospel at Rome in the presence of certain of Caesar's knights and was putting forward many testimonies concerning Christ, being requested by them that they might be able to commit to memory the things which were being spoken, wrote from the things which were spoken by Peter the Gospel which is called according to Mark.[47]

The gospel of Luke was written by the same author as the book of Acts as indicated by (1) the similarity in structure and language and addressed to the same person (Theophilus), and (2) the many references using the pronoun "we"[48] to indicate that the author was traveling with Paul at the time the events described in these references occurred. In his letter to the Colossians, written about AD 60 (approximately thirty years after the crucifixion) Paul corroborates Luke's presence with him, as he writes, "Luke, the beloved physician, and Demas greet you."[49] Similarly, in his letter to Philemon, written about the same time, Paul acknowledges Luke's presence with him, apparently during his imprisonment in Rome, as he writes: "Epaphras, my fellow prisoner in Christ Jesus, sends greetings to you, and so do Mark, Aristarchus, Demas, and Luke, my fellow workers."[50]

Irenaeus's writing at the end of the second century also corroborates the tradition of the times: "Matthew also issued a written Gospel among the Hebrews in their own dialect, while Peter and Paul were preaching at Rome, and laying the foundation of the Church. After their departure, Mark, the disciple and interpreter of Peter, did also hand down to us in writing what had been preached by Peter."[51]

The earliest recorded tradition in the early church was that Matthew had written his gospel when Peter and Paul were preaching at Rome. Accordingly, this writing would then have had to been done prior to their probable executions under Nero, which, as noted above, most likely occurred in the mid-60s.

4.5 ARCHAEOLOGICAL EVIDENCE INDICATES THAT THE GOSPEL WRITERS WERE CONCERNED WITH HISTORICAL ACCURACY.

The archaeological evidence and the style and testimony of the gospel writers indicate that they were very concerned with writing an accurate description of the events of Jesus' life. For example, Luke, in the very beginning of his gospel, gives us a testimony of his attempt at writing a careful and authentic description of the history of Jesus' earthly existence:

> Since many have undertaken to set down an orderly account of the events that have been fulfilled among us, just as they were handed on to us by those who from the beginning were eyewitnesses and servants of the word, I too decided, after investigating everything carefully from the very first, to write an orderly account for you, most excellent Theophilus,

so that you may know the truth concerning the things about which you have been instructed.[52]

Archaeological evidence provides further indication of historical accuracy in the gospel. For example, references in the gospel of John with descriptions of geographical locations have consistently been shown to be accurate. As Blomberg writes, "Archaeologists have unearthed the five porticoes of the pool of Bethesda by the Sheep Gate,[53] the pool of Siloam,[54] Jacob's well at Sychar,[55] the 'Pavement' (*Gabbatha*) where Pilate tried Jesus,[56] and Solomon's porch in the temple precincts."[57] Other evidence includes: an inscription verifying that Pilate was the prefect of Judea during Jesus' lifetime; an ossuary with the bones of a man crucified with nails driven through his ankles, as the gospels describe Jesus' execution; the burial grounds of the high priest Caiaphas, who tried and convicted Jesus of blasphemy.[58] This evidence indicates that the New Testament accounts contain reliable historical information in their description of matters for which physical evidence remains.

4.6 THE LETTERS OF THE YOUNG CHURCH (THE EARLIEST CHRISTIAN DOCUMENTS IN OUR POSSESSION) CORROBORATE THE GOSPEL ACCOUNTS.

Bruce Metzger noted that many New Testament scholars fail to notice the strong corroborative evidence for the accuracy and reliability of the canonical gospel accounts found in the mid-first-century New Testament letters. He held that these letters describe significant historical events in the life and ministry of Jesus. The historical data concerning Jesus in these New Testament letters is often overlooked by contemporary New Testament scholars. As Metzger wrote: "Paul's Letters contain a fairly large number of allusions to saying(s) of Jesus, so many, that some scholars have thought it likely that Paul may have had in his hands a collection of Jesus' sayings. . . . In evaluating the weight of Paul's knowledge of Jesus, the historian finds it significant that the Pauline Letters confirm the broad outlines of the testimony of the Gospels."[59]

Paul's letters to the Romans, First Corinthians, First Thessalonians, and Galatians and the letter of James provide corroborative evidence of the accuracy of the New Testament gospel accounts. These Pauline letters were written in the 50s, and James may have been written in the late 40s. Their content indicates the care given to a reliable handing over and delivery of the oral tradition concerning Jesus' sayings. In chapter 2, supra, I noted that the creeds, hymns, and liturgical formulae that preexist any Christian writings in our possession all corroborate the canonical accounts of the life of Jesus. The information contained in these liturgical formulae is significant evidence of the accuracy of the canonical gospels.

New Testament scholar Craig Blomberg is in agreement with Metzger and has given a provocative and substantial summary of some important passages from New Testament writings that were composed prior to the gospels. All of them corroborate the canonical gospel accounts, and none of them is inconsistent with the accounts:

A summary of the biographical information about Jesus that can be pieced together from just the Pauline epistles alone would include his descent from Abraham and David (Gal. 3:16; Rom. 1:3), his upbringing in the Jewish law (Gal. 4:4), his gathering together disciples, including Cephas (Peter) and John, and his having a brother named James (Gal. 1:19; 2:9), his impeccable character and exemplary life (for example, Phil. 2:6–8; 2 Cor. 8:9; Rom 15:3, 8), his Last Supper and betrayal (1 Cor. 11:23–25), and numerous details surrounding his crucifixion and resurrection (for example, Gal. 3:1; 1 Thess. 2:15; 1 Cor. 15:4–8).

More widespread are signs of a fairly detailed knowledge of Jesus' teaching, especially in Romans, 1 Corinthians, and 1 Thessalonians, even if it is not often cited verbatim. In Romans we hear clear echoes of Jesus' words on blessing those who persecute you (Rom. 12:14; cf. Luke 6:27–28), repaying no one evil for evil (Rom. 12:17; cf. Matt. 5:39), paying taxes and related tribute (Rom. 13:7; cf. Mark 12:17), loving neighbor as summarizing the whole Law (Rom. 13:8–9; cf. Gal. 5:14; Mark 12:31), and recognizing all foods as clean (Rom. 14:14; cf. Luke 11:41; Mark 7:19b). Three times in 1 Corinthians Paul more explicitly quotes the words of Jesus from the gospel tradition: on divorce and remarriage (1 Cor. 9:14; cf. 1 Tim. 5:18; Luke 10:7), and extensively on the Last Supper (1 Cor. 11:23–25; cf. Luke 22:19–20). In 1 Thessalonians fairly close quotations appear in 2:14–16 (on the persecution of Judean Christians by their kinfolk—cf. Matt. 23:29-38) and 4:15–5:4 (on the return of Christ—cf. Matt. 24, esp. v. 43). Moving to the epistle of James, one finds allusions to the Synoptic tradition, and especially the Sermon on the Mount, in almost every paragraph, and a more explicit quotation of the saying on letting your yes be yes and your no no in James 5:12 (cf. Matt. 5:37). Even the Book of Revelation draws on and elaborates imagery from the teaching of Jesus, especially his unique use of the title "Son of man." When we realize that all of these books except for Revelation were written before the canonical gospels were compiled and circulated, this is indeed impressive testimony to the pervasiveness of the gospel traditions in their oral stage.[60]

This is an impressive list of passages that match the canonical gospel accounts. The fact that they have dates of composition preceding the dates of composition of the gospel accounts should not be taken lightly. They provide corrobative evidence that the canonical gospels reflect real historical events, persons, and teaching. When one considers the absence of any conflict with the canonical gospels, the burden of providing equally compelling early evidence for an alternate view of Jesus falls upon those scholars who speculate that the canonical gospels are not reliable.

5

THE MEANS OF COMMUNICATION OF THE GOSPEL IMMEDIATELY AFTER THE CRUCIFIXION WAS THROUGH A RELIABLE ORAL GOSPEL TRADITION

5.1 THE TRADITION FROM JESUS AND ABOUT JESUS WAS VERY LIKELY TO HAVE BEEN MAINTAINED AND PRESERVED IN A TRUSTWORTHY MANNER.

Some persons may be concerned at the potential gap of three or more decades from the time of Jesus' crucifixion to the first written gospels. This gap only occurs in the traditional dating. As I noted, the available evidence points to an earlier dating. Even with the later traditional dating, eyewitnesses were still alive and available to correct any false statements. Yet we have no evidence from the first century of any contrary statement or writing. In addition, New Testament letters written within the first decades after the crucifixion also corroborate the gospel accounts. Moreover, the means of communication of the gospel immediately after the crucifixion was through a reliable oral transmission.

Bart Ehrman's analogy of the "telephone game" where one person tells a story to a person seated next to him or her at a dinner party, and the story is whispered and retold by each guest, is not an appropriate comparison to the first-century oral transmission of the gospel. The process of oral information transfer in the first century was more reliable and subject to verification.

German scholar Rainer Riesner, in his text *Jesus als Lehrer*, gives significant information on the process of transmission of oral tradition in the schools, homes, and synagogues in Jewish Palestine during the time of the earthly ministry of Jesus. The young men often memorized long Old Testament passages. The memorization of sacred literature and teachings is difficult for persons in the twenty-first century to understand. For us it is a remarkable phenomenon because we live in a literary and electronic society. First-century Palestine was a society that emphasized memorization of sayings and events, not the written word. Studies of villages in the Middle East where memorization customs are still maintained confirm that the important emphasis in oral tradition is on faithful adherence to the critical and paramount aspects of an event or saying. The emphasis would have been on accurately preserving the significance of Jesus' sayings and actions.[1]

We know for certain that Christians were preaching about Jesus' crucifixion and resurrection within a matter of weeks after his death. His sayings and deeds were constantly being described in this preaching. Jesus' sayings were in all likelihood memorized by his disciples during his teaching ministry prior to his death. This was the normal practice whereby a teacher would require his disciples to learn sacred sayings by memorization. As Oxford Professor Alister McGrath notes:

> It is difficult for twentieth-century readers, who are so used to information being recorded in written or other visual form, to appreciate that the classical world communicated by means of the spoken word. The great Homeric epics are good examples of the way in which stories were passed on with remarkable accuracy from one generation to another. If there is one ability which modern Westerners have probably lost, it is the ability to remember a story or narrative as it is told, and then to pass it on to others afterwards.
>
> As one study of primitive culture after another confirms, the passing down of stories from one generation to another was characteristic of the pre-modern era, including the time of the New Testament itself. Indeed, there are excellent grounds for arguing that early educational systems were based upon learning by rote. The fact that most people in the West today find it difficult to commit even a short story or narra-

tive to memory naturally tends to prejudice them against believing that anyone else could do it; yet it is evident that it was done, and was done remarkably well.[2]

Learning in the first century was accomplished mainly by memorization and repetition.[3] Literature was a means of transmitting information to some extent, but events and news were related principally by the spoken word. Literature was written to be read out loud and listened to by others. Paul's letters, for example, were principally written to be read out loud to members of the young church.

I want to take some time to describe a plausible Scandinavian-British-German scholarly approach to the examination of Jewish and early Christian methods of transmission of tradition in first-century Palestine. In 1961 Swedish New Testament scholar Birger Gerhardsson published *Memory and Manuscript: Oral Tradition and Written Transmission in Rabbinic Judaism and Early Christianity*. In this landmark study, Gerardsson argued that memorization and repetition similar to the rabbinic methods of learning (refined and developed most thoroughly after 135 AD) were a possible example of how the words and deeds of Jesus were passed on by his disciples. Unfortunately, his thesis was attacked in a caricatured and misleading way by Morton Smith and his pupil Jacob Neusner. They accused Gerhardsson of projecting a post-135 AD rabbinic technique into a pre-70 AD period. Many critics (who in all probability did not even bother to read Gerhardsson's book, as they repeated the same misreadings as Smith) relied on Smith's review article and dismissed Gerhardsson's proposition. The unfair treatment of his work, however, was later reversed in part as several critics took a closer look at his writing.

Anyone who actually reads *Memory and Manuscript* will see that the criticism was unjustified. Very rarely in academic circles does a person have the integrity and courage to admit that he has made a mistake and apologize for it. Jacob Neusner turned out to be a man of extraordinary integrity and courage when he admitted that he had followed the lead of Morton Smith without comprehending the nuances of Gerhardsson's writing. I admire Neusner in many ways and for many reasons, even more so when I read his humble and sincere apology for a misrepresentation of Gerhardsson's book. Neusner realized that Smith was motivated by a "violent invective" and criticized him in a Foreword that Neusner graciously wrote for the republication of *Memory and Manuscript* in 1998. In that Foreword he gave an explanation for his mistake and a clear apology. His honesty is commendable. I quote from his Foreword: "Smith produced . . . a corpus of book reviews of supercilious and misleading character. And one of these—alas!—dismissed and denied a hearing to *Memory and Manuscript*, as Gerhardsson says with complete justification, 'in a caricatured and misleading way.' And let me plead guilty to Gerhardsson's indictment: 'This misrepresentation, and Smith's rather simplistic counter-arguments, were repeated, in even more simplified forms, by countless critics.' I was one of these, and I apologize in word and, here, in deed."[4]

As indicated by Neusner, it is important to understand what Gerhardsson actually said in his 1961 book and in his subsequent publications. Many scholars have simply followed Smith's lead and believe that Gerhardsson tried to project the developed rabbinic techniques of post-135 AD back into the period before 70AD. Gerhardsson, however, did not argue that the complete rabbinic methods of the second century could be traced back to before 70 AD. This does not mean that no tradition for the preservation and transmission of sacred sayings existed in first-century Palestine. It is unlikely that the refined rabbinic techniques post-135 AD were completely novel spontaneous creations *ex nihilo*. It is more probable that they were derived from a previous process for the careful preservation of "holy speech." As New Testament scholar Gregory A. Boyd has written: "they no doubt were tapping into an earlier pervasive Jewish attitude of reverence for religious traditions. And while Jesus was technically not a rabbi, he was clearly a teacher, and thus he quite likely made use of similar *teaching methods*. Here, it is important to recognize the place that ancient Jewish educational practice gave to the memorization of both oral and written tradition."[5]

I will return to the theme of Jesus as a teacher, but at this point I want to emphasize that Gerhardsson was not presenting an anachronistic argument. With respect to the comparison with second-century rabbis, he merely was using their procedure of memorization and transmission as an example. Although the refined rabbinic technique was more fully developed in the second and third centuries, one should not presume that there was no earlier, less refined, but important, tradition of preservation and transmission in first-century Palestine. In this regard, Rainer Riesner has given us valuable evidence. For the moment I want to focus on the following quotation from Gerhardsson that clarifies his position:

> The total program for the transmission of material was not worked out during the time of the temple; the pedagogic techniques were refined and made more methodic, efficient, and general after 70 and 135. The individual guiding principles—'the essentials of the rabbinic method of transmission; as I called them—are, however, mostly old, in many cases very old indeed: memorization; the principle 'first learn, then understand;' terseness; abridgment of material into short, pregnant texts; poetic artifices; rhythm; cantillation; mnemonic devices; use of written notes; diligent repetition, and so on. Therefore, it cannot be totally anachronistic to allow the later, fully developed technique to constitute the total picture, but to take the basic principles for transmission one by one and ask if they were not applied already during the period of the temple by early Christian teachers, perhaps even by Jesus himself; as New Testament exegetes we must of course try to force our way back that far. We would not even need to discuss the question if the total scheme existed before the fall of the temple; but of course it did not.[6]

Gerhardsson's interest was principally on the act of transmission of oral material, or what he labled "early Christianity's work with the word of the Lord." He saw this activity as both preservative and creative and both firm and flexible. He held that in the mother congregation in Jerusalem as well as in other very early churches, a collegium of the leaders (not a rabbinic academy) preserved, studied, discussed, and adapted oral tradition based on the Holy Scriptures and on memories of Jesus. The twelve disciples were the circle of authority in this leadership They would have acted to safeguard the tradition as it was passed on in the early church. The existence of such a circle appears to be present when Paul uses the technical language of "passing on" and "receiving" traditions in First Cor. 11:2, 23 and 15:2-3. In a recent article, Gerhardsson appears more convinced than ever that the tradition about Jesus was transmitted in a safeguarded and reliable manner:

> The references we find in the New Testament to both the pharisaic-rabbinic tradition and to the early Christian tradition, both spoke of with the same quasi-technical terminology (*paradidomi, paralambano,*

paradosis). Paul mentions that he himself has both *received* and *passed on* early Christian tradition. *I find it unthinkable that Paul with his proto-rabbinic background would not have used his old terminology for tradition in the same way he had learned it but would have meant instead popular narrating of a quite different kind.*[7]

Although many scholars, including Richard Bauckham, Gerd Theissen, and Martin Hengel have agreed in many respects with Gerhardsson, his work does not answer all of the relevant questions raised in the very complex area of oral tradition and transmission. For example, if the memorization was rote and always precise, why are there diverse details in the parallel accounts in the Synoptic gospels? Jesus was not technically a rabbi so how can the practices of second- and third-century rabbis be used to claim that Jesus followed their methods of advocating memorization and transmission?

I have already indicated that Gerhardsson allows for flexibility in transmission, a fact often overlooked by his critics. So the variance in the Synoptic details is not an insurmountable problem. With respect to the question of Jesus' status as a nontechnical rabbi, Jesus is addressed as teacher (*didaskalos*) in all four gospels. The Aramaic original for this term meant "my great one." The term *rabbi* in the first century was not a fixed title for an academically trained and ordained person. Rabbi meant teacher and only at the end of the first century with the rabbinic construction of Judaism did the term begin to mean an academically trained scribe.

Rainer Riesner's work emphasizes the significance surrounding Jesus' designation as a teacher. His work does not mean that Jesus was only a teacher, but his forensic investigation into first-century education advances part of the groundwork set forth by Gerhardsson. In his book *Jesus als Lehrer*, Riesner described the transmission processes that took place in pre-Christian times in homes, elementary schools and synagogues. His writing refuted Jacob Neusner's earlier theory that the rabbinic methods of transmission were exclusively academic specialties. Evidence from pre-Christian Israel and other pre-Christian locations support the position that the methods of rabbis were principally old devices of transmission that only required refinement. With this evidence he also refuted Neusner's contention that the rabbis after 70 AD created brand new oral teaching and transmission methods without any proto-predecessor methods in previous pre-Christian Jewish practices. In other words, Riesner demonstrated that the teaching tools of early Judaism and Christianity were older than the rabbinic technique. These tools appeared in material dating long before the rabbinic technique and were in use in Jesus' time. Riesner, contra Smith and Neusner, showed that the techniques were not a novel rabbinic academic specialty, but procedures that contained popular devices that previously were applied for centuries in elementary schools, homes, and synagogues.

Riesner's set forth six reasons why Jesus' followers were careful to preserve and transmit his words and deeds: (1) Jesus' sayings were given the status of a prophet; prophets were among the most historically reliable portions of the Old Testament. (2) Jesus presented himself as the messiah, even if at times he vaguely alluded to this status. Because the messiah was expected to be a teacher of wisdom, his disciples would want to safeguard his teachings. (3) In excess of 80 percent of Jesus' sayings are in poetic or easy to remember forms. (4) Jesus encouraged the learning and transmission of his teaching. (see Mark 6:7-13, Mark 9:10; 13:28; Luke 10:1-17; Luke 11:111). (5) In Israel in Jesus' time elementary education was mandatory for boys until age twelve; Jesus and his disciples would have attended school and learned by rote memorization. (6) Almost all teachers in Graeco-Roman societies gathered disciples to be with them, learn their teaching, and perpetuate their teaching and lifestyle; Jesus was a teacher and appears to have followed this pattern.[8]

I want to continue with the focus on Jesus as a teacher and the status of such a position in first-century Palestine. Riesner's study gives us valuable insight into the historical setting for the preservation of Jesus' words and deeds.

5.2 JESUS' STATUS AS A TEACHER WOULD HAVE FURTHERED HIS DISCIPLES' INTERESTS IN MAINTAINING AND TRANSMITTING HIS TEACHINGS IN AN ACCURATE MANNER.

The culture of memorization in first-century Judaism is well documented in the work of Rainer Riesner. He demonstrated that in the first century the educational system for young Jewish boys emphasized rote memorization. Disciples learned the teachings of their masters by heart and trained their minds to memorize enormous quantities of teachings from their masters. There is every indication that Jesus' relationship with his disciples was one of a teacher and his pupils. They not only lived and traveled together, but his disciples held him in the highest esteem and regarded his words as extremely important.

His words had the ring of great authority, and unlike other teachers, he did not cite others for authority but claimed it himself. The unique esteem accorded to Jesus during his earthly ministry sets him apart from other teachers during this time. The focus of the disciples is on Jesus himself. All other teachers quoted other sources, but Jesus speaks as one with his own authority. Matthew 23:8 quotes Jesus' unusual direction to his disciples: "But you are not to be called rabbi, for you have one teacher (*didaskalos*), and you are all students." This esteemed status of Jesus was highly unusual and would have only furthered the interest of his disciples in assuring that they maintained and transmitted his teachings in a precise manner. As Swedish New Testament scholar Gerhardsson reflects:

> If one thinks about this, it becomes extremely difficult to imagine that there ever was a time when Jesus' followers were not interested in preserving his teachings and in committing his deeds to memory. And if we orient ourselves historically, and remind ourselves how students in the Jewish milieu hung on the words of their teachers and attentively followed their activities in order to learn how to live properly, it then becomes difficult to believe that Jesus' disciples could have been less concerned to hear their master, to observe his way of doing things, and to store up all of this in their memories.[9]

In all probability the disciples were reluctant to modify and distort words that had the aura of authority. I find implausible the suggestion that disciples so devoted to their master's teaching would radically alter his teaching during the relatively short period between the crucifixion and the first written record of his sayings. In reference to the reluctance of disciples to modify and distort the words of their masters, Gerhardsson notes: "The implication is that the words and works of Jesus were stamped on the memories of these disciples. Remembering the attitude of Jewish disciples to their master, it is unrealistic to suppose that forgetfulness and the exercise of a pious imagination had too much hand in transforming authentic memories beyond all recognition in the course of a few short decades."[10]

Bruce Metzger noted the presence of eyewitnesses (Luke 1:2) who would have corrected any substantial misrepresentation of the words or works of Jesus. Metzger pointed to (1) the method of teaching that Jesus used to facilitate his disciples' memorization of his words, and (2) the complete absence of parables in the book of Acts or any of the letters of the New Testament. The second point indicates that the parables contained in the gospels were not the creation of the early Christian community, and, to use Metzger's words, the first point is consistent with a "high degree of fidelity" in the transmission of Jesus' teaching.[11]

5.3 THE NEW TESTAMENT DOCUMENTS ALLUDE TO THE TORAH TRADITION.

The writings of Acts, the Synoptic gospels, and the letters of Paul all provide evidence that this process of Torah education was part of the tradition in the very earliest Christian church. In Acts 22:3 Paul is quoted describing his education in the Torah tradition under his teacher, Gamaliel. He emphasizes that he was educated according to the exactness of "our forefathers' law" (*ho patrōos nomos*). Similarly, in Acts 28:17 he denies having done anything against the "customs belonging to our forefathers" (*ta ethē ta patrōa*). In his letter to the church in Galatia he also describes his zealous attitude toward "the tradition of my forefathers" (*hai patrikai mou paradoseis*).[12] In addition to Luke's writing in Acts and Paul's writing in Galatians, reference to technical terms of Jewish tradition to the Torah is also found in the gospels of Mark and Matthew. As Gerhardsson notes: "Other terms from the Jewish tradition of a technical or quasi-technical nature also appear: 'to pass on' (as tradition, *paradidonai*, Mark 7:13); "to receive" (as tradition, *paralambanein*, Mark 7:4); "to keep" the tradition (*tērein*, Mark 7:9); "to maintain" the tradition (*kratein*, Mark 7:3, 8); "to uphold" the tradition (*histanai*, Mark 7:9 var.); "to walk according to" (*peripatein kata*, Mark 7:5); "to transgress" the tradition (*parabainein*, Matt. 15:2)."[13]

When one reflects that Paul was raised in a Jewish Torah tradition and uses the technical words for a tradition in First Cor. 11:2 and Second Thess. 2:15, 3:6 (*paradosis, pradoseis*), and also uses the technical description of his "handing over" (*paradidonai*) the tradition of the earliest church and his "receiving" (*paralambanein*) this tradition; one must consider that he is very conscious of the fact that he is engaged in a process of transmitting the sacred tradition of the earliest church. In other words, by using the technical terms regarding the transmission of tradition, Paul is describing a reliable method of preserving and carefully transmitting important information about the earliest church's tradition relating to Jesus.[14]

The similarities in the language of tradition in Paul's writings and in Matthew and Mark are very noticeable. This passing on of tradition as described in the passages from Mark and Matthew above are again used in Paul's writings. Gerhardsson affirms this in his linguistic analysis: "The young Christian congregations are to 'maintain' or 'hold fast to,' or 'uphold' these traditions; the verbs used here are (note similarity to usage in passages to Mark and Matthew quoted above), among others, *kratein* (2 Thess. 2:15), *katechein* (1 Cor. 11:2), and *hestēkenai* (1 Cor. 15:1). We also have the expression 'to walk according to' these traditions (*peripatein kata*, 2 Thess. 3:6)."[15] One should conclude that *the early church was very conscious that it was passing on its own tradition in a reliable manner*. This was an established method at the beginning of the Christian era and prior to the written recording of the gospel accounts. As described in chapter 2, in First Cor. 15:3–8 and in First Cor. 11:23–25, Paul is very conscious and emphatic that he is passing on a tradition from his Christian predecessors. As Richard Bauckham writes:

> Paul uses this terminology to refer to a variety of kinds of tradition that he communicated to his churches when he established them. These certainly include 'kerygmatic summaries' of the gospel story and message (for which the best evidence is First Cor. 15:1–8), ethical instruction, instructions for the ordering of the community and its worship, and also Jesus traditions (for which the best evidence is First Cor. 11:23–25). It is obvious that Paul took over the technical terminology for tradition from the usage with which he would have been familiar as a Pharisaic teacher. But it is therefore important to note that there is sufficient evidence of this terminology in early Christian literature outside the Pauline letters to show that it was not peculiar to Paul or solely derived from Paul's usage (Jude 3; Luke 1:2; Acts 16:4; *Didache* 4:13; *Barnabas* 19:11). The

terminology is of considerable importance, for to 'hand on' a tradition is not just to tell it or speak it and to 'receive' a tradition is not just to hear it. Rather, handing on a tradition 'means that *one hands over something to somebody so that the latter possesses it,*' while receiving a tradition 'means that *one receives something so that one possesses it.*' While this need not entail verbatim memorization, it does entail some process of teaching and learning so that what is communicated will be retained.[16]

When we turn to the gospel accounts, we find evidence that this tradition was continued in the writing of the canonical gospels. For example, Luke is keen to emphasize that he is passing on tradition. In his prologue to his gospel, he uses the technical language noted in italics below.

At Luke 1:1–4, the author writes:

> Since many have undertaken to set down an orderly account of the events that have been fulfilled among us, just as they were handed on [*paradidonai*] to us by those who from the beginning were eyewitnesses and servants of the word [*autoptai kai hypēretai tou logou*], I too decided, after investigating everything carefully from the very first, to write an orderly account for you, most excellent Theophilus, so that you may know the truth concerning the things about which you have been instructed.

Note that Luke uses the verb *paradidonai* as he also indicates he is passing on a tradition during the first century. In referring to eyewitnesses, he is alluding to the twelve who were the center of the mother congregation in Jerusalem and those present with Jesus during his earthly ministry. Gerhardsson notes how Luke is passing on a tradition that began with those who formed the mother congregation of Christians in Jerusalem and who were closest to Jesus during his earthly life:

> Luke is primarily thinking of the Twelve. They form the nucleus of those who were present "during all the time that the Lord Jesus went in and out among us" (Acts 1:21), and subsequently devoted themselves to "the ministry of the word" (*diakonia tou logou*, 6:4). They preach and teach and heal "in Jesus' name" (Acts 3:6; 4:10, 18; 5:28, 40, etc). They appear as Jesus' witnesses, witnesses above all to his resurrection. It is the "apostles teaching" (*hē didachē tōn apostolōn*, Acts 2:42) which holds the believers together, and the early Christian community in Jerusalem—the mother congregation itself—grows around a nucleus composed of the Twelve and Jesus' mother and brothers.[17]

5.4 JESUS' ROLE AS TEACHER AND HIS PARTICIPATION IN THE SYNAGOGAL TEACHING ENVIRONMENT OF FIRST-CENTURY PALESTINE CONSTITUTES ADDITIONAL EVIDENCE OF MEMORIZATION OF HIS SAYINGS.

As discussed above, Jesus was often called "rabbi" by his disciples and is addressed as "teacher" (*didaskalos*) in all four of the canonical gospels. For example, Jesus is called "teacher" in Luke 20:21, Matt. 22:16, and Mark 12:14 when the Pharisees say to him, "Teacher, we know that you are sincere, and teach the way of God in accordance with and show deference to no one; for you do not regard people with partiality" (Matt. 22:16). German New Testament scholar Rainer Riesner points out the fact that Jesus was seen and addressed as a teacher. This constitutes evidence that Jesus in some manner acted as Jewish teachers acted in the first century.[18]

In this section I want to focus on the fact that Jesus was known to have taught in the synagogues. All four canonical gospels refer to his teaching in the synagogues.[19] Mark 1:21–39 gives a description of a tradition in which Jesus enters the synagogue in Capernaum and teaches. Those in attendance are astounded at his teaching because he teaches in a manner of one having authority and not as a scribe normally taught. Scribes quoted other sources of wisdom. Jesus referred to himself as the source of authority. The passage goes on to describe his activities in Capernaum, including the healing of Peter's mother-in-law, curing of sick, and a very early morning time of solitude and prayer, followed by the statement that he went throughout Galilee "proclaiming the message in their synagogues."

Riesner follows Joachim Jeremias in holding that the tradition described in this passage of Mark "ultimately goes back to the personal recollections of Peter."[20] He emphasizes the significance of Jesus participating in the synagogal educational and teaching system. Synagogues in first-century Galilee and throughout Palestine served as educational institutions that encouraged the memorization and discussion of Scriptures. In the synagogal educational system we see a pattern that is much more true to the form of transmission of oral tradition and eventually oral gospel tradition than the comparisons to the transmission of folklore or other stories in modern forms of oral transmission, such as those described by John Dominic Crossan. Modern methods of transmitting folklore by the spoken word are a far cry from the tradition and process that was established in the syna-gogues of first-century Jewish culture. Riesner notes that the zealots of Masada, when confronted with a last stand that was certain to end in death from the siege of a Roman legion, decided to build a synagogue for the purpose of opening a school for the teaching and transmission of Torah tradition. Riesner discusses the importance of the synagogal background for an understanding of the reliable nature of the form of passing on and receiving oral tradition in the time of Jesus' earthly ministry:

> In my opinion one cannot overstress the importance of the synagogal teaching system as a background for the formation and transmission of the Gospel tradition. The synagogues provided even in small Galilean villages such as Nazareth a kind of popular education system. Many Jewish men could read and write and were used to memorizing and expounding the Scriptures. Jesus could presuppose a knowledge of the Old Testament, a fact that explains why he seldom cites the Scriptures explicitly but only alludes to certain passages. In comparison with the academically-trained scribes in Jerusalem, most of the Galilean followers seemed ill-educated (cf. Acts 4:13), but in comparison with other peoples of the Roman empire the level of Jewish education was rather high. . . . The first life-setting of the Jesus tradition was not popular folklore and romance but a teach-and-learn situation.[21]

5.5 JESUS' DISCIPLES WERE LEARNERS, MEMORIZING AND RETELLING HIS TEACHINGS DURING HIS MINISTRY IN GALILEE AND JERUSALEM.

The disciples of Jesus considered themselves to be learners (*mathētai*), a word which made the memorization and retelling of the teaching of Jesus their serious business.[22] Jesus frequently called members of his inner circle of followers his "learners" or "disciples."[23] When Jesus sends out the messengers, it is significant to understand that they were to deliver his message as they had received it. As Riesner points out: "An important part of the old Semitic customs and laws for messengers was to deliver the message in the words used by the sender."[24] This is also why Luke in the prologue to his gospel asserts that his account of the events of Jesus' life are given so that Theophilus might have *certainty* about the things in which he was instructed.[25]

Gerhardsson appears to agree with this position and credits the work of Heinz Schurmann in demonstrating that the disciples of Jesus were engaged in an oral transmission process prior to Easter. As students of Jesus, they may have been engaged in memorizing his words during his Galilean and Jerusalem ministries. Reflecting on an essay by Heinz Schurmann, Gerhardsson notes:

> The author has emphasized that even from a purely form-critical point of view one must reckon with the fact that *Jesus' followers began to preserve a tradition of sayings* already *before Easter.* He refers among other things to the fact that according to the Gospels, Jesus, during his ministry in Galilee, sent out his disciples to preach and to heal. This sending has such a strong anchoring in the tradition that, all things being considered, it cannot be dismissed as a simple backdating of the early Christian missionary activity after Easter (Mark 6:7–13 and parallels; Luke 10:1–16). Schurmann points out that Jesus must have given these immature and unlearned disciples certain instructions about what they were to preach before he sent them out. Here then is a situation in which we must assume that Jesus imprinted his teaching in the minds of his disciples. . . . Nothing suggest that these words (the words of Jesus) were of interest only after Easter. On the contrary, everything suggests that devoted disciples memorized them already at the time their master taught them during his ministry in Galilee and Jerusalem.[26]

5.6 WHEN JESUS' SAYINGS ARE TRANSLATED BACK INTO ARAMAIC, THEY TAKE ON A DISTINCT POETIC FORM.

Joachim Jeremias credited Matthew Black with being the first to discover that when the sayings of Jesus are translated back into his Aramaic language, they have extraordinary qualities of alliteration, assonance, and paronomasia. These artistic devices further increase the ability of the listener to remember the sayings. The poetic form that he employed is much easier to memorize than mere prose. When one looks at all of the artistic styles of the sayings of Jesus, one finds a remarkably memorable method of communicating and transmitting his sayings. Gerhardsson notes that Jesus' sayings are not as difficult to memorize as a sermon or a discourse on doctrine, but are made in such a manner so that his students (disciples or learners) can remember them and pass them on to others:

Rather they consist of brief, laconic, well-rounded texts, of pointed statements with a clear profile, rich in content and artistic in form. The artistic devices show through clearly even in the tradition's Greek form: picturesque content, strophic construction, *parallelismus membrorum*, verbatim repetitions, and so on. These features can be seen all the more clearly if one translates back into Aramaic. Then one sees in the sayings of Jesus such characteristics as rhythm, assonance, and alliteration as well. It is obvious that we are dealing here with carefully thought out and deliberately formulated statements.[27]

Jeremias demonstrated to our class at Princeton that when one translates the Greek of these teachings back into Aramaic, the form of Jesus' sayings is such to enhance the ability of his listeners to memorize his words. The memorizable form and poetical structure of Jesus' sayings become very apparent when retroverted back into Aramaic. As Gerhardsson confirms, in Galilean Aramaic, which is the language Jesus spoke, his sayings have an abundance of *parallelismus membrorum*, with other poetical techniques such as alliteration, assonance, rhythm, and rhyme. These qualities would make his words more easily memorized. Riesner noted how the poetical structure of his words were designed for memorization by the disciples and his followers:

> The poetical structure of the words of Jesus made them, like the meshalim of the Old Testament prophets, easily memorizable so one could preserve them intact. Even the form of the sayings of Jesus included in itself an imperative to remember them. It seems that the use of mnemonic devices is very seldom studied from the point of view of the psychology of the memory, but our own experience demonstrates how easy it is to learn and even to reconstruct large bodies of material, if they are in poetical form.[28]

As anyone who recites poetry or sings using rhyme well knows, the regular pattern allows for more easy memorization. We experience this daily in singing popular songs and hymns of worship. This was a mark of Old Testament poetry, and Jesus, who knew the Old Testament well, would find the use of poetry such that it would enable his disciples to memorize his sayings more easily and accurately. In the words of F. F. Bruce:

> Another interesting fact which comes to light when we try to reconstruct the original Aramaic in which our Lord's sayings in all the Gospels were spoken is that very many of these sayings exhibit poetical features. Even

in a translation we can see how full they are of parallelism, which is so constant a mark of Old Testament poetry. When they are turned into Aramaic, however, they are seen to be marked by regular poetical rhythm, and even at times, rhyme. This has been demonstrated in particular by the late Professor C. F. Burney in *The Poetry of Our Lord* (1925). A discourse that follows a recognizable pattern is more easily memorized, and if Jesus wished His teaching to be memorized, His use of poetry is easily explained. Besides, Jesus was recognized by His contemporaries as a prophet, and prophets in Old Testament days were accustomed to utter their oracles in poetical form. Where this form has been preserved, we have a further assurance that His teaching has been handed down to us as it was originally given.[29]

When one combines the memorizable form of Jesus' sayings with the synagogal educational environment of first-century Palestine, the imperative to remember the sayings becomes even more obvious. This stress on memorization and the poetic nature of the words of Jesus indicate an accurate oral tradition for passing on his sayings even prior to Easter.

This conclusion is shared by New Testament scholar Richard Bauckham, who recently emphasized the memorable nature of Jesus' teachings:

> In a predominantly oral society, not only do people deliberately remember but also teachers formulate their teachings so as to make them easily memorable. It has frequently been observed that Jesus' teaching in its typically Synoptic forms has many features that facilitate remembering. The aphorisms are typically terse and incisive, the narrative parables have a clear and relatively simple plot outline. Even in Greek translation, the only form in which we have them, the sayings of Jesus are recognizably poetic, especially employing parallelism, and many have posited Aramaic originals rich in alliteration, assonance, rhythm, rhyme, and wordplay.[30]

5.7 JESUS FREQUENTLY USED APHORISMS, MESHALIM, AND PITHY SAYINGS THAT COULD BE EASILY REMEMBERED.

The distinctive use of aphorisms and meshalim by Jesus was recognized by Gerhardsson and Riesner. Aphorisms and meshalim also appear designed to facilitate memorization and rote learning. Jesus' use of picturesque forms of speech to convey his message, such as parables and pithy statements, is similar to proverbs. The book of Proverbs in the Old Testament contains these kinds of pithy statements, which in Hebrew are called *meshalim*. Jesus used meshalim forms in his teachings even during his earthly ministry. Riesner refers to this phenomenon in the pre-Easter oral gospel tradition:

> Jesus condensed the main points of his theological and ethical teaching in summaries, the aphoristic meshalim. These were uttered, not spontaneously, but consciously pre-formulated. If Jesus created a deliberate formulation and poetical form of a teaching, then it was done not to make his hearers forget but to make them memorize. This would have been possible through the highly poetic form of most of the sayings and supported by some rote learning, either encouraged by Jesus himself or spontaneously done. . . . That Jesus encapsulated his main view in basic sayings, which he repeated deliberately, is stressed by experts on ancient rhetoric such as George A. Kennedy. The unique non-responsorial *amen* may have served as another pointer to statements of special, that is, revelatory character.[31]

5.8 JESUS' SAYINGS FREQUENTLY HAVE DISTINCT RHYTHMIC PATTERNS THAT ENCOURAGE MEMORY.

When Jesus sends out his disciples as messengers during his earthly ministry as described in the tenth chapter of Matthew, Jeremias noted that the Aramaic words of instructions are given in a four-beat line. This rhythm is the rhythm that Jesus used so often in the instruction of his disciples.[32] When one considers the sayings of Jesus as translated back into the Aramaic language (to be more precise, Jeremias concluded that the mother-tongue of Jesus was a Galilean form of western Aramaic),[33] they have a rhythmic form, similar to the sayings of several prophecies in the Old Testament. C. F. Burney discovered three rhythmic patterns to Jesus' sayings: a four-beat, three-beat, and the *kinā* meter; Jeremias also noticed a two-beat rhythm. Each of the rhythms were used in a different mood and in a specific area of thought.[34] For example, the two-beat rhythm appears in the Aramaic translation of the saying of Jesus found in Matt. 11:5–6 and in Luke 7:22–23. Matthew reads as follows: "Jesus answered them, 'Go and tell John what you hear and see:

the blind receive their sight, the lame walk, the lepers are cleansed, the deaf hear, the dead are raised, and the poor have good news brought to them. And blessed is anyone who takes no offense at me.'"[35]

A saying with such a rhythm is more easily remembered and transmitted to others. As noted above, Jesus' sayings also are frequently short and decisive with words that rhyme in Aramaic. This further increases the ability of the listener to remember the sayings. For example, when he commissions the disciples and sends them out, the command has a steady beat with words that rhyme in Aramaic. This terse rhyming form appears in the charge in Matt. 10:8: "Heal the sick, cleanse the lepers, raise the dead, cast out demons. Freely you have received, freely give."[36]

Jeremias gave many examples of the two-beat rhythm in the sayings of Jesus. In Matt. 25:35–36, this two-beat rhythm is seen in a sequence of an enumeration of six works of love: " . . . for I was hungry and you gave me food, I was thirsty and you gave me something to drink, I was a stranger and you welcomed me, I was naked and you gave me clothing, I was sick and you took care of me, I was in prison and you visited me."

Jeremias gave reasons why some of the qualities of the two-beat rhythm in Aramaic increase the ability of the hearer to transmit Jesus' words more accurately: "Because of its brevity, the two-beat line necessitates terse and abrupt formulations, whose sparseness and monotony lends them the utmost urgency. A further look at the themes of the examples given above will immediately show that Jesus used the two-beat line . . . to impress upon his hearers *central ideas* of his message."[37]

An increased ability to transmit Jesus' words accurately is also present when one examines the characteristics of Jesus' sayings in three-beat lines. The three-beat lines were used in the wisdom literature of the Old Testament and demonstrate that Jesus was employing methods of Jewish traditional transmission of holy texts when he conveyed his thoughts. This style is especially effective in conveying aphorisms, meditative thoughts, and proverbs, and was the most frequent rhythm used by Jesus. Jeremias commented on the effectiveness of the three-beat rhythm in oral transmission: "It is the most frequent rhythm to be used in the sayings of Jesus; it serves *to drive home sayings and maxims.*"[38]

Jeremias noted that the *kinā* rhythm was used by Jesus in Aramaic "to express *strong inner emotion.*"[39] This appears not only in admonitions, but also in the beatitudes and in comforting statements about salvation. Jeremias emphasized that one can only appreciate the strength of these rhythms when one reads the sayings of Jesus in the original

CHAPTER 5

Aramaic, but in that language they indicate *a distinctive way of speaking by one person even in different gospel accounts. Despite the differences in the accounts, they are consistent with the interpretation that they have the same source in the style of one man's speech.* This is even true for the gospel of John. Moreover, this style and rhythm appears to be very ancient. As Jeremias concluded:

> To sum it up: it may be affirmed that the accumulation of rhythms in the sayings of Jesus allows us to draw the conclusion that we have to do with a distinct characteristic of his. In addition, they indicate a Semitic background and provide an important pointer towards the antiquity of the tradition. A comparison of the parallel traditions shows that much of this rhythmic language was lost when the sayings were translated into Greek, and while they were being handed on in a Greek milieu.[40]

5.9 MORE ATTENTION SHOULD BE DIRECTED TO THE SCHOLARSHIP CONCERNING THE ARAMAIC FORM OF JESUS' SAYINGS; THERE IS A NECESSITY FOR NEW TESTAMENT SCHOLARS TO REEXAMINE JESUS' ARAMAIC FORMS OF SPEECH.

New Testament scholar James Dunn has written a fine summary of much of the work on the oral tradition of the gospels. In his book *Jesus Remembered*, Dunn notes that the work of Birger Gerhardsson and Jeremias has presented evidence concerning the oral tradition that has not been considered adequately by many scholars. Those attempting to dismiss the orthodox evidence from the oral tradition have failed to develop a model of oral transmission that is consistent with a first-century Palestinian background.

For example, Bultmann and his descendant pupils begin with questionable presuppositions that determine their answers. Although they differ in some respects, their *presuppositions* determine the outcome of their examination of the evidence. Bishop Robinson noted in his comparing Bultmann with his contemporary Jeremias that a scholar's determination of whether Jesus actually said or did something depends to a great extent on where a scholar places the burden of proof:

> Thus, in the contemporary German scene, the great New Testament scholar Rudolf Bultmann tended to start with the question that leads to

123

a negative conclusion, laying the burden of proof on those who would claim that such and such a saying, for example, "You are Peter, and on this rock I will build my church" (Matt. 16:18), has its origin in Jesus rather than the Christian community. The equally great New Testament scholar Joachim Jeremias tends to start with the question that leads to the positive conclusion, noting the Palestinian background to the phrasing and asking why it should not be dominical.[41]

Almost half a century has passed since Jeremias provided effective arguments against the form-critical school led by Rudolf Bultmann. Despite certain existentialist tendencies, Bultmann embraced Kant's inadequate and overly restrictive theory of knowledge that required empirical verification through the senses. (See my discussion on Kant in *A Case for the Existence of God*.) Bultmann's work was based on a presupposition against the supernatural that required a "de-mythologizing" or "demythologization" of the Scriptures. Jeremias called into question this *presupposition* and demonstrated that Bultmann ignored the remarkable character of the sayings of Jesus that allowed them to be more easily memorized and retold among the disciples during Jesus' lifetime.

There is much work remaining for scholars to do concerning the oral tradition of Jesus' sayings. Forty-three years have passed since I studied with Jeremias in his Princeton class; his work should be considered again in the depth of analysis it deserves. His thorough scholarship, coupled with the work of Birger Gerhardsson, Rainer Riesner, James Dunn, and Richard Bauckham, is extremely relevant to the contemporary scene, which is replete with speculations congenial to questionable presuppositions concerning the incarnation. A purely human Jesus is much more acceptable to a pluralistic culture. But one's scholarship should attempt to reflect an honest investigation of history rather than revisionism from a contemporary zeitgeist.

Contemporary scholarship concerning the Jesus tradition may be faulted for a lack of vigor and depth in its consistent failure to examine the Aramaic form of the teachings of Jesus of Nazareth.[42] To attempt to understand the manner in which Jesus communicated with his disciples, any review of his methods and sayings should include an examination of the Aramaic language that he employed. Jeremias emphasized the importance of understanding that Jesus' sayings are most authentic when considered in the light of the Aramaic language:

The discovery that the sayings of Jesus are to be set against an Aramaic background is of great significance for the question of the reliability of the gospel tradition. This linguistic evidence takes us back into the realm of Aramaic oral tradition. It also confronts us with the task of comparing not only the content of the sayings of Jesus (as has so often been done), but also their language and style with the characteristics of Semitic language current in contemporary Judaism.[43]

Dunn agrees with this conclusion and emphasizes the Aramaic oral tradition and the need to give more weight to the observations of Jeremias and reconsider his profound scholarship:

We may start by recalling that the tradition as it has come down to us has already been translated once, from Aramaic to Greek. Here is another curious blind spot in most work on Jesus' teaching, in all phases of the "quest for the historical Jesus." I refer to the repeated failure to ask about the Aramaic form which Jesus' teaching presumably took. Without such inquiry any assertions about earliest forms of the teaching tradition are bound to be suspect in some measure. . . . What is of more importance for us here are the important observations by Aramaic experts with regard to the character of the teaching tradition. All have noted that the tradition, even in its Greek state, bears several marks of oral transmission in Aramaic. . . . Joachim Jeremias climaxed a lifetime's scholarship by summarizing the indications that many of the words appearing in Jesus' teaching had an Aramaic origin, and that the speech involved had many characteristic features, including "divine passive," as well as the features already noted by Burney and Black.[44]

Jeremias was an unusual scholar, with his understanding of Aramaic beginning early in his life and continuing throughout his work. As noted above, Jeremias's father was the pastor of the Church of the Redeemer in Jerusalem, which gave Jeremias an opportunity to learn Aramaic when he lived in Jerusalem with his family from the ages of ten to fifteen. His knowledge of this ancient language allowed him to reconstruct the Aramaic substratum underlying the words of Jesus and to find the actual voice of Jesus (*ipsissima vox*). He used this knowledge to argue for the necessity of New Testament scholars to recover Jesus' Aramaic forms of speech as a foundation for theological study. In his remarkable and thorough scholarship he examined the use of Aramaic in the first century with extensive study of the Dead Sea Scrolls, the Hebrew Bible, the Apocrypha, and rabbinic works of the time. His findings were well described in all of his works, including the *Central Message of the New Testament, The Parables of Jesus, The Eucharistic Words of Jesus, The Prayers of Jesus*, and his *New Testament Theology*. These works are worthy of careful study. Serious scholars approaching the question of the historical Jesus and the authenticity of his sayings should not ignore the Aramaic form of Jesus' original words.

5.10 JEREMIAS EMPHASIZED JESUS' UNIQUE WAY OF SPEAKING AND OUR ABILITY TO DETERMINE HIS ACTUAL VOICE (*IPSISSIMA VOX*).

As indicated above, in our class Jeremias frequently emphasized that Jesus had his own unique way of speaking and that the style of Jesus' teachings were consistent with the same person speaking throughout the Synoptic gospels and even the gospel of John. He noted that, despite the *same* saying of Jesus being transmitted to us in *different* Greek forms, the inflection, pattern, and other peculiarities were consistent with the same person as the source of the saying. In other words, Jesus had his own particular way of speaking, and the sayings in the different New Testament gospel accounts may indicate that one man with his own style of speech was behind the different wordings given to Jesus' teachings in the different gospel accounts.

In one class during a question-and-answer period following a lecture in which Jeremias emphasized these points, another graduate student objected to Jeremias's conclusion, stating that he could not see the similarity of pattern and peculiarities in Jesus' sayings among the Synoptic gospels and the gospel of John. Jeremias politely asked him in which language he had read the gospel accounts. The student proudly stated that he had read them in the original Greek. Jeremias gently chided that in order to see the stylistic similarities one had to read the sayings in Galilean Aramaic because Jesus spoke Galilean Aramaic.

Jeremias's lectures were later published as *The Central Message of the New Testament*. He noted how fruitful the study of Galilean Aramaic can be in New Testament scholarship, the high degree of probability in retranslating Jesus' words into this dialect, and the efficacy of a retranslation to confirm the New Testament's accuracy in recording the actual words of Jesus. Jeremias was convinced that we could draw closer to the historical Jesus by studying the Aramaic forms of the Jesus tradition, including his awareness of his close association with God in his use of the familiar *Abba* address and his unique use of the Aramaic term *Amen*. Jeremias wrote:

> But the studies (of Galilean Aramaic) made so far have already demonstrated how rewarding such meticulous philological research can be. It is only necessary to recall in how many cases one and the same sayings of Jesus has been transmitted to us in different Greek forms. In most of these cases we are dealing with translation variants, which constitute a reliable aid in reconstructing the Aramaic form of the saying underlying the various versions. For example, the Lord's Prayer, the Greek renderings of which in Matthew and Luke show many divergences, can by this means be retranslated into Jesus' mother tongue with a high degree of probability.
>
> Anyone who has ever had anything to do with translations is aware that translations can never take the place of the original and will be able to assess how important it is that we should be able to get back, with a high degree of probability, to the original Aramaic underlying the Greek tradition. It must of course be remembered that the earliest Christian community spoke Aramaic too; so not every Aramaism is evidence of authenticity. At any rate, however, we are drawing nearer to Jesus himself when we succeed in rediscovering the pre-Hellenistic form of the tradition. In this connection it is of special importance to note that this kind of study reveals peculiarities in the utterances of Jesus that are without contemporary parallels. As a form of address to God, the word "*Abba*" (Father) is without parallel in the whole of late Jewish devotional literature. Similarly, there is no contemporary analogy to Jesus' use of "*Amen*" as an introduction to his own utterances. It may be maintained that these two characteristics features of the "actual voice" (*ipsissima vox*) of Jesus contain, in a nutshell, his message and his consciousness of his authority.[45]

The insight of Jeremias's work concerning the accuracy of the oral tradition and the recording of this tradition in the gospel accounts of the New Testament is important additional evidence that we can trust the accuracy of these accounts. He was certain that one could determine with substantial reliability the *ipsissima vox* (the very voice) of Jesus if not his *ipsissima verba* (his very words).

Dunn concurs with Jeremias's assessment that the particular way of speaking of Jesus of Nazareth as passed down through the oral tradition is likely from the voice of one person (Jesus) and not from a multitude of various persons subsequently fabricating words and sayings that they put on the lips of Jesus.

> This evidence should be given more weight than has usually been the case. Of course, such features are common to written as well as oral tradition. And an Aramaic phrase may only be evidence of an early (post-Easter) stage of transmission when the tradition was still circulating in Aramaic. But if the tradition is *consistently* marked by *particular* stylistic features, as the Aramaic specialists conclude, then it has to be judged more likely that these are *the characteristics of one person*, rather than that the multitude of Aramaic oral tradents had the same characteristics. The possibility that we can still hear what Jeremias called "the *ipsissima vox*" (as distinct from the *ipsissima verba*) of Jesus coming through the tradition should be brought back into play more seriously than it has in the thirty years since Jeremias last wrote on the subject.[46]

Jeremias presented a plausible and powerful argument that needs to be reconsidered today in contemporary New Testament scholarship. Jeremias observed that the liturgy of the early church preserved the sayings of Jesus, as they were used in worship. These sayings, such as the Lord's Prayer or the record of the words spoken at the Last Supper that were repeated in liturgical worship in the young church, reflect an authenticity that takes us back to Jesus himself. In other words, as we worship today and pray the Lord's Prayer, and participate in the eucharist, we are most likely repeating the words of Jesus in our own language. The oral tradition represented by these sayings predate the crucifixion and were passed on through the regular communal liturgical worship celebrations. Contrary to some speculative contemporary New Testament analysis, the thorough work of Jeremias, J. D. G. Dunn, Rainer Riesner, Birger Gerhardsson, Richard Bauckman, and others confirms the authenticity and trustworthiness of the New Testament gospel accounts. As Dunn concluded, "What we today are confronted with in the gospels is not the top layer (last edition) of a series of increasingly impenetrable layers, but the living tradition of Christian celebration which takes us with surprising immediacy to the heart of the first memories of Jesus."[47]

For his part, Gerhardsson became convinced that one could hear Jesus' voice in the New Testament gospel accounts. He emphasized the devoted commitment of Jesus' followers who wanted to preserve the message they had received from their master so that others "might know as much possible as about Jesus Christ, the crucified, resurrected, and living Lord of the church."[48]

5.11 THE EVIDENCE INDICATES THAT THE DISCIPLES TRANSMITTED WHAT THEY HAD LEARNED FROM THEIR UNIQUELY ESTEEMED LEADER AS "HOLY SPEECH" THAT WAS UNLIKELY TO BE CHANGED OR INVENTED BY ANOTHER PERSON.

In her book *Oral Poetry: Its Nature, Significance and Social Context* (1977), Ruth Finnegan, an expert on the oral transmission of poetry in ancient societies, held that verbatim memorization and precise oral transmission of religious, ritualized sayings were common in these ancient cultures where the following conditions were present: (1) the author was considered to be divinely inspired; (2) the oral text was fixed in an identifiable form, such as poetry; and (3) the oral text was passed on by a group trained for such a task.[49]

As we have seen, Riesner demonstrated that the last two conditions were fulfilled and in existence during Jesus' earthly ministry. In addressing the first condition, he noted that the authority of Jesus was considered unique, unlike the scribes and other religious leaders. In examining this condition, he agrees with Gerhardsson and others who note that there is no evidence of Jesus invoking the authority of another teacher. The concentration on Jesus as the only teacher, even above the Old Testament, is an important distinction between Jesus and other teachers. His unique use of the Aramaic word *amen* indicates that his sayings are to be regarded as divinely inspired.[50] This uniqueness, coupled with the thought that he was or might be the messiah, made the preservation of his words even more likely. As Riesner concludes, "There was then in his earthly ministry a note of messianic authority that would have occasioned the preservation of Jesus' words and after Easter it became even more important. . . . A word of Jesus was important not only because it could have been useful but also because it was the word of the messiah approved by God himself."[51]

If one considers the resurrection experiences of the original disciples as events that at least they believed to be true, we can understand how the disciples may have interpreted the sayings of Jesus in a new light, but that does not mean that in editing these statements, they created or invented the statements of Jesus. Gerhardsson notes this important distinction: "It is one thing to state that traditions have been *marked* by the milieu through which they passed; another to claim that they simply were *created* in this secondary milieu. The evidence suggests that memories of Jesus were so clear, and the traditions with which they were connected so firmly based that there can have been relatively little scope for alteration."[52]

When one considers that Jesus' teaching was held in the highest regard without any references to any sayings among the most influential of his followers (such as Peter or John), one can understand that his words received special attention so that their memorization and transmission would be at the most careful level of tradition. This means that speculations among certain contemporary scholars that attempt to draw parallels to modern oral transmission are not comparable or informative in considering how the disciples transmitted what they had learned as "holy speech" from their uniquely esteemed teacher.

I want to be clear that I am not arguing that we have a word perfect reproduction of all of Jesus' sayings or deeds. I do not think that such a reproduction is necessary for the reliability of the core doctrine of the Christian faith. I am saying that this core was passed on to us in a reliable, trustworthy manner and that this core is sufficient to sustain the substance of an orthodox Christian faith.

5.12 THE EVIDENCE POINTS TO A CENTRAL FOCUS ON JESUS IN THE FIRST CONGREGATION WITH NO AUTHORITY GIVEN TO ANYONE TO ADD TO OR ALTER JESUS' TEACHINGS; THE CONCEPT THAT ANYONE COULD INVENT TRADITIONS CONCERNING JESUS AND PLACE WORDS IN HIS MOUTH RUNS COUNTER TO OUR KNOWLEDGE OF THE LEADERSHIP AND AUTHORITY OF THE MOTHER CONGREGATION IN JERUSALEM.

Further evidence for the special care given to the maintenance and transmission of Jesus' teaching is demonstrated in the reverence given to Jesus by the original mother congregation of the church in Jerusalem consisting of "the twelve" and the mother of Jesus. The acknowledged three pillars of that church of the first century were Peter, James, and

John. Yet these men are never given the esteem or authority given to Jesus. From the very beginning the young church is Jesus centered. Jesus is the "one teacher" and no other. Not one of the pillars is given the authority to add to or alter his teaching.

Gerhardsson makes the point that the closest disciples to Jesus and his family had positions of leadership in the very early history of the Christian church as witnesses and persons holding the traditions of Jesus' sayings and actions. The speculative concept that another person could invent traditions concerning Jesus and place words in his mouth that he had not said runs counter to our knowledge of the leadership and authority structure of the mother congregation in Jerusalem:[53]

> The sources indicate that Apostle-traditions grew up in the early Church. But when these great men come to be compared with Jesus Christ, then no more is heard of their authority, their maturity, their knowledge, their wisdom and their insight. Never for one moment are we allowed to forget the distance between the "only" teacher and these others. It would be well to keep this in mind in face of skeptical scholars' attempts to show that the tradition of Jesus is a free compilation on the part of the early Church: that they took up sayings which were in circulation, and placed them in the mouth of Jesus; that they themselves freely created "sayings" of Jesus'; that they projected sayings of early Christian prophets back into the life of Jesus; and the like.[54]

In other words, the followers of Jesus were willing to transmit several of his sayings that would be embarrassing to the early church, such as his attitude toward children and animals. Metzger was convinced that the gospel traditions were passed on in a faithful, accurate manner. He was convinced that the earliest Christian community did not invent sayings of Jesus to deal with their problems:

> A consideration of the actual state of the evidence will lead one to the conclusion that there was no large-scale introduction of extraneous materials into the Gospels. . . . A simple test can be made to determine the extent to which extraneous materials have been taken into the Gospels. One of the most influential figures in the early church was the apostle Paul. His Letters, which date from the time when many of the Gospel traditions were taking shape, abound in pithy sentences and spiritual insights that could easily have been transferred to Jesus and presented as oracles of the Lord. If it be asked how many times this has happened, the answer must be *Not once!*[55]

In his recent book *Jesus and the Eyewitnesses*, New Testament scholar Richard Bauckham presents a compelling, meticulous argument that eyewitnesses to Jesus' life and teachings (including his closest disciples) were the authoritative sources and guarantors of the sacred oral tradition of Jesus' actions and words. This tradition was controlled in the mother congregation in Jerusalem by these eyewitnesses, who were also concerned to preserve the tradition faithfully in the Christian communities developing in other geographical areas. These eyewitnesses had an extensive influence on these developing churches. These young churches comprised a close network of communication with leaders and participants in geographically dispersed communities frequently traveling to visit and encourage each other. Moreover, the early Jewish Christians continued the practice of attending Jewish festivals centered in Jerusalem, and consequently, had the opportunity to hear the twelve discuss their lives with Jesus and his resurrection appearances. These visits to Jerusalem would also provide a means of preserving and controlling the passing on of the liturgical traditions concerning Jesus.[56]

Bauckham emphasizes that the individuals closest to Jesus were most likely to have controlled the transmission of the sacred oral tradition. The twelve leaders in the Jerusalem church would have insured a discipline of handing over the formulated traditions about Jesus. In first-century Jewish synagogal education patterns, this tradition would be preserved and faithfully passed on in a much more careful manner than some contemporary form critics allow.

5.13 THE TIME PERIOD BETWEEN THE CRUCIFIXION AND THE WRITING OF THE CANONICAL GOSPELS IS VERY SHORT, AND THE PATTERN OF WORSHIP OF JESUS WAS SUCH THAT THE PILLARS OF THE FIRST CONGREGATION (PETER, JAMES, JOHN) HAD AUTHORITY TO PRESERVE HIS WORDS WITHOUT ALLOWING ANY SIGNIFICANT CHANGES OR THE INVENTING OF WORDS OF JESUS *DE NOUVEAU*.

The period of time between the crucifixion and the writing of the gospel accounts was quite short. Most likely all of the canonical gospels were written within a few decades of the events they describe. We are not considering accounts written a hundred years after the events (as with the gnostic gospels, such as the gospel of Thomas). Eyewitnesses were still living, tradition was passed on in a reliable manner, and the leaders of the inner circle of Jesus' followers who constituted the mother congregation in Jerusalem (such as Peter) were in communication with Luke and Mark. These leaders likely passed on the tradition in the manner indicated by those who handled sacred tradition during this time in Jerusalem and Palestine.

The evidence indicates that the disciples continued the tradition of reliable oral transmission. When the records of the Jesus tradition, including his teaching and instructions, were finally written and recorded in documents, they followed from a Jewish framework of "delivering" and "receiving" tradition. Gerhardsson reminds us that in examining the relatively short time of exclusive oral transmission between the crucifixion and the writing of documents concerning the Jesus tradition, we cannot forget the pattern of worship of Jesus (see my discussion in chapter 2). He points to two facts which anyone considering the path of the Synoptic tradition must consider:

> There are two facts one may not lose sight of: (1) That in the eyes of early Christianity Jesus was a unique and incomparable figure, King of kings and Lord of lords; and we may add: Prophet of prophets, Teacher of teachers, Messiah, Son of God, *Kyrios*. No one was considered his equal. (2) That it was not Jesus the wisdom teacher, prophet, or miracle worker who was the center of early Christian convictions, but Jesus the crucified, the risen and living Lord, the exclusive Redeemer and Savior of the world.[57]

Of course this does not mean that the disciples had reached a clear understanding of Jesus prior to Easter. Only after Easter did they understand the meaning of his life, work, and resurrection. After Easter they had an increased clarity about Jesus, and this increased clarity influenced their interpretation of the sayings of Jesus and his tradition. But this increased clarity only enhanced the stature of the leaders of the mother congregation in Jerusalem. The need to preserve and transmit the sayings of Jesus in a very accurate manner would have received more emphasis in the light of Easter. The communication of this tradition was not done by communities without leaders who had positions of authority. The twelve, including Peter, James, and John, were central authorities in the young church. The evidence indicates that the gospel accounts reflect material that was preserved with great care and respect and under the authority of these leaders. Gerhardsson emphasizes the probability of the closest disciples of Jesus taking care to preserve his saying, parables, and activities, even during Jesus' own lifetime:

> The sources give us no reason to believe that just anyone in the early Christian period could say that Jesus had said anything whatever. I maintain that Jesus' closest disciples—Peter, James, John, and the group known as the Twelve—must be suspected of having had much to do with the oldest stages of the synoptic tradition. They preserved Jesus' meshalim—logia (sayings), parables—and began to tell of his activities even while he was conducting his own ministry before Easter.[58]

The material in the gospel accounts come from the time of the earthly life of Jesus. As noted above, they may have been clarified and given some interpretation by the early Christian leaders in the light of the resurrection of Jesus. The resurrection was an event that allowed them to see the person of Jesus in a greatly clarified and exalted manner, but changes in interpretation is a long way away from placing words in Jesus' mouth that he did not say. If anything, their conviction of the resurrection event and the appearances of Jesus after the resurrection would only have encouraged them to hold fast to the actual words he spoke during his earthly ministry so as to preserve them in a more careful manner. It is one thing to say that they could interpret his sayings in the light of Easter, but an entirely different thing to accuse them of inventing words of Jesus *de nouveau*. Creating words with no relation to his actual sayings would be highly unlikely given the holy and exalted light in which they now viewed his person.

5.14 THE EVIDENCE SUPPORTS THE POSITION THAT THE COMMUNITY AND LEADERS OF THE EARLIEST CHURCH WOULD CORRECT ANY INACCURATE RETELLING OF A STORY OR SAYING OF JESUS; THE CENTRAL CORE WOULD REMAIN FIXED THROUGH THE MONITORING OF THE ORAL TRANSMISSION PROCESS.

As noted above, the evidence indicates that the oral communication of the words of Jesus began during the period of Jesus' ministry in Galilee. Kenneth Bailey, in reflecting on his experience of more than thirty years in analyzing the oral tradition of Middle East villages similar to the villages of first-century Galilee, concluded that the village culture of Galilee in the earliest Christian community exercised control in an informal fashion over the retelling of stories. He noted that this control allowed for some flexibility on matters outside the central core of the story, but that the central points and words of the story were not changed. In his experience of life in such a village, we have a witness to the oral transmission process that appears to be similar to an experience of the oral tradition at the time of Jesus' life. Because of the significance of Jesus' role in his disciples lives, we can assume from what we know of first-century oral communication that the community of earliest disciples around Jesus would have been concerned to exercise some control over the retelling of the words and acts of Jesus.[59]

Richard Bauckham appreciates Bailey's insights but argues persuasively that Bailey's emphasis on the *community* exercising control over the oral tradition overlooks the importance of the *eyewitnesses* in the early Christian movement. These were the persons who were present with Jesus "from the beginning" of his ministry and who experienced the significant events and words in his life. Bauckham argues that Bailey's emphasis on the Christian community in general as the controller of the oral tradition ignores the leadership in the church accorded to those closest to Jesus. He follows Gerhardsson's reflections and presents significant evidence that the leadership of the twelve, including the pillars of the Jerusalem mother congregation, exercised more control over the sacred oral tradition than the Christian community in general.[60]

5.15 THREE EXAMPLES DEMONSTRATE THAT WE CAN TRUST THE ORAL TRADITION TO MAINTAIN THE CENTRAL CORE OF THE DEEDS AND SAYINGS OF JESUS AND THE ACTS OF THE APOSTLES.

I have argued from many sources of historical evidence that the likelihood of the disciples altering the central threads of a story or saying is more remote than presupposed by some New Testament scholarship. The work of Bailey, Gerhardsson, Riesner, Dunn, Bauckham, and Jeremias all points to a conclusion that the central or core elements would remain fixed through the monitoring of the oral transmission of sayings and stories. This is consistent with the story of Saul/Paul's conversion, which is recorded three times in the Acts of the Apostles. The three records of the event appear in Acts 9:1–22, 22:1–21, and 26:9–23. Although Luke relates the event in three different ways, the central threads of the story are all the same: Saul is on a journey to Damascus to persecute members of the young church; a light from heaven shines or flashes around him; a voice says to him, "Saul, why are you persecuting me?"; Saul responds, "Who are you, Lord?"; The response is "I am Jesus whom you are persecuting." The voice then says to him to "get up."

In all three records of the event, the words describing the dialogue between Saul and the risen Jesus are precisely the same, even though the details of the three records vary in the less central details. This supports the conclusion that the central core of a story or saying would be a precisely fixed element with flexibility in the story permitted in the supporting details.[61] As Dunn demonstrates, placing these stories side by side with the same words indicated in italic, bold print vividly discloses that Luke tells the same story in a different way, but with the core of the story exactly the same in each of the three versions.

Table 5.1. Saul/Paul's Conversion

Acts 9:3–6	Acts 22:6–10	Acts 26:12–16
[3]Now as he **was going along** and approaching **Damascus**, suddenly a **light from heaven** flashed **around him**. [4]He **fell to the ground** and **heard a voice saying** to him, **"Saul, Saul, why do you persecute me?"** [5]He asked, **"Who are you, Lord?"** The reply came, **"I am Jesus, whom you are persecuting. [6]But get up and** enter the city, and you will be told what you are to do."	[6]"While I **was on my way** and approaching **Damascus**, about noon a great **light from heaven** suddenly shone **about me**. [7]**And I fell to the ground** and **heard a voice saying** to me, **'Saul, Saul, why are you persecuting me?'** [8]I answered, **'Who are you, Lord?'** Then he said to me, **'I am Jesus of Nazareth whom you are persecuting.'** [9]Now those who were with me saw the light but did not hear the voice of the one who was speaking to me. [10]I asked, 'What am I to do, Lord?' The Lord said to me, **'Get up and** go to Damascus; there you will be told everything that has been assigned to you to do.'"	[12]" . . . **I was traveling** to **Damascus** with the authority and commission of the chief priests, [13]when at midday along the road, your Excellency, I saw **a light from heaven**, brighter than the sun, shining **around me** and my companions. [14]When we had all **fallen to the ground**, I **heard a voice saying** to me in the Hebrew language, **'Saul, Saul, why are you persecuting me?** It hurts you to kick against the goads.' [15]I asked, **'Who are you, Lord?'** The Lord answered, **'I am Jesus whom you are persecuting.** [16]**but get up** and stand on your feet . . .'"

Dunn has written an interesting book on the oral traditioning process, and an exhaustive summary of his research and findings would only be duplicative of his serious effort to convey the significance of this tradition. A few of his examples, however, should suffice to demonstrate the importance of his work and the need for contemporary scholarship to give more attention to understanding the reliability and authenticity of oral tradition in the first century.

To some extent, Dunn's analysis calls into question the reliance of Matthew and Luke on Q and the conventional assumption that Mark was the first recorded document. Q is a hypothetical written collection of sayings that most scholars think was used by Matthew and Luke. If such a document existed, it probably consisted of about two hundred verses common to Luke and Matthew. I do not think it is a major issue for the theme of this book, and I can see arguments for and against its existence. Dunn asks why we should assume that the non-Markan material contained in both Matthew and Luke should be attributed to Q. Given what we now know of the accuracy required in the central core of oral tradition and the flexibility allowed in the nonessential details, the assumption that Matthew and Luke's sole source for their common non-Markan discussion of Jesus was Q may not be valid. In many respects, the oral traditioning process is sufficient to explain the differences in wording without the need to postulate a Q document.

In presenting three of Dunn's examples, I will modify his method of presenting the Synoptic texts in parallel columns by italicizing and marking the closest parallel words. For the first example I turn to the story of the healing of the centurion's servant done by Jesus as he entered Capernaum. Matthew and Luke give the following differing accounts with their matching language indicated in bold italics.

Clearly the core and essentials of the story are identical as demonstrated by the common bold, italicized language. As Jesus enters Capernaum, a centurion asks him to heal his servant. The centurion's response to Jesus is word for word the same, as is Jesus' response to the centurion's words. The story only differs in the details. The central core is the dialogue between the centurion and Jesus.

For the second example, consider the story of Jesus' stilling of the storm from Mark, Matthew, and Luke. Again the identical words are marked in bold italics.

The central core is the same: a storm occurs; the disciples wake Jesus and say "we are perishing"; Jesus gets up and rebukes the wind and

Table 5.2. Healing of the Centurion's Servant in Capernaum

Matt. 8:5–10	Luke 7:1–9
5When *he entered Capernaum, a centurion came to him*, appealing to him and saying, *"Lord, my servant is lying at home paralyzed, in terrible distress." And he said to him, "I will come and cure him."* 8The centurion answered, *"Lord, I am not worthy to have you come under my roof, but only speak the word, and my servant will be healed. For I also am a man under authority, with soldiers under me; and I say to one, 'Go,' and he goes, and to another, 'Come' and he comes, and to my slave, 'Do this,' and the slave does it." 10When Jesus heard him, he was amazed and said* to those who *followed him. "Truly I tell you,* in *no* one" *in Israel have I found such faith*.	1After Jesus had finished all his sayings in the hearing of the people, *he entered Capernaum.* 2*A centurion* there had a slave whom he valued highly, and who was ill and close to death. 3When he heard about Jesus, he sent some Jewish elders to him, asking him to come and heal his slave. 4When they came to Jesus, they appealed to him earnestly, saying, "He is worthy of having you do this for him, 5for he loves our people, and it is he who built our synagogue for us." 6And Jesus went with them, but when he was not far from the house, the centurion sent friends to say to him, "*Lord*, do not trouble yourself, for *I am not worthy to have you come under my roof;* therefore I did not presume to come to you. *But only speak the word, and let my servant be healed.* 8*For I also am a man set under authority, with soldiers under me; and I say to one, 'Go,' and he goes, and to another, 'Come,' and he comes, and to my slave, 'Do this,' and the slave does it."* 9*When Jesus heard this he was amazed* at him, and turning to the crowd that *followed him*, he said, "*I tell you, not* even *in Israel have I found such faith.*"

there was calm; and the disciples wonder who is Jesus that even the wind and the sea or water obey him. Flexibility exists in the details but not in the essential points of the story. Although acknowledging that Matthew and Luke may have only edited Mark's account, Dunn is more convinced that the explanation for the differences could better be explained by variations in the oral tradition that allowed flexibility on the nonessentials of the story but strict adherence to its key points.[62]

The final example also demonstrates the faithfulness of the oral tradition in maintaining the essentials of an account in the recording of the last supper of Jesus with his disciples on the night before he was betrayed. When we compare the accounts in Matthew, Mark, and Luke with the account given by Paul in First Corinthians, we again see that

Table 5.3. Stilling of the Storm

Matt. 8:23–27	Mark 4:35–41	Luke 8:22–25
[23]And when he got into the boat, his disciples followed him. [24]A windstorm arose on the sea, so great that the boat was being swamped by the waves; but he was asleep. [25]And they went and woke him up, saying, "Lord, save us! We are perishing!" [26]*And he said to them, "Why are you afraid, you of little faith!"* Then he got up and rebuked the winds and the sea; and there was a dead calm. [27]They were amazed, saying, *"What sort of man is this, that even the winds and the sea obey him?"*	[35]On that day, when evening had come, he said to them, "Let us go across to the other side." [36]*And leaving the crowd behind, they took him with them in the boat, just as he was. Other boats were with him.* [37]A great *windstorm* arose, and the *waves beat into the boat*, so that the boat was already being swamped. [38]But he was in the stern, *asleep on the cushion*; and they woke him up and said to him, *"Teacher, do you not care that we are perishing?"* [39]He woke up and rebuked the wind, and said to the sea, *"Peace! Be still!"* Then the *wind ceased, and there was a dead calm.* [40]He said to them, *"Why are you afraid? Have you still no faith?"* [41]And they were filled with great awe and said to one another, *"Who then is this, that even the wind and the sea obey him?"*	[22]One day he got into a boat with his disciples, and he said to them, "Let us go across to the other side of the lake." So they put out, [23]and while they were sailing he fell asleep. A *windstorm* swept down on the lake, and the boat was filling with water, and they were in danger. [24]They went to him and *woke him up* shouting, "Master, Master, *we are perishing!"* And *he woke up and rebuked* the wind and the raging waves; they ceased, *and there was a calm.* [25]He said to them, "Where is your faith?" They were afraid and amazed, and said to one another, "Who then *is this, that he* commands even the winds and the water, and they *obey him?"*

the central elements are fixed with the Corinthians account showing the precision that was carried out by the early church as they celebrated the eucharist. As we have noted before, in First Cor. 11:23 Paul states that he received this tradition from Jesus and uses the technical language we discussed above for passing on oral tradition ("received" or in Greek *parelabon*; "handed on" or *paredōka*).

The assumption that the account of the Last Supper was only communicated through a written tradition is questionable. A more obvious

Table 5.4. The Last Supper

Matt. 26:26–29	Mark 14:22–25
[26]*While they were eating,* Jesus *took a loaf of bread, and after blessing it he broke it*, gave it to the disciples, *and said, "Take*, eat; *this is my body."* [27]*Then he took a cup, and after giving thanks he gave it to them*, saying, "Drink *from it, all of you;* [28]for *this is my blood of the covenant, which is poured out for many* for the forgiveness of sins. [29]*I tell you, I will never again drink of* this *fruit of the vine until that day when I drink it new* with you *in my Father's kingdom."*	[22]*While they were eating*, he *took a loaf of bread, and after blessing it he broke it*, gave it to them, *and said "Take; this is my body."* [23]*Then he took a cup, and after giving thanks he gave it to them*, and *all* of them drank *from it.* [24]He said to them, *"This is my blood of the covenant, which is poured out* for *many.* [23]Truly *I tell you, I will* never again *drink of* the *fruit of the vine until that day when I drink it new* in *the kingdom of God."*

Luke 22:17–20	First Cor.11: 23–26
[17]Then he took a cup, and after giving thanks he said, "Take this and divide it among yourselves; [18]for I tell you that from now on I will not drink of the fruit of the vine until the kingdom of God comes." [19]Then *he took a loaf of bread, and when he had given thanks, he broke it* and gave it to them, saying, *"This is my body, which is* given *for you. Do this in remembrance of me."* [20]And he did *the same* with *the cup after supper, saying, "This cup* that is poured out for you is *the new covenant in my blood . . ."*	[23]For I received from the Lord what I also handed on to you, that the Lord Jesus on the night when he was betrayed *took a loaf of bread,* [24]*and when he had given thanks, he broke it and* said, *"This is my body* that is *for you. Do this* in *remembrance of me."* [25] In *the same* way he took *the cup* also, *after supper, saying, "This cup is the new covenant in my blood.* Do this, as often as you drink it, in remembrance of me." [26]For as often as you eat this bread and drink the cup, you proclaim the Lord's death until he comes.

answer may be that the early Christian church knew this account because it was part of their liturgical worship pattern and part of the oral tradition process. As Richard Bauckham concludes: "The close verbal parallelism between 1 Cor. 11:23–25 and Luke 22:19–20 cannot plausibly be explained by a literary relationship between the texts, since Luke's Gospel cannot have been available to Paul and Luke shows no acquaintance with Paul's letters. Only strict oral tradition (memorized in Greek) can explain the high degree of verbal resemblance."[63]

For purposes of accuracy and reliability, it may not matter whether Q existed or not. The oral tradition process gives us sufficient reason to trust the accounts in the New Testament. If Q existed, it had to be composed at a very early date that may have preceded the composition of Mark. In any event, we have great reason to trust the oral tradition process in the very earliest church and to trust the written documents; they are consistent in presenting the core of the deeds and saying of Jesus.

Prior to Dunn's questioning the existence of a written tradition, Joachim Jeremias hypothesized that Q only had a form in an oral tradition. Part of the reasons for his inclination to treat Q as an oral source was the difficulty that exists in the reconstruction of Q in a literary form. Although he acknowledged that a majority of scholars support the two-source theory concerning the similarities among the Synoptic gospels, Jeremias thought that the theory was based on questionable grounds. The idea that the two sources were Q and Mark seemed to him an oversimplification of the problem. He demonstrated that this was obvious given the likelihood that the material in Luke did not come from an independent setting but was developed into the Lucan material earlier than it could have been solidified in a written Q document.[64] For Jeremias there was considerable doubt that Q existed as a written document.

In addition, Jeremias noted that 20 percent of the sayings in Matthew and Luke are almost word for word, but in most instances these sayings are easily memorized, consisting of short parables, antithetic parallelisms, and metaphors. In other words, the word for word sayings are the kinds of sayings that were normally formulated in Jewish tradition to be passed on in memorized verbatim form.

Another aspect which made Jeremias somewhat skeptical about the existence of a written Q document was the sequence of the sayings that diverge widely in Matthew and Luke. This contrary nature of the sequences of the sayings in the two gospels "could equally well have developed in an oral tradition."[65]

Jeremias combined this finding with a demonstration that frequently the same saying of Jesus in Matthew and Luke was "connected by a different linking word." Because the use of such a linking word is a common technique found in first-century writings, serving as a mnemonic aid to assist in memorization, this association technique indicates an oral tradition source for the saying. Jeremias gave several examples of different linking words used by Matthew and Luke. In essence, Matthew would use one word as a linking mnemonic device in a saying of Jesus and Luke in a parallel saying would use a different linking word to aid in memorization. This is significant because the difference in many of the parallel sayings in Matthew with their counterparts in Luke in all likelihood would have developed prior to any editing by the authors of the two gospels. As Jeremias noted concerning the differences in linking words in parallel sayings of Jesus: "This conclusion is important because it does not allow the ascriptions of the differences in the version of the *logia* [sayings] in Matthew and Luke to the redactional [editing] work of the two evangelists without linguistic proof. Most of the differences developed much earlier in the course of the tradition."[66]

This means that the common saying material in Matthew and Luke *may* have come from oral tradition and not from a written Q document. We do not know for certain, and Jeremias himself did not make a major point of it. However, one has to consider the question whether Q might never have existed in written form. What we do know, however, is that the words of Jesus were treated by the authors of Matthew and Luke with the greatest reverence and that Luke's technique of working in "blocks" of material in the composition of his gospel demonstrates that he refrained from making great alterations to the materials he received. This is well documented by Jeremias's examination of the verse by verse, almost word for word, parallel between passages in Luke and many "blocks" of Markan materials.[67]

In summary, the dating of the canonical gospels to a time when there were eyewitnesses available to correct any errors, coupled with the evidence for the reliability of the accurate oral transmission of stories and sayings of Jesus, presents a solid foundation for the trustworthiness of the canonical gospel accounts.

6

THE RESURRECTION IS A PLAUSIBLE EVENT

6.1 WHY DID THE CHRISTIAN FAITH EMERGE SO QUICKLY AND POWERFULLY IN FIRST-CENTURY JERUSALEM AT A TIME ALMOST CONTEMPORANEOUS WITH THE CRUCIFIXION OF JESUS OF NAZARETH?

Today we see an enormous number of persons proclaiming the Christian faith around the world. As I have tried to demonstrate, the evidence is clear that this faith traces its origin back to first-century Jerusalem to a time almost contemporaneous with the crucifixion of Jesus of Nazareth. What gave rise to the new faith? Why did this new faith emerge so quickly and powerfully, with its adherents willing to risk their lives by proclaiming that Jesus of Nazareth rose from the dead? This is an inescapable historical question. As N. T. Wright has made clear, when we look at the weekend in which the Christian faith began, we are confronted with two convictions of the first congregation of the Christian faith in Jerusalem: (1) the tomb of Jesus was discovered empty on Easter morning; and (2) Jesus then appeared to his disciples alive in bodily form. If one takes away either of these two convictions, the belief of the very earliest Christians becomes inexplicable.[1]

In the following pages I will examine whether we have sufficient evidence to hold a plausible, rational belief in the resurrection of Jesus of Nazareth. A dead man rising to new life may involve a challenge to one's worldview. Nevertheless, if a resurrection is the best historical explanation of the known phenomena surrounding the origin of the Christian faith, then perhaps our futures are not so gloomy after all, despite our knowledge about the eventual end of the universe *as we know it now.* There is hope for a new creation with a first-century resurrection serving as a prototype model. As noted earlier, the relevance of the resurrection to the question of Jesus' claim to be divine is that if it occurred, it presents a "signature" of God on the life, teachings, and claims of Jesus of Nazareth.[2]

6.2 ONE'S OPENNESS TO THE POSSIBILITY OF RESURRECTION DEPENDS UPON ONE'S ASSUMPTIONS AND PRESUPPOSITIONS CONCERNING THE POSSIBILITY OF GOD'S EXISTENCE.

To believe in the resurrection, one must be open to the possibility of supernatural events. To be open to this possibility, one must be open to the possibility that God exists and can be active in the physical world. In *A Case for the Existence of God* I discussed the requirement of a necessary being holding and preserving in existence every contingent being or thing, including the universe (or multiverse). When one considers the constant activity of God in preserving our very existence and realizes that every breath we draw requires God's sustaining activity, the concept of divine action in the world is not strange at all.

One problem with believing in the resurrection of Jesus of Nazareth is that a resurrection is outside our experience in ordinary life. Many persons reject the resurrection accounts on the presupposition that "dead men don't rise." German theologian Rudolf Bultmann held this position, partly because he began his inquiry with a presupposition against supernatural events in history. Applying this presupposition to the issue of the resurrection of Jesus, he began with the assertion: "A historical fact which involves a resurrection from the dead is utterly inconceivable."

If one assumes the existence of God, there is no compelling reason for holding a presupposition against the possibility of divine action in history. To make such a presupposition a priori, prior to a review and examination of the evidence, dismisses the legitimacy of historical research. Rather than starting with a questionable presupposition against the possibility of any divine activity, an objective examination of the evidence should be open to following the evidence wherever it may lead. An objective inquiry does not allow one to conclude where the evidence can lead prior to even beginning an examination of the evidence. This was part of the error made by David Hume, who assumed that no amount of evidence would allow one to believe in a resurrection of a dead man. Grounded in a now outdated Newtonian physics, Hume made this statement a priori, prior to the examination of any evidence. By denying that a dead man can come to life again, Hume ruled out any examination of the evidence. Having denied that God can and does intervene in human history, Hume ruled out in advance any belief in a resurrection in history.[3]

If one denies the possibility of God's existence and insists in following the very narrow epistemology of Hume by maintaining that we can only have knowledge about matters subject to our five physical senses, he or she is a priori committed to naturalism and automatically excludes anything above nature, regardless of the evidence. If we follow this epistemological presupposition, we will always come to a dead end in a dead universe with no energy and no ultimate meaning, even though the fine tuning in the universe and the arrival of conscious life give us reason to think that life has an ultimate purpose. We are then left with the conclusion that the appearance of purpose is an illusion and no action of anyone has any lasting value.

But we need to recognize that one arrives at that meaningless conclusion, not by certainty, but *by faith*. The position of complete naturalism is a worldview that one can arrive at only *by faith* in an epistemological presupposition. In other words, just as there is no compelling argument for God's existence, there is also no compelling argument against God's existence. If one believes in God's existence, it is done by faith. If one believes only in the existence of nature and excludes anything above nature, it is done by faith. These mutually exclusive worldviews are based on faith, not on certainty. They involve choices made by the free will of each person. Practically speaking, one must decide whether there is any ultimate meaning in the universe by a leap of faith. But, for all the reasons set forth in *A Case for the Existence of God*, for the theist this is a leap into the light rather than into the dark. There is evidence to consider and that evidence supports a plausible belief in the existence of God. The evidence does not compel one to believe in God, but it does allow that such a belief may be plausible and rational.

If one hypothesizes the existence of a God who brings a finely tuned universe into being out of nothing, one can also consider the possibility that such a being could also intervene in history to perform other remarkable events. And if contingent beings such as ourselves require a necessary being who continuously preserves, sustains, and holds the universe and all contingent beings in existence, then one can rationally hypothesize that such a being could be active in an event in human history. Given these premises, the resurrection of Jesus of Nazareth is a possible or plausible event. The key question is not, therefore, whether miracles can occur, but whether the evidence supports the hypothesis that a miracle occurred. Specifically, we need to examine the evidence to see whether a belief in Jesus' resurrection is a plausible, rational belief. Where does the available historical evidence lead us?[4]

Is the concept of a resurrected body really so difficult for contemporary intellects? There is scarcely a cell in your body that existed five years ago. Your body is not a static thing. It is a dynamic, constantly renewing, and changing entity that has continuity through its information-bearing pattern that is transferred from old and dying cells to new cells. Your body is made of fat and protein and many physical chemicals, but the cells that contain and exchange these physical chemicals are constantly changing, dying, and renewed. Henry Lodge, a Manhattan medical doctor, notes the constant change and replacement of the cells (and atoms) that constitute the matter of our bodies:

> The muscle cells in your thigh are completely replaced, one at a time, day and night, about every four months. Brand-new muscles, three times a year. The solid leg you've stood on so securely since childhood is mostly new since last summer. Your blood cells are replaced every three months, your platelets every ten days, your bones every couple of years. Your taste buds are replaced every day. . . . *This is not a passive process.* You don't wait for a part to wear out or break. You destroy it at the end of its planned life span and replace it with a new one. . . . Biologists now believe that most cells in your body are designed to fall apart after relatively short life spans, partly to let you adapt to new circumstances and partly because older cells tend to get cancer, making immortal cells not such a great idea. The net result is that you are actively destroying (and replacing) large parts of your body all the time.[5]

You are not the same matter you were five years ago. The matter in the cells of your body is different matter than the matter constituting your body five years ago. This raises the question of what is actually "you." From a scientific, mathematical perspective what is continuous about "you" is your information-bearing pattern, which is transferred in the instructions in the DNA of the dying cells in your body to the newly formed DNA in the new cells replacing these cells in your body. Generation after generation of new cells in your body, replacing the dying cells in your body, receive the information or instructions that constitute the continuity of "you" as distinguished from someone else.

If our bodies are constantly replacing atoms and making new cells (with perhaps the exception of certain heart and brain cells) throughout our lives, there is no reason to refrain from believing that a God responsible for the existence of matter could also instantly give a person a completely transformed body. We are still uncovering the mysteries of what constitutes matter. Quantum physics discloses that "empty" space and strange characteristics of probabilities and nonmaterial information underlie the existence of what we perceive as solid matter. (See my discussion in *A Case for the Existence of God*.) The God behind these bizarre aspects of our physical nature must have considerable ability to make changes that could conceivably result in a resurrection. Why are we so amazed at the concept of a bodily resurrection when our science has given substantial verification to a model of a surreal network of probabilities and nonmaterial information underlying the existence of all physical things? Why should we so limit our understanding of what is possible, given the very strange nature of the extremely successful model of quantum physics?

Jewish New Testament scholar Rabbi Pinchas Lapide, who believed in the resurrection of Jesus, understood that the hope of resurrection is a "reasonable faith" that one cannot dismiss in an a priori manner:

> Is not every tree, every flower, and every child a wonder of God? But through the rust and verdigris of everyday life, we have become so hardened that we need a Shakespeare, a Johann Sebastian Bach, and a van Gogh in order to learn astonishment anew. Why should the resurrection of a personal ego after passing through death be more miraculous than the gradual awakening of a human being out of the lifeless matter of a fertilized ovum? And if the physicists affirm that in this inexhaustibly large universe not a single ounce of substance is lost but just changes

its form, why should the most precious gift that God wanted to give us, a spark from his fire, the breath from his spirit, disappear without a trace after our earthly decease? To argue otherwise would not only give the lie to all confidence of salvation but would also contradict the elementary logic of natural science. Thus the hope of resurrection is a reasonable faith which should be sufficient for a meaningful, fulfilling life on earth.[6]

The earliest Christian creed in our possession, formed and repeated by the members of the church no later than a few years after Jesus' crucifixion, stated that "Christ died for our sins in accordance with the scriptures, that he was buried, and that he was raised on the third day in accordance with the scriptures, and that he appeared to Cephas, then to the twelve."

The first followers of Jesus of Nazareth, who led the mother congregation in Jerusalem, claimed that something like the replacement and creation of new cells in our bodies occurred suddenly with his dead body on Easter weekend. The consistent and uniform affirmation of the earliest Christianity was that three days following the crucifixion of Jesus of Nazareth, God raised him to a new, transformed *physical* existence. The resurrection of Jesus was seen as a *bodily* resurrection. As I shall discuss, this is consistent with pre-Christian Jewish thought, which interpreted the term resurrection (*anastasis*) to mean a *bodily* rising from the dead. This was the dominant hope in first-century Judaism. Only in second-century texts, such as those found in 1945 in the Nag Hammadi Library and other gnostic texts, does the historian begin to encounter the concept of resurrection radically changed from this first-century concept to include a "spiritual" experience rather than a rising from the dead in a transformed body. But, as I shall discuss in chapter 7, this is second-century thought and not part of the thinking in the earliest church and in the pre-Christian Jewish context that dominated the first century.

6.3 IF GOD EXISTS, RESURRECTION IS A POSSIBILITY, EVEN IF A PERSON RISING FROM THE DEAD IS CONTRARY TO NORMAL EXPERIENCE.

Once one assumes the existence of God, we find a base for moral values, a base for ultimate meaning, and a base for the possibility of miracles. If

God exists and caused the universe to exist, then any miracles described in the New Testament are feasible, especially if Jesus of Nazareth was the incarnation of the divine being behind all that exists.

Yes, in our normal experience, "Dead men don't rise." But in our normal experience, universes finely tuned for life don't just pop into existence either. We can speculate that they do, but it is not part of our experience. If God is behind the existence of the universe, then a resurrection of a man who claimed to be God, if his claim is true, is clearly possible. It is unusual and contrary to our experience in everyday life, but it is possible. And given the need for a nonfinite existence to give meaning to life and the universe, the resurrection narrative is consistent with the sense of purpose that we see in the fine tuning of the universe and the actions of the laws of physics and chemistry that allow for the existence of life.

People living in the first century also knew that dead persons don't rise. This is not a modern concept. A contemporary reader in the twenty-first century cannot make an accurate assertion that these were superstitious people, and that bodily resurrection is clearly an impossibility to twenty-first-century thought. The ancient world was well aware of the fact that people who have died remain dead in their graves. The idea of a person rising bodily from the dead was as controversial an idea in the first century as it is in the twenty-first century. As N. T. Wright notes, "The discovery that dead people stay dead was not first made by the philosophers of the Enlightenment."[7] What one has to explain historically is why a group of discouraged followers of a first-century Jew insisted that he had risen to a transformed, bodily existence.[8]

6.4 RESURRECTION IN FIRST-CENTURY JUDAISM REFERRED TO A PHYSICAL, BODILY RESURRECTION, NOT TO A VAGUE SPIRITUAL EXPERIENCE.

We have already discussed reasons why the New Testament documents and the oral tradition underlying these documents, including the ancient hymns, creeds, and liturgical formulae incorporated into the New Testament, are reliable and bear the ring of truth. As I noted, the primitive Christian community conceived of resurrection in the first century as a physical, bodily resurrection. Some current New Age and modern gnostic thinking distorts the Christian meaning of resurrection. A few contemporary thinkers hold to a vague, fuzzy position consistent with Jesus' body remaining in the ground with his bones somewhere in Jerusalem. But the idea of resurrection in first-century Judaism and in the primitive Christian community referred to a physical transformation of a dead body, not to some mystical, "spiritual" ascension.

6.4.1 First-century Judaism and the primitive church conceived of resurrection as a physical, bodily transformation.

For Jews at the time of Jesus' crucifixion, the main focus of the resurrection was the bones of the corpse. In the first-century Jewish concept of resurrection the *body* of the individual was to be resurrected. This was not the same as the Greek concept of a disembodied soul surviving death. God would reuse the body to form a person in the general resurrection at the end of time. This was the reason for the Jewish practice of gathering the bones of the deceased and placing them in an ossuary, a practice in first-century Judaism now well documented by archaeological discoveries. The idea was described in Ezekiel's vision of the valley of the dry bones having sinew and flesh put on them and becoming alive again with new bodies that had continuity with the body a person had prior to his or her death. The flesh was considered perishable, but the bones of the deceased were collected and placed in an ossuary waiting for the resurrection that was to occur at the end of the world.

The resurrection proclaimed by the followers of Jesus was not a resuscitation of a dead body. Lazarus allegedly had a resuscitation of his corpse, but the concept of resurrection was a transformation of a dead body into a new mode of physical existence. Resurrection was also not a translation where one is taken bodily into heaven as described in the Old Testament for Elijah and Enoch. The Old Testament claims that these men did not die but were translated into heaven. In Jewish thought, this was not a resurrection. The distinctions among resuscitation, translation, and resurrection were very clear and precise in first-century Judaism.

Contemporary thinkers who argue that the faith in the resurrection of the earliest disciples was a faith in the risen Christ who lives "in the faith of the disciples" are greatly mistaken and are espousing a position completely inconsistent with first-century Judaism. The world of first-century Judaism would never use the word *anastasis* to describe a fuzzy spiritual belief; resurrection meant the physical coming alive again of a dead body. As Oxford scholar Peter Walker writes:

> "Resurrection" (*anastasia* in Greek) was a word which had already developed a clear meaning. It referred to the physical raising back to life within this world of those whom God chose—the "resurrection of the just" "on the last day" (cf. Matthew 22:28; John 11:24). So when the disciples claimed Resurrection for Jesus, they were claiming that God had done for *one* man what they were expecting him to do for *all* his faithful people at the end of time (what Paul refers to as the "hope" of Israel [Acts 23:6; 26:6]). If they had meant merely that Jesus was a good fellow who did not deserve to die and whose effect on people would surely continue beyond his death, they would have used some other word. They would not have dared to use this word, which meant one thing and one thing only—God's act of raising from physical death. That is what they meant. And that is what they would have been heard to mean.[9]

N. T. Wright also points out that the earliest Christians had a very sharp and focused meaning for the term "resurrection." Resurrection meant a bodily resurrection but also a transformation into a new kind of bodily life, not simply a return to a previous kind of bodily existence, such as the Scriptures describe with respect to persons raised to life by Elijah.[10]

6.4.2 In First Corinthians 15:42–50 the Greek term for "spiritual body" meant a physical body inhabited by the spirit of God.

Despite the clear meaning of *anastasis*, there is a mistaken assertion among a minority of scholars that the resurrection of Jesus was not a bodily resurrection but more of a "spiritual" occurrence and that the earliest Christians believed more in Jesus' glorification and ascension to heaven in some special way. Only later, they hypothesize, did they use the term "resurrection" to convey their meaning. And only after that did they start to talk about his empty tomb or his appearances after his death. These appearances are then explained as hallucinations or something like hallucinations and the bottom line is that the body of Jesus was not raised from the dead.

Some of these scholars refer to a passage in First Corinthians where Paul describes the characteristics of the resurrection of the dead. From this passage in the fifteenth chapter, verses forty-two to fifty, much confusion concerning the nature of the resurrection has been spread because of a lack of understanding of the meaning of the original Greek phrases. Several scholars who should know better have argued that the term "spiritual body" means a nonphysical body, but careful analysis demonstrates that the term means a transformed body not subject to death or decay because it is inhabited by the spirit of God.[11]

The Greek term for "spiritual body" is *soma pneumatikon*. The term *soma* means a physical body; it is not a denial of physicality but an emphasis on the transformed nature of the new body and its indwelling by the spirit of God. The distinction that is being made is not between a spiritual nonbodily existence and a bodily existence, but between a resurrected body transformed by the spirit of God and one that is only physical and not so transformed.[12]

The Greek term for "physical" is *psychikon*, which means soul or life. It may be translated as "natural," as contrasted with "spiritual" where the Greek term is *pneumatikon*. The distinction is between a person who is animated only by the natural life and not by the Spirit of God.[13] In other words, the distinction is between (1) bodies with a natural, human life and (2) resurrected bodies transformed and animated by the Spirit of God. This latter animation has continuity with the person who died and yet is animated by and with the Divine Spirit.[14]

The passage from First Cor. 15 refers to a physical body transformed by God's Spirit, not a merely spiritual existence. The passage notes that the transformation is necessary because, as noted in the last sentence of the passage (v. 50), the present physical body (flesh and blood) is unfit for eternal life with God and needs to be transformed by the Spirit into a resurrected, immortal body. As verse 53 of the chapter reads: "For this perishable body must put on imperishability, and this mortal body must put on immortality."[15]

In the Jewish concept of resurrection in first-century Judaism, one could not completely separate the bodily life of Jesus pre-Easter from the bodily life of Jesus post-Easter. The Jewish concept of resurrection entails continuity in the body, as Paul describes in his discourse about the seed being planted. The model for the future resurrection body then is the *transformed* physical body of Jesus of Nazareth. This body has similarities with the previous body so that there is continuity and dissimilarities in the transformed body.

In emphasizing that Jesus' resurrection was a bodily transformation, New Testament scholar Rabbi Pinchas Lapide criticized scholars who maintain that the earthly body of Jesus is what matters and that his resurrection was only a "spiritual" one. Lapide believed that the resurrection of Jesus was a real historical occurrence and not an event only in the hearts and minds of his disciples.[16] He emphasized that the concept of resurrection in first-century Judaism does not allow one to separate the bodily life of Jesus prior to Easter from the bodily life of Jesus after Easter. The Jewish concept of resurrection entails a continuity in the body. In emphasizing the physical, bodily resurrection of Jesus and its continuity with his pre-Easter bodily life, Lapide also noted Jesus' affection for Israel after his crucifixion and his exclusive appearance to Jews:

> The oldest reports in the New Testament about the resurrection of the Nazarene give the lie to this widespread opinion. Repeatedly they emphasize not only the *bodiliness* of the Risen One, but also his unbroken identity with the same Jesus of Nazareth whose life and strife was devoted to his people of Israel. And finally, after his death on the cross, he appeared exclusively to Jews, for there are no Gentiles among the numerous witnesses of the Risen One. . . . The Risen One came in order to bless Israel. . . . Easter faith came into Existence—just as Jesus himself—in the midst of the people of Israel and spread from there over the whole world. In order to do justice to this Easter faith and to discuss its historical origin properly, it is necessary to go back mentally into the time and environment of the Nazarene. Only a re-presentation of its Jewish setting can bring that resurrection in Jerusalem, which has become the birth certificate of the church, close to us.[17]

6.5 THE GENERAL DISTINCTION BETWEEN JEWISH AND GREEK CONCEPTS ON THE NATURE OF A HUMAN BEING AND ON LIFE FOLLOWING DEATH AND THE DEVELOPMENT OF THE CONCEPT OF RESURRECTION IN JEWISH THOUGHT SUPPORT THE IDEA OF THE RESURRECTION AS A PHYSICAL, BODILY RESURRECTION.

6.5.1 In the first century there were variations in pre-Christian beliefs about life after death.

Although the *earliest Christians* were in complete agreement regarding the resurrection of Jesus as a bodily resurrection, there were variations in *pre-Christian* Jewish thought on what happens to a person after he or she dies. It is an oversimplification of history to state that all Greeks believed in an immortal soul and that all Jews believed in a resurrection empowered by God. There were considerable variations of belief on what happened after death in Greek thought and in Jewish thought. Although a general distinction between ancient Jewish and Greek thought on the nature of a human being and life after death may always be too simplistic, it may still be useful to set forth some general, but not absolute, differences between Jewish and Greek concepts concerning resurrection and immortality.

6.5.2 In Greek Platonic philosophy a person is composed of a body and an immortal soul; ancient Judaism defined a person as a psychosomatic unity or an animated body.

In Greek Platonic philosophy a person is composed of a body and an immortal soul. The Platonists did not consider the body evil (as did second-century gnostics), but the body was thought to be an impediment to the more important development of the soul. In Platonic Greek thought, the body was a temporary dwelling, and the real world was the noumenal, permanent world. This was the eternal reality that the soul joined upon the death of the body.[18] Plato gave a rather precise definition of the doctrine of the immortal soul in his writing about the death of Socrates in the *Phaedo*, where he argued that the soul is distinct from the body and eternal. Oscar Cullmann summarized Plato's perspective in his Ingersoll Lectures given at Harvard University: "Our body is only an outer garment which, as long as we live, prevents our soul from moving freely and from living in conformity to its proper eternal essence. It imposes upon the soul a law which is not appropriate to it. The soul, confined within the body, belongs to the eternal world. As long as we live, our soul finds itself in a prison, that is, in a body essentially alien to it. Death, in fact, is the great liberator. It loosens the chains, since it leads the soul out of the prison of the body and back to its eternal home."[19]

In Jewish belief, the Hebrew word for "soul" is *nephesh*, which refers to the life or vitality of a person. In general, the Jewish concept defines a person as an animated body rather than a dualistic combination of an immortal soul imprisoned in a physical body. In other words, a person's soul or *nephesh* is considered to be his or her living nature. In Jewish thought a person consists of a body that is animated and has vitality.

The physical aspects of being are considered good and beneficial, not something that confines the person.

6.5.2.1 A general resurrection was to be an event on the last day of history.

When the concept of resurrection emerged in Judaism, it emerged as a concept of a general resurrection on the last day of history where Israel would be completely and powerfully restored. It was an eschatological concept concerning the hope of the resurrection of the righteous on the last day. There was no concept of a resurrection that had or would take place prior to the end of the world. First-century Jews conceived of the resurrection, not as an event for an individual in human history, but as a general event for all of God's people at the end of the age. In his lectures at Princeton, Joachim Jeremias emphasized to our class that the concept of a resurrection as an event *in* history was completely unknown to Jesus' contemporary Jews; the resurrection was to be a group event, a resurrection of the righteous to take place *at the end* of history, not an event for one dead man during the course of history.

6.5.2.2 First-century Judaism contained a variety of beliefs on the nature of personhood and life after death.

As indicated above, there were a wide variety of views of the nature of personhood and life after death for the Jews in the first century. The following passage in Daniel 12:2–3, although referring to a bodily resurrection, gives us an insight into the broad array of Jewish beliefs about the afterlife that developed prior to the first century: "Many of those who sleep in the dust of the earth shall awake, some to everlasting life, and some to shame and everlasting contempt. Those who are wise shall shine like the brightness of the sky, and those who lead many to righteousness, like the stars forever and ever."

By the first century, the variations of the Jewish perspective on life after death were very broad. The Sadducees denied that there was any life after death, others thought of an existence somewhat similar to Greek thought, and the Pharisees believed in a full physical bodily resurrection at the end of time. In between and among these diverse views were a considerable variety of concepts.[20]

In these views the dominant perspective was the Pharisaic position where a person's hope for eternal life depended upon his trust in God to overcome death, rather than the immortality of an incarnated soul. This trust meant that the person's eternal existence *ultimately depended upon the power and mind of a loving God*. The Jewish confidence was that death could not sever the person's friendship or fellowship and communion with the God behind the universe. Death did not mean the end of a person's existence.

6.5.2.3 In the dominant first-century Jewish perspective, life after death depended upon God and was based on trust in God.

Rather than depending upon an inherent immortal soul, the dominant first-century Jewish perspective on life after death depended upon faith in God. Gregorian University theologian Gerald O'Collins described the Jewish convictions that led to the belief in a resurrection of the dead at the end of time: "The Israelites pinned their faith to Yahweh as the God of life, justice, power and fidelity. In many forms God gave and restored life to the individual and the people. Yahweh was also believed to have consistently revealed himself to be supremely just, powerful and faithful. These ancient convictions about God, possibly supported by beliefs coming from other sources, eventually led many Jews to expect a bodily resurrection at the end of time."[21]

Thus the Jewish hope of resurrection was based in trust in the One who stands behind, forms, and sustains the universe and all contingent things. God is able to call the dead back to life, just as he brought light out of darkness. The Jewish context for a resurrection hope is based on a belief in the power of God and his steadfast care for his people. The devout first-century Jew relied on the omnipotence of God as the foundation for all reality. The universe would vanish if God withdrew his sustaining power. The goodness of life, including food for the birds of the air and the blooming of flowers, depended upon the sustaining will of God.[22]

God was clearly more powerful than death, and one's friendship and communion with God could not be abolished by one's physical death. One's existence from beginning through the future depended entirely upon God, whose presence is available to his people forever.[23] This trust in God as the basis of an afterlife is quite different from the Platonic Greek concept of an immortal soul. In Jewish thought one's present and future existence depends upon the constant love and faithfulness of God as the ground of one's hope rather than one's own immortal nature.[24]

6.5.2.4 Ancient Judaism had a perspective on a state of existence immediately following death, but resurrection meant a bodily life after life after death.

The emphasis on the bodily nature of the resurrection in the meaning of the term *anastasis* in the first century does not mean that there was not any belief in a state of existence immediately following death. Despite the denial of resurrection among the Sadducees, which were a minority group in Judaism, in the broader Jewish population there was a widely held belief in an intermediate state that meant a "life after death."[25]

In the intermediate state, the dead are presently like angels, spirits, or souls held in being by the power of God, resting in the hand of God, in the paradise of God's presence in a temporary state prior to their reembodiment, which will take place through the power of God when he completes his purposes for Israel and the world.[26] The Jewish belief about resurrection then was not the modern view of a person dying and going to heaven. There was an intermediate state for a person after death but prior to resurrection (*anastasis*). Resurrection required physical reembodiment.

Within the variety of Jewish beliefs concerning the intermediate state for a person after death, some Jews believed in a period of disembodied existence after death and some in a period of disembodied nonexistence. In either belief the disembodied period would be followed by a reembodiment at the resurrection at the end of the age.

For those believing in a period of disembodied existence after death, the understanding of the nature of a person was that a complete person was composed of a body and an immaterial soul that could exist for a period of time without a body. This disembodied existence was an incomplete form of existence that would only be complete at the end of history when God would raise a person's body in a transforming way and reunite the body with the soul, making a complete and transformed person who has continuity with the person who died. The essential distinctions between this type of disembodied existence in Jewish thought and the Greek Platonic concept of the immortal soul were the necessity of a reembodiment for a person's completeness, a view of the body as something good rather than a prison for the soul, and an emphasis on the disembodied existence depending on the power and faithfulness of God rather than a natural, immortal property inherent in the soul.[27]

In the development of the concept of resurrection in Jewish thought, the ancient Jewish discussion moved from what happens after death and existence in Sheol to what happens after life after death. N. T. Wright's scholarship is particularly useful in emphasizing that resurrection (*anastasis*) in the first century uniformly meant life after a certain period of being dead; it meant "life *after* life after death," and this final life was perceived as a bodily life. Resurrection involved a future state in which the dead would again be alive with a physical body.

6.5.2.5 In the first century resurrection also was used as a metaphor for Israel's restoration.

In the first century the term "resurrection" was not only concerned with the restoration and reembodiment of an individual, it was also concerned with the restoration of Israel. In second-Temple Judaism the concepts of Israel's restoration and a new bodily life for all of the people of Israel's God were closely connected. These great events were to take place at the end of history. At that time the martyrs who had died for the Torah and for the God of Israel would be raised, together with all of God's people, and Israel would be vindicated.[28]

To a great extent, the language of resurrection emerged as a metaphor for Israel's restoration and return from exile. The fall of Jerusalem left the Jewish people dispersed and downcast. The oracle in Ezekiel gave a message to the Jewish people that Israel would be revived and its land restored. The hope for resurrection was in metaphorical language concerning this restoration in Ezekiel 37:1–14, where in a valley full of dry bones, the bones are covered with flesh and return to life. This passage is to be a proclamation to the people of Israel that they will be brought out of their graves and restored to their land:

> The hand of the Lord came upon me, and he brought me out by the spirit of the Lord and set me down in the middle of a valley; it was full of bones. He led me all around them; there were very many lying in the valley, and they were dry. He said to me, "Mortal, can these bones live?" I answered, "O Lord God, you know." Then he said to me, "Prophesy to

these bones, and say to them: O dry bones, hear the word of the Lord. Thus says the Lord God to these bones: I will cause breath to enter you, and you shall live. I will lay sinews on you, and will cause flesh to come upon you, and cover you with skin, and put breath in you, and you shall live; and you shall know that I am the Lord."

So I prophesied as I had been commanded; and as I prophesied, suddenly there was a noise, a rattling, and the bones came together, bone to its bone. I looked, and there were sinews on them, and flesh had come upon them, and skin had covered them; but there was no breath in them. Then he said to me, "Prophesy to the breath, prophesy, mortal, and say to the breath: Thus says the Lord God: Come from the four winds, O breath, and breathe upon these slain, that they may live." I prophesied as he commanded me, and the breath came into them, and they lived, and stood on their feet, a vast multitude.

Then he said to me, "Mortal, these bones are the whole house of Israel. They say, 'Our bones are dried up, and our hope is lost; we are cut off completely.' Therefore prophesy, and say to them, 'Thus says the Lord God: I am going to open your graves, and bring you up from your graves, O my people; and I will bring you back to the land of Israel. And you shall know that I am the Lord, when I open your graves, and bring you up from your graves, O my people. I will put my spirit within you, and you shall live, and I will place you on your own soil; then you shall know that I, the Lord, have spoken and will act.'"[29]

The prophecy in this passage was a metaphor for the rebirth of the people of Israel rather than an emphasis on individual resurrection.[30] The passage concerns Israel's return from exile and the restoration of its land. The hope of the Jewish people was that their nation would be restored and that those loyal to God and his Torah would be raised from the dead and participate in the restoration of Israel. In the first century the Jewish perspective on resurrection was mainly on exile and restoration. The sufferings of the martyrs who were tortured are rewarded by receiving back restored physical bodies. The God of Israel was to restore his people and reward those loyal to the Torah.

6.6 THE CONCEPT OF A RESURRECTED MESSIAH WAS UNKNOWN IN JUDAISM.

To appreciate the radical nature of the disciples' claim concerning the resurrection of Jesus, one needs to grasp the unprecedented character of the new proclamation and so it is worth repeating that the disciples and crowds who followed Jesus never conceived of a resurrection within history. Resurrection was to be a group event to take place at the end of the age. Bearing this in mind, we can understand the confusion of the disciples upon discovering the empty tomb of Jesus. The concept of a resurrected messiah was completely foreign to Judaism.[31] The proclamation of the resurrection of one individual prior to the end of history was a new concept to Jews. There was no concept of resurrection in the role of the messiah; Jewish expectation was only that that there would be a general resurrection at the end of history. No Jewish group had ever contemplated a resurrection by the messiah, a resurrection of one individual occurring before the end of the age.[32] This brings us to the question of why the followers of Jesus, who had no concept of a resurrection in history and no concept of a resurrected messiah, came to proclaim that Jesus of Nazareth had been resurrected on Easter weekend and was the messiah. Why did they change their concept of the resurrection and live and die for their belief that the body of Jesus had been resurrected prior to the anticipated resurrection at the end of the world? Why did they change their concept of the messiah? What caused the radical shift in their thinking and the transformation of their character into bold, confident proponents of Jesus' resurrection?

6.7 THE FIRST-CENTURY JEWISH CONCEPT OF MESSIAH WAS ONE OF AN INVINCIBLE, CONQUERING POLITICAL KING.

The Jewish concept of messiah was one of an invincible, conquering, victorious political king, descended from David, not a suffering servant who dies a humiliating death under the authority of pagan Romans. From his disciples' perspective, Jesus, as the messiah, was to conquer the Romans by force and restore Israel to power in God's kingdom. He was certainly not to be a person who was defeated and crucified like a common criminal. The physical submission, torture, and death of Jesus were completely contrary to the Jewish concept of a victorious messiah who would lead and restore the people of God to power.

The disciples and followers of Jesus of Nazareth were dejected and dismayed because the passages in the Old Testament that were regarded as prophecies of the messiah indicated that he would crush anyone who opposed him and bring peace to the entire world. With supernatural strength, this messiah would destroy all of Israel's political enemies and bring Israel to power in an earthly kingdom of God based in Jerusalem. He would be a forceful political leader and remove the pagans who were corrupting Jerusalem. The messiah was not to be a person who would suffer and die a humiliating death on a Roman cross. Yes, there was a passage in Isaiah 53 about a suffering servant, but this passage was never interpreted in Judaism to refer to the messiah.

This is why Jesus' disciples deserted him when he was taken captive. Their minds were so completely imbued with the idea of a conquering messiah whose role was to destroy his enemies that when they saw him scourged, bleeding, and a helpless prisoner of the Romans being nailed to a cross to die the death of a common criminal, their hopes that he was to be the invincible conquering messiah were destroyed. Jesus' arrest, flogging, and crucifixion were inconsistent with the idea of the messiah who was to bear the destiny of Israel, defeat the pagans, and physically reestablish God's kingdom in Jerusalem. As the messiah, Jesus was to overthrow the pagan occupiers by physical force. When it appeared that Jesus would not fulfill that role, the disciples fled. Totally disillusioned and shattered by his death, they were not expecting his resurrection.

They hid in Jerusalem for fear that a similar fate could befall them, but a relatively short time after this display of cowardice and fear, they were willing to suffer and die for the bold proclamation of the resurrection of Jesus. And they did this right in the middle of the city in which he had been crucified. Something must have happened to them to create a powerful, heroic faith in them that Jesus was alive and had conquered death and was the messiah. What were the events that transformed them from disillusioned, frightened, disheartened persons into bold, courageous proponents of a new faith for which they were willing to risk torture and death? What happened to change their concept of the messiah so that they were proclaiming this new concept in a hostile and dangerous environment? How does one account for such a dramatic transformation in the disciples?[33]

New Testament scholar Rabbi Pinchas Lapide was convinced that the historical evidence affirmed Jesus' resurrection. Part of this evidence is the transformation of the disciples, which is difficult to explain if one rules out the resurrection. Lapide reasoned as follows:

> When this scared, frightened band of the apostles which was just about to throw away everything in order to flee in despair to Galilee; when these peasants, shepherds, and fishermen, who betrayed and denied their master and then failed him miserably, suddenly could be changed overnight into a confident mission society, convinced of salvation and able to work with much more success after Easter than before Easter, then no vision or hallucination is sufficient to explain such revolutionary transformation. For a sect or school or order, perhaps a single vision would have been sufficient—but not for a world religion which was able to conquer the Occident thanks to the Easter faith. . . . If the defeated and depressed group of disciples overnight could change into a victorious movement of faith, based only on autosuggestion or self-deception—then this would be a much greater miracle than the resurrection itself.[34]

The evidence of the disciples' transformation is rather compelling. James did not consider Jesus more than his brother and a roaming teacher whom, at least on certain occasions, James opposed. One can see from the accounts that Jesus did not just appear to those who believed in him. The accounts indicate that he appeared to Thomas, James, and Paul, none of whom were believers prior to his appearance. The evidence from history and the very origin of the church with James assuming a leadership position in the mother congregation in Jerusalem point to the resurrection.

6.8 UNANIMITY IN THE CHRISTIAN PROCLAMATION OF THE MEANING OF RESURRECTION IN THE MIDST OF A VARIETY OF JEWISH BELIEFS ABOUT RESURRECTION SUPPORTS THE DISCIPLES' ASSERTION OF THE NAZARENE'S RESURRECTION AS THE CENTER OF THE EARLY CHRISTIAN FAITH.

As noted above, first-century Judaism had a wide variety of beliefs concerning life after death. As Wright emphasizes, one would then think that since the Christian faith emerged from this context of a wide variety of beliefs about what happens after one dies, the new faith would also have a corresponding wide spectrum of beliefs about life after death. But this is not what one finds in the early Christian congregations. Instead we encounter a uniformity and unanimity about life after death. Wright asks the question, "How does it happen that we find virtually no spectrum of belief about life after death, but instead an almost universal affirmation of that which pagans said could not happen, and that which one stream (albeit the dominant one) of Judaism insisted would happen, namely resurrection?"[35] The earliest Christians had a *uniform* perspective on life after death. They consistently centered this belief in a conviction of a bodily resurrection. They did not have a chaos of diverse beliefs. Wright concludes:

> With the early Christians, who came from every corner of Judaism and every corner of paganism, you might well have thought that over the first two centuries we would find evidence of all sorts of beliefs about life after death held by different Christian groups. The extraordinary thing is that we do not. From Paul, on through the New Testament, through the Apostolic Fathers and through the great theologians at the end of the second century (e.g., Irenaeus, Tertullian, and Origen), we find a remarkably consistent set of beliefs about what will happen to God's people ultimately after death. . . . The early Christians held firmly to a view of a future hope that focused on resurrection. They did not simply believe in a life after death in some platonic sphere, . . . the focus is not where you will be instantly after death. The focus is on where you will be in God's new world, in the new creation, in the new heavens and the new earth. The answer given is that, in that world, you will be a newly embodied self. The early Christians held firmly, as did the Pharisaic Jews, to a two-step belief about the future: first an interim waiting period, and second a new bodily existence in a newly remade world. Let me stress again, there is nothing like this in paganism.[36]

It is particularly important to understand that the very earliest Christians centered their beliefs on the resurrection of Jesus. More than anything else, the early Christian faith was a faith in the resurrection. The cross was extremely important, providing atonement for sins. But the major focus was on the resurrection. Resurrection was the epicenter of the volcano that came forth in the weeks following the crucifixion of Jesus of Nazareth, and the meaning of resurrection was quite specific, precise, and uniform in the earliest congregations.

Pinchas Lapide maintained that the two fundamental pillars of the Christian faith are the crucifixion and the resurrection. However, he was convinced that the resurrection is by far the most important. Lapide reasoned that without the resurrection, the crucifixion of Jesus would have been forgotten, just as innumerable crucifixions of Jews carried out by the Romans were forgotten. He cited Flavius Josephus, a Jewish eyewitness to the mass crucifixions under Titus during his siege of Jerusalem, as he described the magnitude of the killings: "So the soldiers out of the wrath and hatred they bore the Jews, nailed those they caught, one after one way, and another after another, to the crosses, by way of jest; when their multitude was so great that room was waiting for the bodies. . . ."[37]

Lapide noted that no one remembers the names and lives of any of these Jews, even though they were all killed in a manner similar to Jesus. According to Lapide, what is distinctive about Jesus is his coming to bodily life again on the third day after his crucifixion. For Lapide the Christian faith "stands or falls" not with the crucifixion of Jesus, but with the experience "on the third day."[38] This experience is the resurrection of Jesus.

Lapide's insight is confirmed when we look at the evidence from the earliest church. We can see that the resurrection of Jesus is the central foundation for the mother congregation in Jerusalem. The resurrection is not just one of many equal beliefs in this early community but the central cornerstone of their message. The center of the earliest proclamation was not about the great teachings of Jesus but about his resurrection. His resurrection is the linchpin of the whole beginning of the new community.[39] As New Testament scholar George Ladd wrote: "It is clear that not the life of Jesus, not his teachings, not even his sacrificial death, was the central emphasis in the earliest Christian proclamation; it was the resurrection of Christ."[40]

6.9 WHEN ONE EXAMINES THE EVIDENCE SURROUNDING THIS CENTRAL FOUNDATION OF THE MOTHER CONGREGATION IN JERUSALEM, THE PROBABILITY OF THE TWO MAIN CONVICTIONS OF THIS CONGREGATION BEING TRUE IS QUITE HIGH.

When one examines the evidence concerning what happened on Easter weekend, the accounts given in the gospels (corroborated in the preexisting creeds incorporated into the earliest New Testament letters) appear to be the source from which the early church originated, rather than the product of theological reflection within the church. Indeed, the probability of the previously mentioned two main convictions of the mother congregation in Jerusalem being true is quite high. Again, these two convictions are: (1) the empty tomb of Jesus on Easter morning; and (2) the appearances of Jesus alive in bodily form.[41] I shall now turn to the evidence for the empty tomb and then discuss evidence concerning the appearances.

6.9.1 The evidence for the empty tomb of Jesus of Nazareth is quite strong.

6.9.1.1 There is a high probability that Jesus was buried in the well-known tomb of Joseph of Arimathea, an actual member of the Jewish Sanhedrin at the time of the crucifixion.

One of the principal causes behind the transformation of the disciples was that Jesus' tomb was empty on Easter morning. We have good evidence that the tomb was empty because if his body still lay in the tomb, the Jewish leaders who had worked so diligently to put an end to his life and ministry could have stopped the origin of the church and the proclamation of his resurrection merely by producing his dead body. The gospels describe how Joseph of Arimathea placed the body of Jesus in a tomb. Joseph was described as a wealthy man and a member of the Sanhedrin, an institution of seventy men who were leaders in Jerusalem. It is likely that Joseph of Arimathea was. (1) a member of the Sanhedrin and (2) the person who buried Jesus because all of the members of the Sanhedrin were well known in Jerusalem. If Joseph was a fictitious character, one would expect to see some evidence of a quick and emphatic denial of his position on the Sanhedrin by those opposing the early Christian community and the story of his having placed the body of Jesus in a tomb.

It is far more probable that Joseph of Arimathea actually was the member of the Sanhedrin who placed the body of Jesus in the tomb and that the site of his tomb was well known in Jerusalem. In Matt. 28:11–15 we find an early narrative stating that the authorities in Jerusalem created an explanation for the empty tomb by spreading the story that the disciples had stolen the body of Jesus. If the tomb was not empty, there would be no reason for the creation of that story or for its continued assertion during the life of the earliest church.

6.9.1.2 The meaning of the term "resurrection," the absence of any evidence of a dispute about whether the tomb was empty, the existence of a hostile polemic asserting that the disciples had stolen the body of Jesus, and the failure to produce his body to stop the proclamation of his resurrection point to an empty tomb.

As noted above, in proclaiming the resurrection of Jesus, the disciples were using the term *anastasis*, which referred to a bodily resurrection, not a fuzzy spiritual experience. As I have discussed, first-century Jews were very specific about this point: the resurrection was a reembodiment, a transformed physical existence.[42] Consequently, when Paul, trained as a Pharisee, said that Jesus rose from the dead in First Cor. 15:3–5, he could not have meant that Jesus' body remained in the tomb. The creed Paul incorporates into his writing describes the death, burial, and resurrection of Jesus, events completely inconsistent with the body of Jesus remaining in the tomb. By stating that Jesus was buried, the creed implies the empty tomb. This is very early evidence that Jesus' body was not in the tomb on Easter morning.

There is no evidence, however, of any argument in the very earliest of Christian times concerning whether the body of Jesus was absent from the tomb. There is no evidence from any source of any dispute concerning whether the tomb was empty. The disagreement was over the explanation for the empty tomb. The question of debate was why, not whether, the tomb was empty. This can be clearly seen from the polemic in the passage in Matt. 28:11–15:

> While they were going, some of the guards went into the city and told the chief priests everything that had happened. After the priests had assembled with the elders, they devised a plan to give a large sum of money to the soldiers, telling them, "You must say, His disciples came by night and stole him away while we were asleep. If this comes to the governor's ears, we will satisfy him and keep you out of trouble." So they took the money and did as they were directed. And this story is still told among the Jews to this day.

This polemic was an attempt to explain the empty tomb and was given at the beginning of Christian origins. The mere existence of this explanation is evidence that the tomb was empty. If the tomb had not been empty, there would have been no reason for this story. The existence of a Jewish polemic explaining the absence of the body of Jesus is substantial evidence that the body was not in the tomb.

Moreover, if the tomb was not empty, why did no one produce the dead body of Jesus? Producing his body would have stopped anyone from believing in the proclamation by the disciples of Jesus' resurrection. The church would not exist today because the whole movement would have ceased with the production of the body. No one could believe in a physical resurrection of a dead body if the dead body was shown in public. The evidentiary force of the polemic found in Matthew, the lack of any evidence of any dispute questioning whether the tomb was empty, and the failure to produce the dead body of Jesus demands an explanation.[43] The spreading of the Christian resurrection faith was a great incentive for the Jewish authorities to produce the body of Jesus. This new movement challenged the establishment of the time and disrupted the city of Jerusalem.[44]

6.9.1.3 The probability that the disciples stole the body of Jesus is quite low.

One cannot take the idea of the disciples stealing the body of Jesus very seriously. If the disciples had done so, it would be very unlikely that all of them would continue to maintain a conspiracy that a resurrection had occurred when they knew differently. In the face of torture and martyrdom, someone would have exposed the hoax to prevent his own torture or death. As I heard William Starr emphasize, "I don't know about you, but if someone was about to stone me or drive nails into my hands, and I knew that person had stolen the body of Jesus, I would have at least given an indication that I was not so certain that Jesus rose from the dead in order to save myself from great pain and death."[45] But we have no record of any disciple doing anything of the sort. On the contrary, history is well documented that many of the proponents of the resurrection of Jesus suffered and died rather than deny the resurrection. John Stott notes that modern psychology discredits the theory that the disciples could have removed the body of Jesus and then been willing to suffer torture or death for the purpose of promulgating a fantasy which they knew was false.[46] Walker agrees and maintains that the evidence requires the conclusion that the disciples were convinced of the resurrection of Jesus:

> Is it likely that they would have persisted with it all the way to their death? For in the coming years many of those first disciples would suffer a great deal—including, for some, martyrdom. Was all this the result of a prank? Was their newfound courage based on a palpable lie? Is it not likely that one of them, when under pressure, would spill the beans and divulge the secret? No. What turns a coward into a person of courage is not a demonstrable lie but a conviction based on an assured fact. Others might think them wrong, but the disciples who preached the Resurrection of Jesus were themselves convinced that they were right.[47]

6.9.1.4 If the concept of the empty tomb was a creation of fiction, why did the first-century gospel authors create a story where women were the witnesses when women had no legal status as witnesses in first-century Judaism?

Another aspect to the resurrection narratives that bears a distinct ring of truth is that women were the witnesses to the empty tomb. In first-century Judaism, women were not allowed to act as legal witnesses.[48] If the accounts were fabrications created by myth makers, why would the authors uniformly assign the role of witnesses of the empty tomb to women? Anyone wanting to invent a credible story would be much more likely to give the role of a witness to a male.[49]

It is also unlikely that the women went to the wrong tomb. If they had gone to the wrong tomb and found no body, the Jewish authorities could simply have stopped the proclamation of the resurrection by going to the correct tomb and producing the body of Jesus. Yet the resurrection account thrived in the earliest days right in Jerusalem where thousands joined those who believed in Jesus' resurrection.[50]

6.9.1.5 The probability that Jesus did not die but revived in the tomb is quite low.

The evidence for the resurrection also cannot be denied by asserting that Jesus was not really dead when he was taken down from the cross. The idea of a person who suffered flogging and crucifixion three days later appearing to his disciples as one worthy of worship as Lord is simply not feasible. His appearance would be that of a beaten, half-dead, weakened, suffering man, not a glorious, transformed conqueror. This was the conclusion of D. F. Strauss, who was emphatically not a Christian.[51]

6.9.1.6 The earliest creed known to us describes the postresurrection appearances of Jesus; this creed was received by Paul, probably from the mother congregation in Jerusalem whose leaders were eyewitnesses to the Easter weekend events.

We have discussed the creed which preexisted Paul's writings and is found in First Corinthians 15:3–8. This creed appears to have been received by Paul in a reliable process for transferring important oral tradition. Because of the very early nature of the evidence presented in this tradition and its references to Jesus' death, burial, resurrection, and appearances, it is worth quoting this creed once again in connection with our discussion of the resurrection:

> For I handed on to you [*paradidomi*] as of first importance what I in turn had received [*paralambano*] that Christ died for our sins in accordance with the scriptures, and that he was buried, and that he was raised on the third day in accordance with the scriptures, and that he appeared to Cephas, then to the twelve. Then he appeared to more than five hundred brothers and sisters at one time, most of whom are still alive, though some have died. Then he appeared to James, then to all the apostles. Last of all, as to one untimely born, he appeared also to me.

Without entering into the question of whether the last three sentences are part of the creed, the important and universally accepted conclusion among scholars is that the beginning of this passage is the earliest reference to the life of Jesus in our possession. This is also the earliest tradition of the death and resurrection of Jesus. It was first passed on in oral form among Jesus' contemporaries and then incorporated into Paul's writings, which are the earliest documents in our possession. In using the terms *paradidomi* and *paralambano* Paul is giving technical words for delivering and receiving oral tradition.

We have good reason to conclude that the most likely source of the creed is the earliest congregation in Jerusalem, a congregation that included many of the closest followers and disciples of Jesus, persons who were eyewitnesses to the events of Easter weekend. As noted above, learning at this time was not mainly by literary means but by memorization of oral tradition. The language of this creed supports the conclusion that it did not originate with Paul. Again, the phrases "for our sins," the "third day," "he appeared," and "the twelve" are un-Pauline phrases that, together with the use of the Aramaic "Cephas" instead of Peter's Greek name, point to Jerusalem as the place of the creed's origin. Paul most likely received this creed in the early 30s when he visited Jerusalem after his conversion. The ancient age of this creed and its closeness to the mother congregation in Jerusalem required the renowned German scholar Wolfhart Pannenberg to conclude that the appearances of Jesus were actually experienced by a number of the members of that Aramaic-speaking initial congregation in Jerusalem.[52]

All the evidence points to the conclusion that Paul most likely received this creed directly from the congregation of Peter and James in Jerusalem. The creed is consistent with the words ascribed to the disciples/apostles as they proclaimed the resurrection in Jerusalem as set forth in the book of Acts. The consistency of the content in this creed, the gospel accounts, and the sermons in Acts is remarkable and unvaried at their core. This is no doubt testimony from eyewitnesses. No matter what dates we ascribe to the gospels and to Acts, this is eyewitness testimony that corroborates the gospel accounts. This appears to be the confession of members of the Jerusalem mother congregation who actually saw the resurrected body of Jesus, formulated this creed as their testimony to the events they witnessed, and passed this creed on to Paul. We need not become embroiled in a debate over dates for the gospels; this eyewitness testimony takes us back to a time almost simultaneous with the events of Easter weekend and corroborates the core of the New Testament gospel narratives concerning that weekend.

In referring to the content of this creed, N. T. Wright concludes that this account stands alongside and is consistent with the accounts given in the four canonical gospels. In his words, it is a "fifth witness" to the events of Easter weekend.[53] Here we are at the bedrock of the foundation of the first Christian congregation. This creed is not to be taken lightly or casually as the terms *paradidomi* and *paralambano* indicate the seriousness of the process of transferring important oral tradition. It is very unlikely that the creed was changed in any significant way in the transmission process. As Wright concludes: "This is the kind of foundation story with which a community is not at liberty to tamper. It was probably formulated within the first two or three years after Easter itself, since it was already in formulaic form when Paul 'received' it. We are in touch with the earliest Christian tradition, with something that was being said two decades or more before Paul wrote this letter."[54]

6.9.1.7 The appearances of Jesus were not likely to be hallucinations.

It is improbable that the appearances of Jesus to his disciples and the five hundred persons described by Paul in first Cor. 15 were illusions or hallucinations. There were multiple appearances at different times and in different places. Clearly, the disciples believed that Jesus had appeared to them, as did Saul of Tarsus, who completely changed his life and promulgated a gospel that he had previously sought to terminate. His opposition to the gospel was not a part-time task for him. He was willing to hunt down and even kill those who proclaimed the resurrection of Jesus. Yet something changed his life and turned him into the apostle Paul who spread the gospel throughout the Hellenic world. Hallucinations do not occur in such varied circumstances at so many different places and times.

Moreover, hallucinations are known to have a basis in expectations. But the disciples, as noted above, had the expectation that, as the messiah, Jesus would physically throw the pagans out of Jerusalem and restore Israel to power; they had no expectation of a crucified and humiliated messiah. Nor did they have any expectation of a resurrection by the messiah. The concept of a messiah and the concept of resurrection had never been linked together.

Further, the resurrection was to be a general resurrection at the end of time, not a resurrection by one person in history. They were not expecting the resurrection of the individual Jesus. This is why they were bewildered at the empty tomb. Hallucinations are not the explanation for the appearances of Jesus. Nevertheless, even if one assumes that the disciples were deluded by some inexplicable reason, one still has to explain the empty tomb of Jesus. Why was the tomb empty and why did the disciples' concepts of resurrection and messiah change so radically and so quickly from the concepts they had held prior to Easter morning? What was behind the undeniable volcanic explosion that gave birth to the primitive Christian church?

6.10 DESPITE SOME INCONSISTENCIES IN THE GOSPEL ACCOUNTS, THE EXTREMELY EARLY EVIDENCE FROM PREEXISTING CREEDS FROM ORAL TRADITION CORROBORATE THE ACCOUNTS THAT AGREE ON ALL OF THE IMPORTANT EVIDENCE SUPPORTING THE RESURRECTION OF JESUS OF NAZARETH.

From time to time one may hear the criticism that because the gospel accounts vary and are not precisely the same, they must be relating completely different stories and therefore, the core of the story cannot be true. But this ignores the remarkable agreement among the accounts in the writings of Paul (including the preexisting creeds that he incorporates) and the gospel accounts. The inconsistencies among the gospel accounts should not deter anyone from considering the accounts to be historically valuable sources with a general agreement that bears the ring of truth. The most significant aspects of the canonical accounts contain a remarkable unity. Wright notes the importance in their agreement among the accounts:

> In fact, the accounts all tell a story which, in general terms, can be summarized without doing violence to any of them. All four agree that the key events took place early in the morning on the first day of the week on the third day after Jesus' execution. All four agree that Mary Magdalene was at the tomb: Matthew, Mark and Luke agree that another woman was there too, and Mark and Luke add others. All agree that the stone presented an apparent problem, but that the problem was solved without the women having to do anything. All agree that an unusual stranger, an angel or near equivalent, met and spoke to the women. Matthew and John agree that Mary Magdalene then met Jesus (Matthew, of course, has the other Mary there too). All except Mark agree that Mary (and other women, if they are mentioned) go off to tell the male disciples: Luke and John agree that Peter and another disciple then go to the tomb to see for themselves.[55]

New Testament scholar George Ladd argues that the canonical gospel accounts agree on important points that the reader may consider historically reliable. These points are: Jesus died and was buried. His disciples did not expect his crucifixion but expected him to become a political messianic king. His disciples were confused by his humiliating death. His tomb was found empty on Easter morning. Mary thought his body had been stolen. The disciples claimed to have experienced appearances of Jesus risen from the dead. The disciples proclaimed his resurrection in the city of Jerusalem where he had been crucified.[56]

In summary, an examination of the evidence surrounding the four canonical resurrection accounts and the development of the church, including the creeds, hymns, and ancient formulae that were part of the worship pattern of the earliest Christian communities, point toward two events that appear to be undeniable: the empty tomb and the appearances of Jesus. An honest assessment of the evidence indicates that these two events bear the mark of authentic history. One cannot explain the birth of the Christian faith without them.[57]

THE NEW AND OLD GNOSTICISM
ARE BASED ON FANTASIES,
NOT ON HISTORICAL EVENTS

One remarkable phenomenon in a number of relatively recent publications is the promotion of a gnostic-type "alternative Christianity." The idea advanced is that the traditional, orthodox faith and the documents of the New Testament represent only one of a variety of equally valid faiths that one can choose to pursue as an authentic form of Christianity. These alternative faiths are basically represented by certain texts discovered in the last century and are usually gnostic in character. To evaluate the authenticity of this new view, I shall review some of the most significant evidence relating to this phenomenon, which I will call "the new and old gnosticism."

7.1 THE NEW AND OLD GNOSTICISM ARE BASED ON MID-TO LATE SECOND-CENTURY FANTASIES DISTORTING A CORE FIRST-CENTURY ORTHODOX BELIEF; THEY ARE NOT SUPPORTED BY ANY DOCUMENTS RELATING TO JESUS OF NAZARETH THAT CAN BE INDUBITABLY TRACED TO THE FIRST CENTURY.

7.1.1 Central themes are clearly detectable in gnostic thought.

Gnosticism is a modern term that refers to a broad variety of religious teachings that emphasize *gnōsis*, a Greek word for knowledge from personal acquaintance. In gnosticism, this kind of knowledge is a secret comprehension of one's divine origins or an inner divine spark. In most gnostic literature, this *gnōsis* is not something available to everyone, but only to an elite few who without it remain ignorant of their divine spark. This knowledge is more mystical than intellectual. It is similar to the knowledge by personal acquaintance that I discussed in *A Case for the Existence of God* concerning Kierkegaard's writings. *Gnōsis*, in other words, is a participatory, inner, existential knowledge. The distinction between the *kendskab* knowledge[1] of orthodox Christian faith described by Kierkegaard and the *gnōsis* of the gnostics is that *kendskab* is a knowledge by acquaintance with the "wholly other" God. In gnosticism, however, the emphasis for *gnōsis* is a knowledge of one's own inner divinity. In orthodox Christianity and Judaism, the emphasis is on the God of Israel; in gnosticism it is on one's own divine nature.

In her book, *What Is Gnosticism?* Karen King proposes that "gnosticism" was too diverse to be defined.[2] Most scholars believe, however, that it had some central themes that allows one to describe a document as gnostic in character. Simone Pétrement, a renowned historian of classical philosophy and ancient Christianity, acknowledges the difficulty in describing gnosticism as a single doctrine. She agrees with King that the term "gnosticism" is a modern term, notes a variety of differing "gnostic" movements, but then joins the consensus of scholars who hold that despite a broad spectrum of beliefs, gnosticism has a discernible theological core:

> Gnosticism was not a single doctrine. This name covers a large number of widely differing doctrines. It is modern scholars who speak of Gnosticism; the ancients spoke of Simonians, of Menandrians, of Sturnilians, of Basilideans, of Carpocratians, of Valentinians, of Marcionites, Ophites, and Sethians, to name a few. Nevertheless, there is a justification for this single name because despite great differences, the doctrines of all these sects betray certain common traits. Insofar as they have these features in common, they can be placed in the same genre and under the same name.[3]

King has a valid point in stressing the extremely broad variety of thought in gnosticism, but central themes clearly are detectable. One central theme is the opposition of the spiritual world to the evil physical world. Gnostic teaching is quite different from orthodox Judaism or Christianity. In gnosticism the physical world was not made by a God who is the ultimate reality, but by a lesser god, often known as the demiurge. This lesser god was quite incompetent and made many mistakes in creating the physical world. He intended to make the world immortal and without pain, ignorance, or decay, but could not get it right. In spite of his incompetence, this lesser god wants humans to worship him. Gnostics frequently equate the Jewish God, *Yahweh*, to this lesser god so they do not worship *Yahweh*. In some gnostic teaching, Sophia (wisdom) is blamed for the inherently evil physical creation. The real God is an ultimate reality completely ineffable, beyond any human knowledge, and abhorrent of anything physical.

The Jewish God, *Yahweh*, the God of Israel, described in the Old Testament, is rejected by the gnostics. On balance, gnostics were anti-Judaism and considered the God of Israel to be a bungling and sometimes even malevolent being. In the gnostic myths, the Jews of orthodox Judaism are completely wrong. Gnostics rejected their Scriptures and the Old Testament, including the Psalms. Bart Ehrman describes the "overriding point" of the various gnostic myth: "This world is not the creation of the one True God. The god who made this world—the God of the Old Testament—is a secondary, inferior deity. He is not the God above all who is to be worshiped. Rather, he is to be avoided, by learning the truth about the divine realm, this evil world, our entrapment here, and how we can escape."[4]

In gnostic thought one of the mistakes of the lesser god in creating the world was to leave traces of divinity or small sparks of the divine in certain human beings and their descendants. Since these human beings are made of matter that is considered evil, the saving knowledge or *gnōsis* is brought about by these elite human beings discovering the divine spark within them and nurturing their own divine nature. For the elite few who have this divine spark left by a bungling lesser god, his or her bungling was to their advantage as they, if they gain knowledge (*gnōsis*) about their inner bit of divinity, can increase the spark into a flame and become more divine.

As noted, in gnosticism divinity is not available to everyone; only a certain elect few are considered to have a spark of the divine within. The rest of humankind are relegated to ultimate annihilation or worse. As Henry Chadwick of Cambridge University described the elite nature of gnostics: "A dualism of spirit and matter, mind and body, was joined with a powerful determinism of predestinarianism: the gnostics (or 'people in the know') are the elect, their souls, fragments of the divine, needing liberation from matter and the power of the planets. The huge majority of humanity are earth clods for whom no hope may be entertained."[5]

If one is among the fortunate few human beings to have a trace of divinity accidentally left within them, the process of salvation is one of self-actualization, beginning with the discovery of the divine spark. If they fulfill this self-actualized goal, these select few can escape their evil physical bodies and ascend to a union with the real God, provided they can ascend through the realms of demonic spirits. Because in gnostic thought matter is considered evil, this would be a completely spiritual ascension, not a physical resurrection. A resurrection of the body makes no sense to a gnostic worldview because one's goal is to escape from evil physical matter.

The role of Jesus in the gnostic salvation story is one of a person who descended from the spiritual world and teaches the message of self-actualization or redemption as a mystical experience. He was not sent by the bungling *Yahweh* but descended from a level above *Yahweh* and closer to the God of ultimate reality. He did not die on the cross because he was too spiritual to become actually one who had a material body. Matter was too evil and too beneath one of his spiritual level. Because he did not really have a physical body, or only used a physical body prior to his crucifixion, his "resurrection" was a spiritual one. (As discussed in chapter 6, the concept of a spiritual resurrection is an oxymoron in first-century Jewish thought. For the first-century Jew, resurrection implied *physical* resurrection of a body.)

Jesus is seen as a divine revealer to tell an elite few of their hidden inner divine spark and help them fan it into a flame of a fuller divinity. In gnostic myths Jesus is considered to be the divine emissary from the spiritual realm. The exact nature of this divinity is not well described.[6]

Contrary to the earliest creeds and liturgical formulae discussed in chapter 2 above, Jesus' death is not seen as redemptive. The crucifixion, atonement, and resurrection are not his purpose in coming to earth. He visited earth only to give the elite the *gnōsis* or inner knowledge of their hidden divinity.

This view of Jesus, of course, is quite different from the orthodox view, which holds that he was the Son of God and the Son of Man, fully divine *and* fully human. In the orthodox view, he suffered and died on the cross for the forgiveness of all the sins of humankind and was resurrected bodily. In our earliest Christian documents the orthodox view is that he was God *incarnate*, that is, God indwelling fully a human body. His body was raised to life three days after his death. Those who believed in Him and followed in his way looked forward to a physical resurrection of a glorified, perfect body. Jesus' resurrection can be seen as the prototype of this kind of physically resurrected body. This is the classical traditional teaching of the Christian faith.

Gnosticism may be considered a form of self-worship or self-deification. It is attractive because it appeals to the idea that one can be divine and be like God. This was part of the message in the story of the first sin in the Garden of Eden where the temptation was to eat fruit of the tree that was in the middle of the garden. The serpent told the woman that to eat of it would open her eyes and make her wise and be "like God, knowing good and evil."[7] The desire to be like God is an attractive aspect to gnosticism because the focus is on the hidden divinity of human beings. One can focus on one's divine inner nature. This focus is in essence a worship of one's own divinity. By its nature, gnosticism encourages a self-focused worldview. Some revisionist writings would like to portray the gnostics as an enlightened, loving community, but the evidence is that they were selfish, with an unusual concentration on one's own divinity without a concern for anyone who was not part of the elite. The world was considered evil and something to escape. Gnostics had no concern with changing the world or making it a better place. Physical matter was evil to them. If one was part of the elite, one wanted to focus on his or her inner divine spark and ascend out of the physical realm to the purely spiritual realm.

For the orthodox Christian the temptation to be as God is perverse and dangerous. The distinction between the orthodox and gnostic perspective is that the gnostic considers equality with God as a goal and the orthodox Christian sees the desire for such equality as a distortion of the core of our being. As James Houston writes: "The desire 'to be as God' (*eritus sicut dei*) is a perversion at the core of our being; it is the refusal to be human. This is the meaning of sin—the perversion of our imagination and actions to be anything but creaturely. . . . Our sinful temptation is to seek superiority over others, to want equality with God, to try to make religious 'deals' with Him, to insatiably desire conspicuous glory."[8]

7.1.2 Bentley Layton's diagram of a classic gnostic myth gives valuable insight into the nature of gnostic thought.

In his book, *The Gnostic Scriptures*, Yale University scholar Bentley Layton draws a useful diagram of a gnostic myth that he entitled "The Classic Gnostic Myth."[9] Layton notes that his diagram depicts a classic gnostic myth that drew upon the myth of creation set forth in Plato's *Timaeus* in combination with certain aspects of Genesis. According to Layton, the gnostics were mainly active in the mid-second century,[10] approximately one hundred years after the writing of Matthew, Mark, Luke, and John.

Because a diagram of the myth is useful for providing a basic framework in which to understand a classic gnostic myth, I will present the essence of Layton's diagram with some comments from his writings to fill in the content of the myth. Later I shall discuss how Layton's diagram, taken from *The Secret Book According to John*, appears to be the basic myth that underlies the recently discovered gospel of Judas.

Bentley Layton summarizes the diagram (see fig. 7.1) of this classical form basically as follows:

1. The first principle of the Entirety or the All is intellect and is ineffable and beyond human comprehension. Essentially, the first principle is consistent with Platonic discussion about god in vogue in the second century. This first principle overflows into a second principle, known as Barbēlo,[11] which emits other beings known as aeons. Aeons are realms or places as well as abstract concepts, such as "eternal life." Sophia (wisdom) is the last aeon and is the mother of a bungling creator who is often associated with Israel's god, Yahweh.

2. The four aeons are luminaries which are realms and characters. These aeons are the dwelling places of four archetypes: Geradamas (Adamas), Seth, the posterity of Seth, and Elēlēth. The aeons complete the purely spiritual universe.

3. After the completion of the spiritual universe, the creator of the physical universe, Ialdabaōth (often equated with Yahweh, the God of Israel), appears. Layton notes that this character is clearly derived from Plato's creation myth. Ialdabaōth copies patterns from the spiritual universe and has offspring, including "powers," "demons," "rulers," and "angels." Although this creator is not

The Classic Gnostic Myth
(Adapted and modified according to Bentley Layton's The Gnostics Scriptures.)

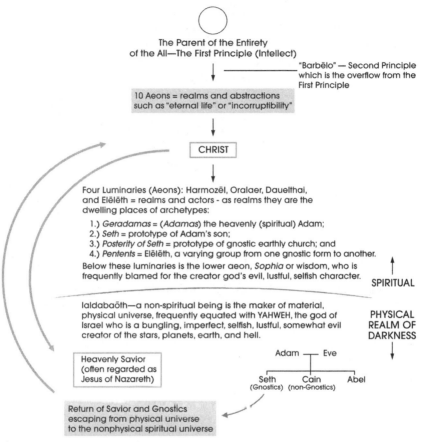

Figure 7.1

completely evil, he is imperfect, self-focused, ignorant, bungling, and lustful. As Layton writes: "He recognizes the goodness of the patterns in the spiritual realm and feels a natural attraction toward them; but this attraction is also experienced as an ignorant, selfish, erotic lust to possess the divine, even to rape it."[12] The imperfection of this creator appears to come from a lustful emotion by the mother of the creator, the aeon Sophia (wisdom).

4. As discussed above, for the gnostics, the Jewish God, *Yahweh*, the God of Israel, is not the ultimate God, but a very imperfect, almost

evil buffoon. As Layton writes: "The gnostics did not identify the god of Israel with the first principle. Rather the god of Israel was equated either with Ialdabaōth, the imperfect craftsman, or with Ialdabaōth's first born offspring Sabaōth."[13]

5. Sophia (wisdom) with the help of other aeons tries to regain for the spiritual universe the power stolen by Ialdabaōth. She does not succeed, and the stolen power dispenses into some of Ialdabaōth's offspring, most notably Seth and his offspring. The offspring of Seth are gnostics who can return to the spiritual universe *if* they obtain *gnōsis* (knowledge) of their inner divine power.

6. The last act of the myth invokes a heavenly savior, often regarded as Jesus of Nazareth, who is sent from the spiritual universe to give this *gnōsis* to the offspring of Seth and to teach them how to escape from the evil, physical world and return to the spiritual universe.[14]

For the most part, gnosticism had a negative perspective on Judaism. Because of its eclectic, syncretic collection of diverse thought, the origins of gnosticism are difficult to trace. Gnosticism took pieces of Greek Platonic and neo-Platonic philosophy with its dualism and rejected the Jewish account of creation and the end times. Although there was a spectrum of gnostic beliefs, my point will be that gnosticism did not present an equally valid historical alternative to orthodoxy but rather a distortion of the earliest portrait of Jesus.

7.2 THREE ARCHAEOLOGICAL DISCOVERIES GIVE US SIGNIFICANT INFORMATION ABOUT SECOND-CENTURY TEXTS PRESENTING AN ALTERNATIVE GNOSTIC VIEW.

One way to begin to understand the current interest in gnosticism is to describe three archaeological discoveries made principally in the last century. The first two discoveries were not considered to have a significant effect upon the New Testament perspective of scholars until the publication of Elaine Pagels's *The Gnostic Gospels* in 1979. Although her perspective was not widely accepted by New Testament scholars, it contained the kind of proposition that was attractive to persons eager to find an alternative to the traditional orthodox view. I shall describe the three discoveries, which begin in 1897 and end sometime around the late 1970s.

7.2.1 In the Oxyrhynchus papyri, modern rubbish may be derived literally from ancient rubbish.

In the late nineteenth century, Bernard Grenfell and Arthur Hunt became close friends as scholarship students at Queen's College in Oxford University. After they received financing from the Egyptian Exploration Society of London, they began an archaeological excavation of the ancient ruins of Oxyrhynchus, a thriving regional capital of the nineteenth province in Egypt's Pharonic Period.[15]

The city has a fascinating history that is relatively easy to uncover because the city's garbage heaps remain preserved due to the lack of rain in the area. Because of the arid atmosphere, even perishables above ground survived well in the thirty-foot-deep rubbish mounds of Oxyrhynchus.

Working in the winter excavating these mounds, shipping their discoveries back to Oxford in biscuit tins, and spending their summers in Oxford, reviewing and clarifying their findings; Grenfell and Hunt exposed the extraordinary life of the citizens of Oxyrhynchus and their substantial literary collection, including fragments of the writings of Sophocles, Euripides, Menander, and Euclid.

The most important discoveries were made in 1897 and 1901 when Grenfell and Hunt found three Greek fragments of different versions of the gospel of Thomas. The fragments preserved 20 of the 114 sayings of the gospel of Thomas. Oxyrhynchus papyrus fragment 1 ("p.Oxy 1") contains sayings 26–30, 77, and 30–31 (an order quite distinct from the Coptic Nag Hammadi version). Saying 77 reads: "Jesus said, 'It is I who am the light (that presides) over all. It is I who am the entirety: it is from me that the entirety has come, and to me that the entirety goes.'"

The following sentences, which are the last sentences in the Coptic version of Saying 77, are part of Saying 30 in p.Oxy 1:[16] "Split a piece of wood: I am there. Lift a stone, and you (plural form) will find me there."

Saying 77 clearly indicates that the author of this saying held the perspective of Jesus as divine. Bentley Layton notes that "the entirety" is purely spiritual: "The entire system of the aeons that are lower than the second principle are part of 'the entirety.'"[17] The entirety is the All or the spiritual universe of divine beings.[18] As noted above, a characteristic of gnostic thought was the perspective of Jesus as a purely spiritual divine being who, if he inhabited a human form at all, did so only temporarily: "The function of Christ was to come as the emissary of the supreme God, bringing 'gnosis.' As a divine being He neither assumed a properly human body nor died, but either temporarily inhabited a human being, Jesus, or assumed a merely phantasmal human appearance."[19]

I will discuss Saying 77 in more detail when examining the Coptic version of the gospel of Thomas, but I want to note for now that our earliest manuscript of a fragment from the gospel of Thomas portrays Jesus as divine, for from him the entirety comes.

The other two Oxyrhynchus papyrus fragments contain the following sayings from the gospel of Thomas: p.Oxy 654 contains Sayings 1–7 and p.Oxy 655 contains Sayings 36–40.

The differences between the Greek and Coptic versions of these sayings are clearly set forth in Bentley Layton's translation in *The Gnostic Scriptures*. Over the years, a general consensus has emerged that the gospel of Thomas was originally composed in Syria, probably in the City of Edessa. Grenfell and Hunt dated the fragments to about 200 CE but, without giving any explanation or evidence to support their dating, assigned a date of 140 CE to the original composition of Thomas. Strangely, this dating has become the operating assumption of most scholars, even though the reason for this dating has never been explained or supported by logical argumentation. This is remarkable given the importance of the dating in addressing the question of whether the gospel of Thomas can give us any historical, authentic, independent information about Jesus of Nazareth.[20]

7.2.2 The texts in the Nag Hammadi Library have a second-century gnostic mythology.

Until 1945 the Oxyrhynchus papyri were the only fragments of the gospel of Thomas in our possession. In December of that year a peasant, digging for fertilizer near a cliff not far from the village of Nag Hammadi in Upper Egypt, discovered a large, red earthenware jar. Inside the jar were twelve codices or books and eight leaves from a thirteenth codex. These codices constituted a library of pagan, Jewish, and Christian writings displaying various degrees of gnostic thought, in forty-five separate tractates (not counting duplicates).[21]

The library has been translated into English by several authors. One useful translation covering the Nag Hammadi material is *The Nag Hammadi Library*, by James M. Robinson, director of the Institute for Antiquity and Christianity at Claremont Graduate School and its Nag Hammadi Research Project. The most highly touted of the Nag Hammadi texts is the controversial gospel of Thomas.

7.2.3 Although discovered in the 1970s, the "gospel of Judas" only received public attention in 2004; however, the overwhelming majority of scholars acknowledge that it is a second-century text with no independent historical information concerning Jesus of Nazareth.

In the mid- to late 1970s, a group of peasants entered a cave in the Jebel Qarara hills near the Nile River in Middle Egypt. Among human skeletal bones they found a papyrus codex (a leather-bound book) written in Coptic. For the next twenty-five years this manuscript had a bizarre history of sales and peculiar storage locations. Although scholars at Yale University identified the manuscript as the gospel of Judas in the late twentieth century, it wasn't until 2004 that the manuscript received much public attention. In that year the National Geographic Society became interested in publishing and disseminating the text.

Ehrman points out that through Irenaeus's writings we have evidence that the gospel of Judas was used by gnostics known as Cainites. Cainites believed that the world was created by an ignorant deity, the Jewish God, *Yahweh*. This inferior deity was not the One True God. Cainites honored persons who defied this inferior Jewish God. They honored Cain, who murdered his brother, Abel, and also honored the men of Sodom and Gomorrah. Their bizarre theology was allegedly supported by a gospel written in the name of Judas Iscariot. Like Cain, Judas was honored as the only disciple who did Jesus' will and understood the mysteries of his teachings. All of the other disciples were dishonored by the Cainite community.[22]

7.3 I WILL DISCUSS THREE IMPORTANT QUESTIONS CONCERNING THE GOSPEL OF THOMAS.

Because the gospel of Thomas is the most highly promoted of the "alternative gospels," I will discuss three important questions concerning this "gospel": (a) Is the gospel of Thomas a gospel in its literary genre? (b) Does it have a gnostic mythology? (c) Does it contain any reliable, authentic information about the historical Jesus that is independent from the canonical gospels?

The evidence will show that it is not a gospel in its literary genre, that it has a gnostic mythology, and that the text does not provide us with any independent, historical, reliable information about Jesus. It is a late second-century composition derived from a Syrian gospel harmony of the four canonical gospels; the claims surrounding this gospel by its proponents are vast exaggerations, unsupported by hard evidence and backed only by inconsistent, compounded speculations designed to place a second-century myth back into the first century.

7.4 THE GOSPEL OF THOMAS IS NOT A GOSPEL IN THE HISTORICAL LITERARY GENRE, CONTAINS A GNOSTIC MYTHOLOGICAL THEME, AND GIVES US NO RELIABLE, INDEPENDENT HISTORICAL INFORMATION ABOUT JESUS.

7.4.1 Is the gospel of Thomas a gospel in its literary genre?

The gospel of Thomas is not actually a gospel in its literary genre. As Bentley Layton wrote: "The use of the term 'gospel' to characterize an anthology is distinctly Christian and within Christian literature it is highly unusual (although GTh is entitled 'gospel' it bears no relation to the biographical genre called by this name, e.g. the gospel of Mark)."[23] This "gospel" is merely 114 sayings without any narrative. More than half of these sayings are similar to Jesus' sayings in the New Testament gospels. The author of *Thomas* appears to have borrowed and modified some of the sayings from the canonical gospels. Designating the gospel of Thomas as a gospel is inaccurate from a literary standpoint.

7.4.2 Does the gospel of Thomas have a gnostic mythology?

John P. Meier, Professor of the New Testament at the University of Notre Dame, in his highly acclaimed study of Jesus, entitled *A Marginal*

Jew, emphasizes that substantial elements of a gnostic myth are implied throughout the gospel of Thomas. Meier describes the implied gnostic myth in some detail:

> In the gnostic myth implied in the *Gospel of Thomas*, the individual spirits originally dwelt in the kingdom of light, the kingdom of the Father, who is the first principle of "the All" (= the spiritual universe of divine beings). By their very nature, these spirits were all united with and of one substance with the divine. Through some sort of primeval catastrophe, some of the spirits entered into the poverty of this material world and are imprisoned in the fleshly garments of human bodies. This fall and imprisonment have caused them to fall asleep spiritually, have caused them to forget their true origin in the kingdom of light; they are like drunkards and blind men in the realm of darkness. The "living" Jesus (basically, the timeless, eternal Son, without any true incarnation in matter, lengthy earthly ministry to the Jewish people in general, real death, or true bodily resurrection) comes into this world to wake these spirits up, to remind them of their true origin and destiny, to free them from the illusion that they belong to this material world of death. . . . The material world and physical body are rejected as evil, and one abstains as far as possible from things material. Sex is seen as an evil, and the female role in bearing new spirits imprisoned in bodies is especially deprecated. By asceticism the spirits already triumph in principle over the body, which will be totally left behind at physical death. . . . Physical death is simply final release from the evil material world.[24]

Meier notes that the strange mixture of polytheism, ascetism, pantheism, and mysticism contained in the myth is the only key that can interpret many of the obscure sayings of Jesus in the gospel of Thomas. As evidence supporting his conclusion of an implied gnostic myth, Meier calls our attention to the following sayings:[25]

> (27) "If you do not fast (abstain) as regards the world, you will not find the kingdom." [In the gnostic myth the "kingdom" is not something above or something to happen in the future, but a spiritual kingdom inside the elite with a divine spark; this spark is part of the All, hence the idea of the divinity of the elite.]

> (29) "Indeed, I am amazed at how this great wealth has made its home in this poverty." [The great wealth is the divine spark inadvertently left in some humans; the poverty refers to the physical matter of the body, which is regarded as disdainful and evil.]

(30) "Where there are three gods, they are gods. Where there are two or one, I am with him." [The elite human beings are divine because they have the divine spark; they are one in divine substance with Jesus.]

(50) "If they say to you, 'where did you come from?', say to them, We come from the light, the place where the light came into being on its own accord and established (itself)." [The elite are from the All or the Entirety, i.e., the purely spiritual universe. They have part of the divine substance, which is now trapped in their physical bodies.]

(77) "It is I who am the light which is above them all. It is I who am the all. From me did the all come forth, and unto me did the all extend. Split a piece of wood, and I am there. Light up the stone, and you will find me there." [Jesus is divine. The Entirety or the All—the spiritual universe, came forth from him and he is present everywhere.]

(108) "He who will drink from my mouth will become like me. I myself shall become he. . . ." [Jesus reveals the true knowledge that the elite are beings who are one in substance with Jesus' own divine being.]

(114) "Simon Peter said to them, 'Let Mary leave us, for women are not worthy of life.'" "Jesus said, 'I myself shall lead her in order to make her male, so that she too may become a living spirit resembling you males. For every woman who will make herself male will enter the kingdom of heaven.'" [Res ipsa loquitur. Saying 114 is the last of the sayings. Despite convoluted arguments proposed to the contrary, the gnostic myth was decidedly antifeminine.]

After reviewing these sayings and the evidence surrounding the text, Meier states that (1) the gospel of Thomas was written with a gnostic intention, (2) the parallels to Synoptic canonical material is given a gnostic distortion, (3) such a thorough gnostic distortion of Christianity was not used until the second century, (4) the Nag Hammadi text of the gospel of Thomas gives us no reliable, authentic information concerning the historical Jesus or the earliest sources of Christianity in the first century, and (5) the gospel of Thomas was composed in the second century as an expression of second-century gnosticism.[26] Meier also proceeds to address whether Thomas could represent a "trajectory" of authentic sayings of Jesus that was independent of the Synoptic tradition and concludes that no such trajectory existed.

Support for Meier's five conclusions is found in Bart Ehrman's recent book *Lost Christianities*.[27] Just as John Meier concludes that the gospel of Thomas could only be understood in reference to an *implied* gnostic myth, Bart Ehrman concludes that a gnostic myth is *presupposed* by the redactor of the gospel of Thomas. He disagrees with scholars, such as Elaine Pagels and Karen King, who perhaps would prefer to avoid the elitism and bizarre nature of such a myth in constructing their interpretation of the gospel of Thomas. Ehrman gives a detailed analysis of the sayings of Thomas that demonstrates clearly the presupposition of a gnostic mythology. Ehrman argues that the gospel of Thomas can only be understood by reference to gnosticism. He begins by quoting Saying 1:[28] "These are the secret sayings which the living Jesus spoke and which Didymus Jude Thomas wrote down. And he said, 'Whoever finds the interpretation of those sayings will not experience death.'"

He then notes that the gospel of Thomas was discovered at Nag Hammadi with other documents that clearly can be "identified under the umbrella term *Gnosticism*."[29] He goes on to state his case that the gospel of Thomas presupposes gnosticism and that the reader needs to interpret the text of Thomas with this gnostic myth in mind.[30] Ehrman claims that if one bears in mind the "presupposed" or, to use Meier's terminology, the "implied" gnostic myth, one can make sense of the sayings contained in this Nag Hammadi text. In support of his position, Ehrman cites and comments on Sayings 1, 3, 4, 11, 28, 29, 36, 37, 40, 49, 50, 56, 110, and 114. The reader with a keen interest in this argument should see Ehrman's thorough discussion on interpreting the gospel of Thomas in pages 59–63 of *Lost Christianities*. He adds to the above described sayings given by John P. Meier and presents substantial evidence of a bizarre syncretic myth underlying the gospel of Thomas.

In the end, however, whether one considers the gospel of Thomas a gnostic text or not may depend upon one's definition of gnosticism. It is possible, of course, to define gnosticism so narrowly that the gospel of Thomas does not match a description of gnosticism. For example, April DeConick has argued for a very narrow definition of gnosticism that appears to require a reference to a malevolent creator. Although such a reference is lacking in the gospel of Thomas (and thus would allow DeConick to consider the text outside the scope of her definition), it contains many references compatible with a gnostic-like myth. Yale's Bentley Layton argues that the presupposed myth underlying the gospel of Thomas is expressed most clearly in another text from the school of Thomas known as the Hymn of the Pearl. Layton notes that the alleged sayings of Jesus can only be understood in the framework of a hellenistic myth. He writes about the interpretive key to the obscure writings and sayings contained in the gospel of Thomas:

> The opening paragraph of GTh [*Gospel of Thomas*] directs the reader's attention to the need of interpreting Jesus' sayings in order for them to be effective: "Whoever finds the meaning of these sayings will not taste death." Without recognition of their hidden meaning, Jesus' sayings are merely "obscure." The interpretive clue to this hidden meaning was provided by references (especially in GTh 18, 29, 50) to a Hellenistic myth of the heavenly origin, fall, incarnation, awakening, and return of the soul. The structure of the myth was known in more coherent form in another work of Thomas scripture, HPrl [*The Hymn of the Pearl*]. Once the myth had been recognized or reconstructed by the ancient reader it would have provided a framework within which the other, more traditional sayings could be interpreted.[31]

In his introduction to the writings associated with Didymus Jude Thomas,[32] Layton sets forth the following summary of the strange myth that is deduced from the Hymn of the Pearl and presupposed in the gospel of Thomas:

> The (1) first principle of (2) the spiritual realm providentially causes (3) the individual soul to descend past (4) the heavenly bodies into (5) incarnate life in a material body, in order to (6) be educated (get salvation). The soul (7) becomes unconscious and inert because of (8) matter. But it (9) disengages itself in response to (10) the savior or message of philosophy (wisdom). It (11) becomes acquainted with itself and its career and (12) is metaphysically reunited with (13) itself (i.e., becomes integral) and with (14) the first principle, (15) gaining true repose.[33]

Craig Evans notes that this "strange myth" underlying the gospel of Thomas may not be an explicit example of a "full-blown gnosticism," but quotes Sayings 36, 37, 38, 39, and 77 as strongly suggesting that the gospel of Thomas is a gnostic writing: "There were, of course, many variations of these Gnostic and mystical ideas. The main thing to see, however, is that Gnosticism was not a neutral variation of general Christian belief but indeed an essentially different and opposing religion that simply borrowed terminology from the New Testament Gospels and changed its meaning. Although not an instance of this kind of full-blown Gnosticism, there is a strong Gnosticizing element in the *Gospel of Thomas*."[34]

Evans's conclusion is supported by an analysis of the gospel of Thomas conducted by Nicholas Perrin, former Canon Research Theologian at Westminster Abbey. Perrin argues that the gospel of Thomas does not give us any independent, new information about the historical Jesus. His evidence points to the conclusion that the text was originally written in Syriac and was composed in a Syriac "Christian" community after AD 170. Perrin's argument is a cumulative one providing substantial evidence that the author of the gospel of Thomas used the *Diatessaron*, a harmony of the previously composed canonical gospels. *Diatessaron* means "through the four." It is a gospel harmony of the four canonical gospels, a harmony written by Tatian after he returned from Rome to Edessa after AD 165.

7.4.3 Does the gospel of Thomas contain any sayings or deeds of the historical Jesus that are independent from the canonical gospels?

Promoters of the gospel of Thomas argue that it should be considered as valid or more valid than the canonical gospels. They even argue that it represents a deeper form of spiritually mature understanding. But the key issue in terms of the validity of the gospel of Thomas is the date of its original composition. If it was not composed until the late second century, it is far away from the life and sayings of the historical Jesus, much farther away than the canonical gospels of the first century. N. T. Wright is quite certain of a late second-century date for its composition. He holds that its sayings are mere fantasies or, at best, distortions of the sayings found in the canonical gospels:

> Take the best known, and one of the longest, of the Nag Hammadi documents: a collection of supposed sayings of Jesus known as the *Gospel of Thomas*. This is the book that has often been suggested could and should be treated as at least equal and quite possibly superior, to the canonical gospels as a historical source for Jesus himself. The version we now have, like most of the Nag Hammadi material, is written in Coptic, a language

spoken in Egypt at the time. But it has been demonstrated that Thomas is a translation from Syriac, a language quite like the Aramaic that Jesus must have spoken. . . . *But the Syriac traditions that Thomas embodies can be dated, quite reliably, not to the first century at all, but to the second half of the second century.* That is over a hundred years after Jesus' own day— in other words seventy to a hundred years *after* the time when the four canonical gospels were in widespread use across the early church.

What's more, despite efforts to prove the opposite, the sayings of Jesus as they appear in Thomas show clear indications that they are not as original as the parallel material (where it exists) in the canonical gospels. Sayings have, in many cases, been quietly doctored in Thomas to express a very different viewpoint.[35]

7.4.3.1 Nicholas Perrin's study is powerful evidence of a very late second-century date for the composition of the gospel of Thomas.

In his book *Thomas and Tatian: The Relationship between the Gospel of Thomas and the Diatessaron*, Nicholas Perrin presents a solution to the question of whether the gospel of Thomas was dependent on the Greek Synoptic gospels. As noted above, Perrin offers substantial evidence that Thomas was dependent on the very first Syriac gospel record, the *Diatessaron*, a harmony of the canonical gospels written by Tatian in about AD 173. To the best of our knowledge, the *Diatessaron* was the only gospel account available in Syriac in the second century.[36]

In the first chapter of her book *Beyond Belief*, Pagels writes: "Let us start by taking a fresh look at the most familiar of all Christian sources— the gospels of the New Testament—in the perspective offered by one of the *other* Christian gospels *composed in the first century* and discovered at Nag Hammadi, the Gospel of Thomas."[37] Perrin's study undermines Pagels's speculation that the gospel of Thomas was composed in the first century. His evidence points to a late *second*-century date for the composition of this text.

Perrin argues that the original composition of the gospel of Thomas was in Syriac. When one reads the gospel of Thomas in the Coptic version of Nag Hammadi, the 114 sayings of Jesus appear in a completely random sequence with no discernible pattern. However, when translated back into Syriac, the work becomes a carefully arranged text with dynamic connecting words that present a structured, distinct literary rhetorical pattern.[38] When one translates the Nag Hammadi Coptic text into Syriac, the gospel of Thomas becomes "entirely interconnected by a complex pattern of word linkages and paronomasia." (Paronomasia refers to clever puns or word-plays.)[39]

Perrin shows that a Syriac translation of the gospel of Thomas uses over five hundred "catchwords" involving sound plays or linkage patterns[40] and is also consistent with "Syriac redaction" (editing) at the compositional level so that one is ineluctably directed toward a Syriac written source for the author of Thomas. Perrin notes that the only written Syriac source available would have been Tatian's harmony of the canonical gospels known as the *Diatessaron*: "Given the frequent and protracted use of catchwords, as well as traces of 'Syriac redaction' at the compositional level, . . . the author of Thomas must have drawn upon Syriac written sources, not the least for his use of synoptic materials. Since Tatian's harmony was presumably the only gospel record available in the Syriac language at that time, the evidence points ineluctably to *Diatessaronic* influence. This conclusion is finally vindicated from historical text-critical, and source-critical perspectives."[41]

Perrin's insights have probative validity, for these catchwords "constitute a technique which, like rhyme or assonance, must be preserved in the original language in order to be effective or recognizable. When catchwords rely on paronomasia, verbal play involving the sounds of words, they are also a linguistically conditional trope."[42] In other words, the sound and meaning of an extraordinary number (502) of catchwords appear to give a special effect and meaning when one translates the Coptic gospel of Thomas back into Syriac. These words create a play on words, an intended literary device of the author in order to amplify and connect their meaning. Catchwords used as paronomasia was a second-century Syriac literary style.[43] An author would use a word similar in sound (in Syriac) in order to achieve a certain meaning. This is similar to one using a pun or play on word sounds to achieve humor or a special effect.

Perrin's analysis demonstrates that the Syriac text of the gospel of Thomas has a "consistent matrix of phonological and semantic catchwords." Perrin meticulously sets out the English text of the gospel of Thomas in a parallel structure with every Coptic, Greek, and Syriac term that could be a catchword. One can follow him saying by saying through the gospel of Thomas and see 502 identifiable catchwords in Syriac, 263 in Greek, and 269 in the Coptic text. When the sound of a Syriac word and its meaning converged within two sequential sayings in the gospel of Thomas, the Syriac translation of the sayings appears to be intentionally connected by this impressive pattern of "catchwords." Out of the 114 sayings that constitute the text, Perrin found catchwords for all but three couplets (and a misunderstanding of the Syriac sounds can explain the lack of catchwords in these three couplets).

Over five hundred catchwords in Syriac is a telling number considering that the gospel of Thomas consists only of 114 sayings. In the Syriac language these catchwords or puns link the sayings in a highly ordered, definite literary pattern. As noted above, such a pattern does not exist in English, Greek, or Coptic.

Perrin's quantitative, statistical evidence is formidable. Although one may argue that he advanced his own point of view in translating the Syriac, there are only so many optional words available to a translator. The vast number of catchwords is statistically relevant. If one is to criticize his translation as "inventing" catchwords, then one must be prepared to show how the number of catchwords in Syriac could be reduced to the number in Coptic or Greek. As Perrin's translation stands, Syriac has about double the number of Greek or Coptic catchwords. If one were able to use other *equally valid* words to translate the gospel of Thomas into Syriac and thereby reduce the number of catchwords by a hundred (a task which I think may not be so easy), Perrin would still have more than four hundred catchwords, a statistically significant number to support his position.

Perrin's evidence shows that the gospel of Thomas is a unified work, not a product of stages of sayings gradually occurring over a long period of time. The unity of the gospel of Thomas places the burden of proof on those who assume its disunity and development through stages of oral tradition. The tightly woven, unified pattern indicates a Syriac *written* source with a carefully arranged sequential order. Perrin shows that the author of the gospel of Thomas is familiar with Tatian's *Diatessaron* and used it in creating his text. Perrin shows where Thomas follows the Syriac text. He combines a combination of literary-historical analysis with this linguistic evidence to demonstrate how the author of the gospel of Thomas edited and modified the *Diatessaron* by purposefully using this pattern of linking catchwords. He concludes that the author of the original composition relied on a Syriac written source and that "for his numerous quotations from and allusions to the synoptic tradition, Thomas could only have used the *Diatessaron*. . . . This conclusion is vindicated on historical, text-critical and source-critical grounds."[44]

As noted above, Perrin's analysis points toward Tatian's *Diatessaron* because it was the only gospel account available in Syriac. The author of Thomas relied on a Syriac text, and when one matches the sequence in the gospel of Thomas with the sequence in the *Diatessaron*, the reliance becomes even more apparent: "It appears that the author of the Gospel of Thomas relied on a text whose sequence of pericopes, though sometimes following the biblical order, more closely followed the order of the *Diatessaron*. . . . It is in the shared sequence of sayings that I find strong confirmation that the Gospel of Thomas is dependent on the *Diatessaron*."[45]

Perrin's work establishes the following five points:

1. The author of the gospel of Thomas wrote the original composition in Syriac.
2. There was only one original author of the Syriac text.
3. The Syriac text displays a unity and coherent pattern that indicates that this author relied on a written Syriac source.
4. The only gospel record available in Syriac that could have been available to the author was the *Diatessaron*.
5. The *Diatessaron* was a gospel harmony dependent upon the canonical gospels.

These five points have great significance. They mean that the gospel of Thomas's original composition could have been no earlier than AD 170, the earliest feasible date for Tatian's writing of the *Diatessaron*. *These points also mean that the gospel of Thomas does not provide historical, independent information concerning Jesus of Nazareth.* Given Perrin's analysis, the arguments of pro-Thomas scholars appear to contain vastly exaggerated claims. The speculations advanced by these scholars concerning a nonorthodox perspective on Jesus of Nazareth lack a valid historical base.

Perrin's evidence places the burden on those who would argue against his position. To support their proposals concerning the gospel of Thomas, pro-Thomas scholars need to provide evidence to counter the points listed above. Until they do so, their promotion of an early date for the composition of the gospel of Thomas or for a basis for that gospel in early oral tradition appears to be without merit. A basis in a previous oral tradition is unlikely because Thomas relied on a *written* Syriac source. Further, in Thomas there is nothing like the evidence from the earliest creeds, hymns, and liturgical formulae found in the New Testament. Distinguished New Testament scholars N. T. Wright[46] and Craig Evans are convinced that Perrin's study provides compelling evidence that the gospel of Thomas was composed in the late second century and that "nothing in *Thomas* can be independently traced back to the first century."[47] Evans notes that from the beginning of the study of the Nag Hammadi text of the gospel of Thomas, many scholars recognized a Syriac style in the text and an agreement in the text with the Syriac version of the canonical gospels or with Tatian's *Diatessaron*. He finds that Perrin's evidence strongly indicates a dependence on Tatian's harmony of the four canonical gospels. Evans is convinced by Perrin's study and summarizes his evidence as follows:

> Perrin is not only able to explain the order of the whole of *Thomas* in reference to catchwords, he is able to show in places the Gospel's acquaintance with the order and arrangement of material in Tatian's *Diatessaron*. The mystery of the order of the sayings that make up the *Gospel of Thomas* appears to have been resolved. Perrin concludes that the *Gospel of Thomas* is indeed dependent on the New Testament Gospels, but not directly. *Thomas* depends on the New Testament Gospels as they existed in the *Diatessaron*, in Syriac.
>
> In my view the principal argument that Crossan and others have advanced in support of the literary independence *of* the *Gospel of Thomas* from the New Testament Gospels has been dealt a crippling blow. It is no longer justified to say that there is no discernible framework or organizing principle lying behind the composition of *Thomas*. There clearly is, when this writing of acknowledged Syrian origin is studied in the light of the Syriac language.
>
> Just as impressive is the number of specific contacts between the *Gospel of Thomas* and Syrian Gospel traditions and other Syrian religious traditions. What we see is that again and again, where *Thomas* differs from the New Testament Gospels, this is where *Thomas* agrees with Syrian tradition. This point has not been sufficiently appreciated by Crossan and others.[48]

Perrin's evidence establishes that the gospel of Thomas gives us no first-century information about Jesus of Nazareth other than information derived from the canonical gospels. It does not represent an equally valid and authentic form of first-century Christian belief. Anyone interested in exploring the evidence further should read Perrin's writings and Evans's careful presentation of his evidence in his well-constructed recent book *Fabricating Jesus*. Evans argues that the evidence supports a conclusion that the gospel of Thomas has a second-century origin and does not contain any independent information about the historical Jesus:

> When all of the appropriate evidence is taken into consideration, I find it hard to avoid the conclusion that the *Gospel of Thomas* originated in the late second century, not in the middle of the first century. Let me make this emphatically clear: This is where all of the evidence takes us: (1) the association of the *Gospel of Thomas* with "Judas Thomas," (2) the arrangement and order of the sayings explained by hundreds of Syriac catchwords that link the sayings, and (3) the coherence of the readings in *Thomas*, which differ from the Greek New Testament Gospels, with the readings either in the *Diatessaron* or other Christian Syriac works from this period compellingly argue for a late-second-century Syrian origin of the *Gospel of Thomas*. In short, it is this flood of factors that point to the Eastern, Syriac-speaking church, a church that knows the New Testament Gospels primarily—perhaps exclusively—through Tatian's *Diatessaron*, a work not composed before A.D. 170, that persuades me that the *Gospel of Thomas* does not offer students of the Gospels early, independent material that can be used for critical research into the life and teaching of Jesus. Reliance on this writing can only lead to a distorted portrait of the historical Jesus.[49]

Evans's "flood of factors" clearly shifts the burden of proof to scholars who argue for an alternative, "gnostic" Jesus. In order to support their speculations they need to answer the powerful evidence that undermines their effort to invent a portrait of Jesus without a verifiable historical foundation. They may wish for such a Jesus to be the Jesus of history, but wishing alone does not make for an authentic, truthful foundation. Those who argue against an orthodox view should produce solid first-century evidence for their speculations, not attempt to transport a second-century distortion back into the first decades of the Christian faith.

7.4.3.2 Other considerations regarding the gospel of Thomas argue against its validity as an independent source of any first-century event or saying.

Many persons have read books containing exaggerated claims about the gospel of Thomas, but not all have taken the time to read the short text of this gnostic writing. I encourage everyone to read it and compare it to the canonical gospels. It is quite short and can be read in its entirety in about fifteen minutes. Bruce Metzger, one of the true giants in New Testament studies, recently died at his home in Princeton where he had worked and written for over seventy years. With respect to the Nag Hammadi codices, including the gospel of Thomas, Metzger wrote: "Even a casual acquaintance, however, of these gospels and their credentials will convince the reader that no one excluded them from the Bible; they excluded themselves."[50]

Phillip Jenkins has emphasized that the key question in terms of the reliability of any Nag Hammadi text in giving us valid information about Jesus or about the earliest days of the Christian faith depends upon the date of the original composition of these texts. If these texts were not written until the second century, they are far away from the sayings or events they purport to describe, much farther away than the four canonical gospels, which were all written in the first century, and even farther away then the hymns, creeds, and liturgical formulae incorporated into the letters and writings of the New Testament. As discussed in chapter 2, many of these creeds hidden in the New Testament date back to a time almost contemporary with the events they describe. These early formulae of the church present an orthodox Christian position. There are no comparable creeds, hymns, liturgical formulae in the Nag Hammadi texts. The texts discovered in Upper Egypt describe a distortion of the Christian faith derived from second-century forms of gnosticism. This distortion represents a worldview that is mutually exclusive to the worldview of orthodox New Testament Christianity.

Jenkins criticizes the idea that the Nag Hammadi texts open a window on earliest Christianity. The validity of the position of pro-gnostic scholars depends upon whether these texts were written in the first century and whether they give us any historically reliable information concerning Jesus of Nazareth that is independent from the canonical gospels. The consensus is that they originated in the second and third centuries. They are not alternative voices of the first followers of Jesus, but works of later dissidents who distorted the earliest tradition of the church: "Far from being the alternative voices of Jesus' first followers, most of the lost gospels should rather be seen as the writings of much later dissidents who broke away from an already established orthodox church. . . . The late character of the alternative texts is critical to matters of historicity and reliability. Historical research is as good as the

sources on which it relies, and to the extent that the latest quest for
the historical Jesus is founded on the hidden gospels, that endeavor is
fatally flawed."[51]

As noted earlier, at least half of the sayings in Thomas appear to
reflect sayings of Jesus in the four canonical gospels, but the differences in the sayings as they appear in Thomas can be demonstrated
to be consistent with the author of Thomas relying on the canonical
gospels and changing certain sayings in the canonical gospels to reflect
a second-century syncretistic gnostic style of mythology. N. T. Wright
concurs with this assessment. One may summarize his analysis with the
following three points:

1. Thomas moves toward a Greek Platonic perspective and away
   from the Jewish environment of Jesus' ministry where Jesus
   inaugurates the kingdom of God, "calling his fellow Jews back
   to a genuine following of Israel's God and the inner meaning of
   the Jewish law." Rather, Thomas in a manner consistent with
   second-century gnosticism, exhibits an anti-Judaism perspective.
   As Wright notes: "This fits very neatly with the largely non-Jewish
   Jesus invented by Rudolf Bultmann and his followers, and rein-
   vented by the now defunct 'Jesus Seminar', but not at all with
   any picture of Jesus which can be produced by serious and sober
   historical scholarship."[52]
2. Thomas does not try to give a narrative about Jesus. Instead, the
   Nag Hammadi text gives teachings attributed to Jesus and ignores
   the Jewish background of the Old Testament that points to Jesus,
   the cross, and his resurrection as the fulfillment of God's plan to
   bring from among the Jewish people the source of salvation of
   humankind.
3. Thomas and the other Nag Hammadi texts see Jesus only as a
   teacher or one who reveals knowledge. For Thomas and these
   texts the message about Jesus is not gospel, that is, not "*good
   news*" about something that happened in history (the atonement
   on the cross and the resurrection), but "*good advice*" from Jesus
   about how to rearrange one's spiritual priorities. (In these texts
   history is unimportant because of the *gnostic* emphasis on one's
   own spirituality with a sharp hope that one is one of the lucky
   few with a divine spark within his or her being. History does not
   matter. What matters is believing that you are one of the few who

have this spark which can be fanned into a real flame of divinity allowing you to ascend to the ultimate God, not the God of Israel.)[53]

Meier agrees with Wright and Jenkins and concludes that the criteria of historicity requires us "to toss the Gospel of Thomas back into the sea."[54] Meier notes that wanting Jesus to be part of the gnostic myth does not mean that in history he actually was part of the myth. For a variety of independent reasons, certain North American scholars appear to want almost anything besides the traditional Christian faith. The result is a strained, convoluted interpretation of the available evidence.

7.5 THE GOSPEL OF JUDAS IS A SECOND-CENTURY TEXT WITH NO INSIGHTFUL NEW INFORMATION INTO THE FIRST CENTURY.

7.5.1 The overwhelming majority of scholars date the composition of the gospel of Judas to the second century

For a lawyer looking at evidence concerning the very beginnings of the Christian faith, the dramatic publicity surrounding the discovery of the text of the gospel of Judas is puzzling. Even the most liberal of scholars hold that the gospel of Judas is a second-century composition that does not give us any independent, historically reliable information about Jesus of Nazareth. As Karen King and Elaine Pagels write: "Because the Gospel of Judas was written sometime around 150 C.E., about a century after Judas would have lived, it is impossible that he wrote it; the real author remains anonymous. *Neither do we learn anything historically reliable about Judas or Jesus* beyond what we already know from other early Christian literature. Instead, the Gospel of Judas opens a window onto the disputes among *second century* Christians."[55]

James M. Robinson,[56] in a more sardonic tone, notes that there is nothing about the gospel of Judas that presents authentic new information about the first decades of the first century, the period during which Jesus lived, died, and, many believe, was resurrected. It was in the early 30s that the church began. To evaluate the evidence regarding the claims of the Christian faith, one must go back to the very earliest worship patterns of the first participants in the Christian movement. This requires an examination of the earliest creeds and liturgical formulae from these first few decades, and that information is only found in the first-century documents regarding the faith. The only first-century documents in our possession are the orthodox documents of the New Testament.

The date of composition of the gospel of Judas was at least eighty years after the gospel of Mark and about one hundred years more recent than the early letters comprising the epistles in the New Testament. Robinson is not an orthodox proponent, but he realizes that it is impossible for the gospel of Judas to give us new, valid information about the first decades of the first century: "Since the *Gospel of Judas* is a Gnostic tractate written in the middle of the Second century, it does not add any new information about what happened in Jerusalem around 30 CE. Though it is an important text for specialists in second-century Gnosticism, such as myself, it has been misrepresented so as to sensationalize it in order to make as large a profit on its investment as possible."[57]

Robinson goes on to quote Hershel Shanks about the hype and sensationalism surrounding the publication of the gospel of Judas: "The idea that this new gospel might be an accurate historical report of the reason for Judas's betrayal of Jesus is arrant nonsense."[58] Actually, we have known about the existence of the gospel of Judas for a long time. There is nothing astonishing about its discovery. Irenaeus wrote about it in detail in 180 CE.

The excitement around the publication of the gospel of Judas is even more difficult to understand after one has the opportunity to read this very short text. Rather than being told what to think about the gospel of Judas, take a few minutes and read the gospel of Judas and make your own assessment of its validity. Compare it to the canonical gospels. You will find that it reflects a gnostic Sethian myth very similar to the myth depicted in the modified diagram of Bentley Layton shown and discussed earlier in connection with *The Secret Book According to John*.

The author of the gospel of Judas is clearly influenced by Plato's *Timaeus* and this gnostic gospel has a strong anti-Judaic worldview. Perhaps a brief tour of some of the main points of the text is worthwhile to show the nature of a second-century gnosticism document. I will try to focus on some major themes. The initial translators of the text present it in three scenes.

7.5.2 Scene 1: The author describes a Jesus who ridicules the God of Israel.

At the beginning of the text, Jesus approaches his disciples and laughs in mockery at their celebration of the eucharist. When they ask him why he is laughing at them for "giving thanks" (*eucharisti*) in the eucharist, Jesus responds by saying that he is laughing because the disciples are not worshipping the ultimate deity, but the ruler of this world (who for a Jew was *Yahweh*, the God of Israel described in the Old Testament). In the Sethian gnostic myth of the gospel of Judas, the creator of this world is the clumsy, second-rate, and even semi-evil "god" of Israel. As we shall see in scene 3 of this text, Jesus sets forth the cosmogony of divine beings from the spiritual realm with a similar list of names as mentioned in the *The Secret Book According to John* reflected in the diagram above. The idea of the eucharist is ridiculed in gnostic thought, partly because the elements of the bread and wine are made of physical matter. In this myth, matter is considered evil. The bungling *Yahweh* clumsily made matter (something which was considered abhorrent to the gnostics). In his bumbling creation, he inadvertently left a divine spark in *some* human beings. These humans are of the generation of Seth, the son born to Adam and Eve after Cain killed Abel. If one is not of the generation of Seth, he or she is a "mere clod" who will cease to exist at death. Human beings of the generation of Seth, however, once they have the knowledge of their inner divinity, can fan its spark into a flame, become more divine, and ascend past the stupid, malevolent *Yahweh* to the Ultimate Reality.[59]

After Jesus ridicules the disciples for celebrating the eucharist, toward the end of scene 1, Judas proclaims that Jesus is "from the realm of Barbēlo." Sethian gnostics considered Barbēlo a primary divine being from the divine realm and Jesus to be son of God (not of *Yahweh*, but of the "Infinite One" or of "Ultimate Reality").[60]

At the close of scene 1 Jesus tells Judas in private that he will explain to him the "mysteries of the kingdom." Jesus tells Judas that someone will replace him. Judas asks when Jesus will tell him these things. Jesus does not respond but abruptly disappears.

7.5.3 Scene 2: Jesus criticizes the priests who serve the inferior Jewish God and alludes to language from Plato.

Jesus appears again to the disciples, stating that he had been in another realm, most likely a spiritual realm that is a "great and holy generation." When the disciples ask him what generation is superior to them, Jesus again laughs at them and tells them that no one of this aeon (generation) will look at that generation. The disciples then discuss the Temple and Jesus gives an allegorical interpretation of activities in the Temple, criticizing the priests who serve an inferior "god" (*Yahweh*, the Jewish God of Israel). As Bart Ehrman emphasizes: "Jesus in this gospel indicates that they (the disciples and proto-orthodox Christians) are completely misled. They do indeed worship the Jewish God. But this god is a reckless fool. He did create this world, but the world is not good; it is a cesspool of misery and suffering. The true God has never had anything to do with this world. This world must be escaped, not embraced."[61]

Later, Jesus states that "each of you has his own star." This appears to reflect language from Plato's *Timaeus* where each soul is assigned a star.[62] Jesus then begins to tell Judas about the distinctions in generations. He further elaborates on this distinction toward the end of scene 3. One of the principal points is that an elite, the generation of Seth, will be the only ones who will ascend to God. The rest of humanity will cease to exist. The last thing a member of the elite (the Sethian generation) would want is a physical resurrection body. Their goal is to escape the body and this world.[63] Jesus distinguishes between "this generation" (the clods) and "that generation" (the elite Sethians). Only the elite will gain eternal existence. Bart Ehrman explains: "Some people belong to this generation, some to that one. Those with the divine element within belong to that one; only they can be saved when they die. When the others—of 'this generation'—die, that will be the end of their story."[64]

7.5.4 Scene 3: Jesus explains the cosmogony of the gnostic myth.

In the final scene of this very short text, Jesus gives an explanation of the cosmogony underlying the gospel of Judas. As noted above, this reflects something akin to the diagram of a classic gnostic myth shown above, using distinctive gnostic terms such as "the Self-Generated," "El" (an ancient Semitic name for *Yahweh*), "Nebro," "Yaldabaoth," "Saklas" (an Aramaic term for "fool" used to describe the "god" of Israel in Sethian texts), "Seth," "Harmathoth," "Galila," "Yobel," "Adonaios" "Adam," "Eve," and "Zoe." Only Judas understands that Jesus is from the realm of Barbēlo, not from the inferior realm of the second-rate, foolish god of Israel.[65]

These are the main themes in the gospel of Judas. One can easily recognize them in the diagram given earlier regarding the cosmogony of *The Secret Book According to John*. Some pro-gnostic scholars strain credulity in attempting to interpret the gospel of Judas outside of the gnostic myth. But the presence of a gnostic myth is obvious and central. Pagels and King admit that it does not give us any authentic, independent information about the historical Jesus.

Pagels, however, has suggested that one should read the gnostic texts together with the canonical gospels, using the gnostic texts for a more advanced level of spiritual comprehension. But the worldview of the gospel of Judas, the gospel of Thomas, and the other gnostic texts is in conflict with the worldview of the canonical gospels. The differences between the gnostic texts and the New Testament are clear and logically irreconcilable. N. T. Wright believes that Pagels fails to appreciate the irreconcilable worldviews among these texts. Gnosticism as portrayed in the gospel of Judas and as implied in the gospel of Thomas cannot be seen as historically, philosophically, or spiritually compatible with the core beliefs of the earliest Christian faith. If gnosticism is true, classic Christianity and Judaism are not:

> Elaine Pagels's statement is quite breathtaking. It could only be sustained by a systematic and sustained rereading, and in fact a misreading, of the canonical gospels themselves. When it all comes down to it, Matthew, Mark, Luke and John believed that Jesus really was Israel's Messiah, and that he had indeed come to bring about the kingdom of the one creator God on earth as in heaven. "Judas," like "Thomas" and the other gnostic texts, believed . . . that Jesus had come to show the way out of Judaism, out of the wicked created order, and off into a different realm altogether. Pagels is actually well aware of this. . . . These two sets of belief are like oil and water; like chalk and cheese. If we cannot see that, we are simply not paying attention to the texts. The idea that there might be a progression from the first to the second, as with basic and advanced teaching of the same subject, is simply wishful thinking, whether in the second century or today.[66]

Like the gospel of Thomas, the gospel of Judas was composed after the middle of the second century. All of the gnostic writings in our possession are from no earlier than the second century. The New Testament documents, on the other hand, are all from the first century.[67] If one is attempting to answer the historical question of the earliest origins of Christianity and the life of Jesus of Nazareth, one needs to focus on the earliest evidence in our possession. These are the first-century canonical documents and the preexisting creeds, hymns, and liturgical formulae found in those documents and discussed above in chapter 2.

7.6 OTHER EVIDENCE SUPPORTS THE VIEW THAT GNOSTIC "CHRISTIANITY" WAS NOT CONTEMPORANEOUS WITH THE EARLIER BEGINNING OF THE ORTHODOX, TRADITIONAL CHRISTIAN FAITH.

7.6.1 Anti-Judaism in the gospel of Thomas and the gospel of Judas is inconsistent with an early beginning to "Christian" gnosticism.

The gospel of Thomas fits the pattern of the classic gnostic myth in rejecting the physical world and the significance of Israel and the Old Testament. Given the distinct anti-Judaism content found in Thomas, it is difficult to see on a historical basis how the sayings of Thomas could be derived from the very earliest church in Jerusalem. We know that the earliest church began in a Jewish environment and continued Jewish tradition.

The earliest Christian believers in the mother congregation in Jerusalem in the first decades of the Christian faith defended Jewish practices such as circumcision and the Jewish food restrictions. It is highly improbable that a community strictly following Jewish customs would have produced a text such as the gospel of Thomas, which diverges so far from Jewish practices and beliefs.[68] N. T. Wright describes the distinction between the worldview of gnosticism and the worldview of Judaism and Christianity:

> Judaism, from Genesis to the rabbis and beyond, believes in the goodness of the created world, and in the special calling of Israel to be the light of that world. Gnosticism believes in the fundamental badness of the created world, the folly of those who take the Old Testament as their

guide, and the special status of the *Gnostics* as the sparks of light who are to be rescued from that world. In particular, Judaism believes that the God of Israel is the good, wise and sovereign creator of all that is, while Gnosticism believes that the God of Israel is the incompetent and malicious demiurge who made this wicked world. If Gnosticism is true, Judaism is not, and vice versa.[69]

7.6.2 Ecological apathy and rejection of the physical world were part of gnostic thought.

Although some would like to attribute an ecological concern to the gospel of Thomas, it is simply not there. One will look in vain in the gospel of Thomas for any concern for the environment of the planet earth. This is consistent with the view of the world in gnostic thought. Matter is seen as evil. There is no concern to protect or redeem the world but rather to escape from it. Gnosticism emphasized a dualism with salvation from matter to a purely spiritual existence. The gnostics despised matter and the physical world.

Unlike those who later followed the gospel of Thomas, Jesus was concerned with this earth and with the coming of God's kingdom on this earth, and he believed that the God of Abraham, Isaac, and Jacob was the one true holy God. In the prayer that he taught, he urged his followers to pray that God's "will be done on earth as in heaven." In traditional, orthodox Christianity, the Christian is to be in the world, and engaged in a loving transformation of the world, which includes, among other things, alleviating the suffering in the world. When Christ calls someone, he does not call them only to a mission of inner self-discovery nor does he call them to abandon the world, to abandon the poor, the needy, the suffering, the victims of injustice, or even the care of the ecological environment. The incarnation of God in Christ, reconciling the world to himself through the atonement of his suffering on the cross, is not an abandonment of the world. It is the rescue of the world and a calling for his followers to engage the world and work in concert to transform it into a place of love, caring, justice, and truth. In traditional, orthodox Christian thought, Christ calls us into a transforming friendship with himself. This friendship includes his all-embracing love and concern for the world.

7.7 PREEXISTING CREEDS AND CONFESSIONS INCORPORATED INTO THE NEW TESTAMENT HAVE NO COUNTERPARTS OR EQUIVALENT VALIDATION IN THE GNOSTIC TEXTS.

As described in some detail in chapter 2, the earliest written sources concerning the Christian faith contain preexisting creeds, hymns, and liturgical formulae setting forth an extremely early core belief consistent with the orthodox, traditional faith. These worship formulae and practices contain summaries of the core belief of the earliest church and can be reliably dated to within the first decades of the church's existence. Bock describes these extremely early liturgical formulae and their core beliefs:

> One compelling element of evidence from this material includes extracts of church confession or short theological statements. These short pieces of theological summary or praise taught people the theological core of the church's teaching. When it comes to the Creation, two ideas are consistently set forth: (1) God is the Creator, not some substitute figure, and (2) Jesus participated in that Creation and is not a creature. . . . The core can be viewed as this: There was one Creator God. Jesus was both human and divine; He truly suffered and was raised bodily. He also is worthy to receive worship. Salvation was about liberation from hostile forces, but it also was about sin and forgiveness—the need to fix a flaw in humanity that made each person culpable before the Creator. This salvation was the realization of promises that God made to the world and to Israel through Israel's Law and Prophets. The one person, Jesus Christ, brought this salvation not only by revealing the way to God and making reconciliation but also by providing for that way through his death for sin. Resurrection into a new exalted spiritual life involves salvation of the entire person—spirit, soul, and body. Faith in this work of God through Jesus saves and brings on a spiritual life that will never end. This was the orthodoxy of the earliest tradition.[70]

As previously noted, in the gospel of Thomas, the gospel of Judas, and the other Nag Hammadi texts, a person redeems himself by gaining knowledge of his or her divinity. It is a process of self-redemption through self-discovery and self-actualization. It may lead toward self-worship and a focus on one's self. This is far different from a redemption that comes from Jesus who died for us all and was an atoning sacrifice, allowing us to become blameless in the presence of God. This concept of an atoning sacrifice is a core belief contained in the earliest sources in our possession and in the oral tradition of preexisting creeds and formulae incorporated in those early sources. In other words, this belief in the redemptive nature of Jesus' crucifixion is part of a core of orthodoxy (proto-orthodoxy or traditional) Christianity that we can trace to within a few years of the crucifixion.

> All the major strands of the earliest traditional texts declare that Jesus' work is a saving sacrifice for sin, something that most new materials did not affirm. This declaration appears in the doctrinal summaries and in the materials that describe the church's worship, including the Lord's Table. That tradition claims that Jesus passed on this teaching Himself. These practices of worship then have roots that we can show are early, coming from the earliest sources we have. We cannot show such solid connections to the earliest era for the distinctive teachings of the new materials [Nag Hammadi texts].[71]

In summary, the suggestion that Jesus was part of the implied gnostic myth in the gospel of Thomas or in agreement with the gnostic portrayal of him in the gospel of Judas places Jesus in a context that is counter to all of the information we have about him from a variety of sources that we can accurately date to the first century. It is counter to the canonical gospels, which were all written within fifty years of his life. It is counter to the portrait of Jesus and the worship of Jesus that we see in the creeds, hymns, and liturgical formulae that were part of the worship patterns of the earliest church within the first two to three decades after the crucifixion. And it is counter to the portrait of Jesus that we have from within the letters of the New Testament, our earliest written texts concerning the Christian faith.

7.8 DID FIRST-CENTURY CHRISTIANITY CONSIST OF A "CHAOS OF DIVERSITY"?

Some scholars maintain that early Christianity was a "chaos of diversity." This statement is an exaggeration and often used to imply that second-century disputes with gnosticism were present in the first century. Speculating on several passages in the New Testament, the proponents of this perspective reinterpret canonical verses as evidence for a first-century gnostic worldview.

One often hears the argument that the gospel of John and certain epistles, such as Ephesians, Colossians, and Hebrews, disclose gnostic tendencies in the first century. But these gnostic tendencies are not in keeping with the kind of gnosticism represented by the gospel of Thomas. This distinction is important and is well described by John P. Meier:

> I do not deny that, to varying degrees, NT books like Colossians, Ephesians, the Epistle to the Hebrews, and especially the *Gospel of John* reflect a "gnosticizing tendency" present in various streams of 1st-century Christianity. But this is not the same thing as the gnosticism of the final form of the *Gospel of Thomas*, where the spirits of the saved are actually preexistent particles of the divine that unfortunately have become divided from their divine source, have tragically entered the evil world of matter and the human body, and are now called back to a knowledge of their divine origin and essence by a Jesus who is really consubstantial with the very people he saves. All this, plus the fierce asceticism that rejects all sexuality and the implication that humans who are not made up of the divine essence are excluded a priori from salvation, is simply not the Christianity represented by any of the admittedly varied views of the canonical books of the NT. One wonders whether even the adversaries of Paul at Corinth, of the author of the Epistle to the Ephesians, or of the author of the First Epistle of John went as far as the redactor of the *Gospel of Thomas*.[72]

Claims that the earliest Christian faith was a chaos of diverse beliefs with all of them having more or less equal value and authenticity are not consistent with our best and earliest evidence. These claims inevitably rely on extracanonical sources that are all from the second century, not the first century. We know that the canonical gospels and Paul's corroborative letters were all written in the first century. To give some legitimacy to their claims, a few scholars hypothesize that the second-century extracanonical gospels had earlier sources in the first century. But they present no substantial evidence for this speculation. They merely assume that their hypothesis is true and then draw conclusions for this hypothesis without presenting any evidence to support their speculations. Evans notes that their claims are often based on assigning first-century dates to writings that were composed in the second century, including the highly touted gospel of Thomas: "Yet these are some of the writings that a few scholars would like to convince us actually were composed in the first century—perhaps in slightly different, earlier hypothetical forms—and reflect ideas older still, perhaps reaching back to the first generation of Christians. As we have seen, there simply is no convincing evidence for the early dating of these extracanonical writings."[73]

There were disagreements and disputes among first-generation Christians, but these did not concern their core beliefs about Jesus of Nazareth. The disputes were limited to questions of the application of the law of Moses to Gentile Christians and possibly to the question of works and justification. The disagreements in the early church would not qualify as an "alternative Christianity."

As I noted in the discussion of the earliest evidence found in the worship patterns of the first generation of Christians, the very first members of the Christian movement had a core belief that Jesus was God's Son, the messiah, who died a redemptive death on the cross and rose on the third day. Early Christians did disagree about whether the law of Moses applied to the Gentiles, *but the disagreements were not about Jesus*. They were unified in their belief about his person and deeds. Their disputes hardly constituted a "divergent Christianity." Other than the controversy concerning whether Gentile converts should be required to observe Jewish law, there is simply no evidence of a material diversity concerning the core beliefs of the earliest Christians. There is no evidence to support the claim that the *earliest* church was a chaos of diverse beliefs. Yes, there were distortions of the core message that came about in the *second* century, but in the first few decades of the Christian church there is a solid core message. Evans writes:

> The point that I want to make here is that there is absolutely no evidence of a significant difference in opinion with regard to the *core message* of the Christian faith. Both Paul and Peter affirm the death and resurrection of Jesus, and the need for a response in faith if one is to be saved. . . . Whereas the first generation of Christians were unified with respect to the core beliefs that Jesus—Israel's Messiah and God's Son—had died on the cross for the sin of humanity and that on the third day he had been raised, there were disagreements over questions pertaining to the validity and application of the law of Moses, either with regard to Jews or Gentiles. . . . The disagreements in the first generation of Christians do not focus on Jesus himself. He is universally regarded among his fol-

lowers as Israel's Messiah, God's Son and the world's savior. The point of disagreement concerns whether non-Jews (or Gentiles) must become Jewish proselytes (or converts) in order to be saved. . . . The differences and disagreements attested in the New Testament writings do not constitute evidence of divergent "Christianities" in the first generation of the church. . . . In short, Ehrman, and others who speak of "lost Christianities" are talking about individuals and groups who moved away from the earlier, widely attested teaching of Jesus and the first generation of his followers. These hypothetical Christianities did not exist in the middle of the first century.[74]

This is the evidence concerning diversity. It is an exaggeration to claim that there is substantial evidence for diverse "Christian faiths" in the first decades of the church. The earliest members of the church held a solid core that was only challenged by writings in the *second* century. As we have seen, these writings were distortions of the core message, not independent traditions dating back to Jesus himself. They tell us nothing about the historical Jesus. There is simply no significant evidence that these extracanonical faiths were around in the first few decades of the church. As Evans concludes: "The only way someone can come up with a divergent 'Christianity' is to import a second-century writing or teacher into the middle of the first century. The examples cited by Bart Ehrman in his *Lost Christianities* are second-century persons and movements. He discusses Ebionites, Marcion and his following, and Gnosticism. All of these individuals and groups arose in the second century."[75]

ONE CANNOT LOGICALLY MAINTAIN
THAT ALL RELIGIONS DESCRIBE A PATH
TO THE SAME ULTIMATE REALITY

8.1 THE DIVINITY OF JESUS RAISES QUESTIONS CONCERNING OTHER RELIGIONS

I have set forth a case for the divinity of Jesus. The crucial evidence surrounds the proclamation of his resurrection by his followers. If their proclamation is true, the resurrection would place God's signature on Jesus of Nazareth. These disciples or apostles testified repeatedly that they were eyewitnesses to his resurrected life. They were imprisoned, released miraculously, and, despite the threat of torture and death, returned to the Temple in Jerusalem to proclaim their faith in the resurrection. They were rearrested, flogged, and ordered not to speak in the name of Jesus. Flogging was an extremely painful form of physical punishment. Many persons died from floggings in the early first century. Yet, the apostles continued to proclaim the resurrection of Jesus. Stephen became the first Christian martyr when he was charged with blasphemy and stoned to death. Undaunted, the apostles continued their resurrection proclamation, and the church grew at a remarkable rate, expanding from the mother congregation in Jerusalem. The evidence supports the conclusion that they believed beyond any doubt that Jesus had appeared in his resurrected life. Why would they suffer so severely for a lie or for even an uncertain belief?

If one accepts their testimony and the evidence I have described for the divine nature of Jesus, what is the effect on one's perception of other religions? In the next two chapters I will discuss some of the delicate issues raised by this question.

8.2 DEFINING THE TERM "RELIGION" IS NOT A SIMPLE TASK.

Defining what one means by the term "religion" is not an easy task. Keith Ward, former Regius Professor of Divinity and head of the theology department at Oxford University, wrote a highly acclaimed five-volume series on comparative religions. In one of his recent books, *The Case for Religion*, he notes that defining the term "religion" is not a simple undertaking: "Many colleges in America and Europe have courses on 'Religion.' These courses usually start with a lecture entitled 'What is Religion?' After running through a few dozen definitions, the lecturer almost invariably concludes that nobody knows what religion is, or is even sure that there is such a thing. The course continues to be called courses on religion, however, because that sounds better than having a course entitled, 'I do not know what I am talking about.'"[1]

Ward notes how the issue of defining religion manifested itself in a government census in 2001 when thousands of British citizens described their religious affiliation as "Jedi Knight." This position may be defendable as a "religion" because Jedi Knights have peculiar clothing; are in communion with "the Force," which is invisible; and recite proverbs from a certain body of oral wisdom knowledge.[2] But a relevant question is whether or not this religion describes any reality.

There is no plausible benchmark for deciding when one can or cannot include a given set of beliefs as a religion. For example, if one attempts to confine the religions that lead to the same reality to the more prominent of the world's religions, one needs to define "prominent." Does this term require a large number of adherents? What does one mean by "large"? At what number of adherents does one exclude a religion as not prominent? One can see the difficulty when one realizes that there are many different religions where there is no communion or fellowship with the divine and that the plethora of religions in the world have many different objectives. For example, witchcraft involves manipulating or placating evil spirits. Imperialistic religions require total allegiance to a political figure, such as a Shinto emperor in Japan, the kings of Egypt, Roman Caesars, or dictators. Hinduism, Buddhism, several New Age faiths, and Gnosticism all are concerned with one's "self-actualization" or the renunciation of all selfhood.

From the beginning of history to the present time, there have been and are an enormous number of world religions. Can all of them be true? The worship of Satan is a religion. Can it be a religion that also leads to the same ultimate reality as Judaism? The Vikings had three major deities: Odin, Thor, and Frey. The Third Reich borrowed heavily from the Norse faith in promoting its "fellowship of the blood." Was this also a religion? If one wants to exclude one of the religions, where does one draw the line and conclude that although all other religions lead to the same ultimate reality, a particular one does not? What are the criteria for making that decision? Upon what higher authority can someone make that decision? Is it merely a matter of personal preference? As noted above, deciding on the basis of the number of adherents won't work because the number of adherents fluctuates, and on what basis do we conclude that the mere number of adherents is a valid criterion?

8.3 THE WORLD'S RELIGIONS HAVE MUTUALLY EXCLUSIVE PHILOSOPHICAL POSITIONS.

The concept that all religions relate to the same ultimate reality is an attractive thought but cannot be maintained logically when one studies the differences among the religions and perceives the depth of historical contradictions and irreconcilable differences among them. For example, Hinduism holds that the ultimate reality underlying existence is an impersonal essence or a polytheistic panoply of gods; Buddhism holds that there is no God or that God is completely impersonal; Islam holds that the underlying reality is Allah, but he is unknowable; and Christianity holds that the ultimate reality is a God who has revealed himself to humankind.

With respect to the view of the nature of a human being, Hinduism holds that the nature of humanity is divine; Buddhism perceives humanity as not having a personal individual essence; Islam holds that God created humans, but that they are not like him; and Christians and Jews hold that God created humans in his image.

With respect to the imperfect human predicament, Hinduism holds that we are caught in a series of reincarnations in an illusory, unreal world because of bad karma; Buddhism holds that we are caught in suffering (*dukka*) in a cycle of rebirth and death, resulting from our desire for existence (*tanhā*); Islam holds that our failure to keep the Islamic law (*shari'a*) places us under Allah's judgment; and Christianity holds that we are under the judgment of God because of sin, which separates us from fellowship with a personal God.

With respect to salvation from the human predicament, Hinduism hopes for extinction after cycles of reincarnations; Buddhism strives for the cessation of suffering by the elimination of all desire and a liberation from the cycle of death and rebirth by achieving an ineffable state (*nirvana*), even though the existence of the individual person is considered an illusion; Islam seeks paradise by strict obedience to the *shari'a* with one's good deeds outweighing one's bad deeds; and Christianity holds that deliverance from judgment is through faith in God's grace and belief in the atoning sacrifice of Christ.

With respect to life after death, Hinduism looks to an extinction into an ineffable state; Buddhism looks to the end of suffering, desire, and the disappearance of the illusion of individuality; Islam looks to paradise or hell; and Christianity looks to heaven or hell.

8.4 HISTORICAL RELIGIONS WITH MUTUALLY EXCLUSIVE FOUNDATIONAL CLAIMS CONCERNING EVENTS IN HISTORY CANNOT ALL BE TRUE.

When we look at the religions that base their beliefs on historical foundations (i.e., events in history), the mutually exclusive nature of the religions becomes even more apparent. When the events claimed in one historically based religion are mutually exclusive with the events claimed by another historically based religion, both religions cannot be true. They can both be false, but they cannot both be true. For example, Islam holds that Jesus did not die on the cross; Christianity proclaims that he did. In history, either he died or he did not; both religions could not be true about their claims about what happened in history.

Ward emphasizes the need to try to treat the belief of persons of other faiths with respect and to extend a spirit of nonjudgmental love. However, as attractive as it might be to treat all religions as holding equally acceptable truths, after a lifetime of studying, teaching, and writing about world religions, he holds that such a position is impossible:

> Nevertheless, it is not possible to believe everything at the same time. Disagreement is part of religion, too, and it is wrong to pretend that every belief can be equally true. . . . There are many disagreements in religious belief. Some believe in reincarnation, whereas others think we are only born once on earth. Some think God is a personal agent, whereas others think the supreme reality does not act in the world. Some think the soul is immortal, while others think that there is no life beyond death. It is not possible for all these beliefs to be correct. So while we can certainly say that God is at work in all human cultures, we cannot say that all human beliefs about God's nature and purpose are more or less equally acceptable.[3]

8.5 BUDDHISM'S BELIEF THAT THE INDIVIDUAL SELF IS AN ILLUSION IS INCOMPATIBLE WITH THE CHRISTIAN CONCEPT OF THE VALUE OF THE INDIVIDUAL PERSON.

When we probe more deeply into the concept of human nature in Buddhism and compare it with the Christian concept of the individual, irreconcilable differences become more apparent. As noted, Buddhism believes that the individual self is an illusion. Christianity emphasizes the value of individual persons, the concepts of repentance and atonement, and fellowship with a personal God. As mentioned above, the first goal of Buddhism is the elimination of suffering (*dukka*) with the ultimate goal of the liberation from the cycle of death and rebirth (*samsara*) to *nirvana*. Ninian Smart summarizes the essence of the Buddhist concept: "The idea of impermanence, the rejection too of a permanent soul in the individual, the concept of universal causation, and the goal of an ineffable ultimate state—*nirvana*—are the bare bones of Buddha's messages."[4]

The fourth of the Four Noble Truths enunciated by Buddha is that the method of eliminating desire (which is the solution to suffering) is to follow the Noble Eightfold Path.[5] The Eightfold Path has three major elements, the first being wisdom (*Panna*), which consists of right understanding and right thought. Right understanding contains the doctrine of *anatta* or nonself. This doctrine holds that the self is an illusion, that the universe is also illusory, and that the "I" does not exist in reality. No person as an individual actually exists. The self is an illusion. John Polkinghorne finds this belief inconsistent with the religions of the Near East and with Christianity in particular:

> Let us begin with the individual human self, seen by all the religions of the Near East (Judaism, Christianity, Islam) as being of infinite value in the sight of the God of Abraham, Isaac and Jacob, and seen by Buddhism, with its doctrine of *anatta* (non-self), as an illusory individualism which produces *dukkha* (suffering). Of course, Christianity recognizes the ambiguous character of the ego apart from God. . . . The Christian diagnosis of the human condition sees sin (alienation from God) as the root of the problem, and a repentant and faithful return to God as its solution. The Christian hope lies not in the attainment of non-desire, but in a purification that leads to right desire, that seeking of the soul for God which is the central thought of Augustine[6]

The Christian faith considers the intrinsic value of each human individual; it is not consistent with a religion that considers the individual an illusion. For the Christian, individuality is not an illusion, nor is the material universe. We have to face up to the dramatic and contradictory nature of the world's religions.

8.6 THE PROPOSITION THAT ALL RELIGIONS ARE TRUE CONTAINS AN INHERENT SELF-CONTRADICTION.

The position that all religions lead to the same ultimate reality is in itself a religious belief held as a matter of faith. One who holds that position cannot prove that it is true, but holds the position as a religious belief. If we assume that the proposition that all religions are true is a true statement, then what can we say to a woman who as a matter of faith (i.e., a religious belief) holds the opposite position that all religions do not lead to the same ultimate reality? If we are to be consistent under the proposition that all religions are true, we must regard her religious belief as also true. But if her religion is true, then the proposition that all religions are true must be false. One can see that the proposition that all religions are true contains an inherent self-contradiction.

8.7 SINCERITY CANNOT BE A MEASURE OF THE HISTORICAL VALIDITY OF ONE'S RELIGION.

One current expression that is popular in Western society is that it does not matter what one believes as long as one is sincere in his or her belief. This rather unreflective position makes sincerity the benchmark for the evaluation of a religious belief. Sincerity, however, cannot be the test of the value of a belief. Right and wrong cannot be established using sincerity as the criterion. The executors in the Nazi death camps may have sincerely believed that they were making a better world, but they actually were committing terrible crimes against humanity. The ancient Greeks sincerely believed that lightning and its resulting thunder were caused by the gods, but they were mistaken. I could sincerely believe that studying for the law school admissions test would prepare me to pass a test for a medical license, but I would be mistaken. Sincerity is not a good criterion for evaluating a belief system. No one will do well in the financial world if he believes that one thousand dollars plus five hundred dollars is equal to three thousand dollars. Similarly, a sincere belief in a religious figure may be honest and committed, but it may be unrelated to reality. The followers of a cult figure who believed that he had divine powers that could protect them even though they drank a poisonous Kool-Aid beverage were victims of a sincere belief system that did not correspond to reality. Truth matters, and by truth I mean that which corresponds with a reality that exists independently of one's belief.

8.8 THE EVIDENCE DOES NOT INDICATE THAT ANY HUMAN AUTHORITY EXISTS THAT CAN VERIFY THAT ALL RELIGIONS HAVE THE SAME UNDERLYING REALITY.

Many proponents of the proposition that all religions have the same underlying reality are fond of a story where a series of blind persons are led to an elephant near the Rajah's palace and asked to touch it and feel the various aspects of the elephant's body. One of the blind persons describes the elephant's trunk as a snake, another feels the tail and describes the elephant as feeling like a rope, and another blind person feels one of the legs and describes the elephant as a tree. All of the blind persons felt the same elephant but had different descriptions of the elephant.

The blind persons then engage in an argument, each one asserting that his analysis was the correct analysis. When their argument
intensifies and becomes so loud that it awakes the Rajah, he walks to
his balcony and shouts in exasperation, "The elephant is a big animal.
Each man touched only one part. You must put all the parts together to
determine what an elephant is like." The blind persons agree that each
one of them only knew a portion of the elephant and to determine the
complete truth they had to put all of their portions together.[7]

This story is often cited in support of the view that each religion is
only a part of a larger truth and that all religions have the same underlying reality. But the fallacy in the analogy is that we humans have no
Rajah who is not blind and who can see that the blind persons were
only touching part of the elephant and that they must put the parts
together to determine what the elephant is really like.

The analogy breaks down completely because human beings have no
Rajah to inform them that all religions lead to the same ultimate reality.
Why are human beings without such a Rajah? Because for a human being to know that the analogy reflects ultimate reality, he or she would
have to have seen ultimate reality, just as the Rajah saw the elephant.
(Remember the symbol for ultimate reality in the story is the elephant,
not the Rajah.) But no human being is in the position of the Rajah and
has seen that all religions are only a part of a larger truth. No one knows
this by experience. If someone were to argue that he is like the Rajah
and can see that all religions are the same, even though the rest of the
world is blind and cannot see what he sees; what evidence is there that
the person making such an argument is right? What evidence indicates
that such a person is in the position of the Rajah who can see that all
religions are the same?

A committed pluralist may argue that our cultural biases blind us to
the larger truth that all religions are the same with the same underlying reality. But for us to know this, someone must see clearly without
any bias and inform us. But the story makes the point that each one
of us is blind and no one knows what the ultimate reality is really like.
On cross-examination one may ask the pluralist: Where are you in this
story? Is the pluralist one of the blind persons or the Rajah? If he is one
of the blind persons, how does he know that everyone else is unable to
see? If he is truly blind, how does he know if everyone else's analysis is
wrong? Only if he is the Rajah can he have such knowledge. But if he is
the Rajah, how does he alone escape the illusion that makes the other

participants in the story blind? It is part of the pluralist's worldview that everyone is blind. But how then do they know that the pluralist's worldview is true?

Upon cross-examination, what is an interesting, appealing story turns out to have unsolvable contradictions that force us to the conclusion that the story fails to give us any reason to believe that its illustration actually describes the way things really are.[8]

8.9 THE FACT THAT A PERSON IS BROUGHT UP IN A CERTAIN CULTURE THAT ENCOURAGES A CERTAIN RELIGION DOES NOT ADDRESS THE TRUTH OR FALSEHOOD OF THAT PERSON'S RELIGIOUS BELIEFS.

If a person is brought up in a culture that encourages a particular faith, she will more likely follow that faith rather than another. I was once asked whether I thought I would adhere to a religion other than Christianity if I had grown up in a Muslim country. My answer was that the probability would be that I would have been raised a Muslim and, unless given reasons to change my belief, I would probably still be a Muslim. But that question and my answer do not go to the question of whether the Muslim faith is true or the Christian faith is true. The fact that a person is brought up in a certain way does not address the truth or falsehood of the content of a person's beliefs. It merely explains how the person came to be a Muslim or a Christian. It does not give evidence concerning whether a person's beliefs are true or not; the question merely addresses the origin of belief, not the validity of its content.[9]

8.10 CHRISTIANS ARE FLAWED AND IMPERFECT, BUT THEIR FAITH IS NOT ABOUT CHRISTIAN BEHAVIOR BUT ABOUT THE PERSON OF JESUS OF NAZARETH.

Christians have not always been the best advertisement for the Christian faith. They have been as flawed as others, even though one can point to saints who lived remarkably beautiful lives. But the Christian faith is not about Christians; it is about the unique nature of Jesus of Nazareth. The Christian claim is unique in asserting that Jesus was in his very nature God and was made in human likeness, being found in appearance as a man. No other religious figure claimed to be God in human form. No other religious figure addressed God as his father in such a familiar manner as Jesus did in using the Aramaic term *Abba*. Jesus even used the word for God given in the Jewish Scriptures and translated as *egō eimi*.

As discussed at the beginning of this book, the claim of Jesus's divinity in the Christian faith is unique among the world religions. Buddha or Confucius would never have made this claim, nor would Mohammed.[10] Ward draws the clear distinction between the incarnation of God in Jesus and any related concept of incarnation in other religions:[11]

This idea of a real human nature united in the closest way to God is not found in the prophetic religions of Judaism and Islam, where prophets always remain distinct from God. And it is not found in the Indian Vaishnava traditions, where the avatars of Vishnu do not suffer the limitations of having a real human nature. In some ways, Gautama the Buddha is more like Jesus, because (at least in many forms of Buddhism) he is a human being who has so perfected his nature that he transcends the human and becomes identical with ultimate reality. But the Buddha is not and has never, by Buddhists, been claimed to be an incarnation of God. Indeed, classical Buddhism has no belief in one creator God. Gautama is said to have attained perfection by his own efforts over many lifetimes. Jesus, however, is believed by Christians to possess a human nature that is perfected by the grace of God, and his loving relation to the Father is rather different from the Buddha's attainment of the perfect calm of nirvana, which seems to have transcended all relationships. So, though there could in principle be many incarnations of God, there is only one realistic historical claim to such an incarnation, and that is the claim made for Jesus.[12]

Many persons are eager to do away with the claim that Jesus was God incarnate. Some of the motivation for such a position is that they think by doing so all the religions will be able to find agreement. By removing the unique claim attributed to Jesus, they hope to eliminate the disagreements. The incarnation appears to be a stumbling block to unity among the practitioners of different religions. Ward's lifetime of reflections on the religions of the world lead him to conclude that denying the incarnation will not remove the disagreements and that no common factor on which to base a world religion is possible. We will have to learn to live with our disagreements and love and care for each other in spite of our differences.[13]

8.11 EVERY WORLDVIEW BY ITS NATURE IS ARROGANT. ONE HOLDS A PARTICULAR WORLDVIEW OR BELIEF BECAUSE ONE CONSIDERS IT MORE VALID THAN OTHER BELIEFS; OTHERWISE, ONE WOULD NOT HOLD THAT PARTICULAR WORLDVIEW. EVEN THOUGH EVERY WORLDVIEW HAS AN ASPECT OF ARROGANCE, EVERY EXPRESSION OF THAT WORLDVIEW NEED NOT BE MADE IN AN ARROGANT MANNER.

Of course when one holds a particular religious belief, for example an orthodox Christian faith, one may be regarded as arrogant, condescending, and unfairly judgmental of other beliefs. But logically such pejorative attributes should also be described of all worldviews because every worldview is a belief. Whether we realize it or not we all have a worldview, a belief system that we hold because we think it accurately represents reality. A person who holds that all religions are equally true is setting forth a religious belief. His or her position that all religions are equally true is itself simply another religion. It is another worldview based on faith and not on certainty. Consequently, it is also arrogant, even though it may not be expressed in an arrogant manner or style.

Since everyone lives by a certain faith, however unarticulated that faith may be, everyone may be faulted for having these pejorative attributes. This is unavoidable. But it does not follow that everyone should then regard themselves as superior to one who holds a different belief. We all have to examine ourselves and see that merely holding a certain belief does not make one a better person than one who holds a different worldview. Keith Ward's insights are again helpful:

> I should never say that my holding specific beliefs makes me superior to other people. On the other hand, it is equally obvious that I must hold that a true belief is in some sense superior to a false belief. It is superior simply in the sense that I should reject the false one in favour of the true one. Of course, it does not follow from this that I am infallible or in a specially privileged position to know the truth. It is just that I cannot hold both conflicting beliefs at the same time. A Christian must think that the belief that Jesus died on the cross is "superior" to the usual Muslim belief that he did not. But equally the Muslim will think that her belief on this matter is "superior" to the Christian one.[14]

The fact that one regards his or her belief as "superior" does not mean that he or she regards one holding a different view as stupid or depraved. We all consider our beliefs more valid than the beliefs we choose not to hold. One holds a particular worldview because one considers it to be more valid than other worldviews. Otherwise, one would not hold that particular worldview.

In the expression of one's belief, Christians are commanded to love everyone. Jesus said even to love one's enemies. For a mature Christian, a person who disagrees with a Christian can never be regarded as an enemy. In our families, among our friends, and in the world in general, with some understanding we are able to love persons with whom we disagree about many things. This is especially required for Christians if they attempt to adopt the mind of Christ toward other persons. Jesus expressed wonderful love toward a Samaritan woman who came from a different faith background. He also did the same with Gentile soldiers. He sets an admirable example for all of us in his ability to communicate unlimited love and truth.

9

HOW SHOULD ONE ENGAGE A PERSON OF ANOTHER FAITH CONCERNING DIVERSE RELIGIOUS BELIEFS?

9.1 HOW SHOULD ONE ENGAGE PERSONS OF OTHER FAITHS IN A MANNER CONSISTENT WITH GRACE AND TRUTH?

The world is becoming a smaller place and our lives are becoming more intertwined with persons of different faiths. How should we live in this environment? How do we remain faithful to our beliefs and yet engage and love those who differ from us? In May 2002, I gave an address at a conference at Windsor Castle and specifically examined these questions. The conference was entitled "The World After September 11: The Political, Economic, Military, and Spiritual Challenge." The remainder of this chapter is the substance of my address.

9.2 THREE CATEGORIES OF RELIGIOUS PLURALISM POINT TO THE NEED FOR HONEST, AUTHENTIC DIALOGUE IN AN ATMOSPHERE OF MUTUAL RESPECT.

I would like to discuss one aspect of the spiritual challenge for the world's religious communities in contemporary society. For Christians the issue can be stated as follows: How do we engage persons of other faiths in a manner consistent with grace and truth? How do we honor their right to practice a religion different from our own, respect them as persons, love them as beings made in the image of God, and yet maintain the integrity of our own faith?

To begin to consider these questions we need to have a better understanding of the term "religious pluralism." This term is in vogue today but has different meanings for different people and frequently is used in an inconsistent and contradictory manner. The confusion around the meaning of this term roils the clarity of our thinking about diverse religious beliefs.

In an attempt to clear some of the muddle, I would like to propose a distinction among three kinds of religious pluralism, which I will define as prohibitive, relativistic, and authentic.

Prohibitive religious pluralism is religious pluralism as a prescriptive prohibition against any religious faith making exclusive truth claims. In other words, this kind of religious pluralism tells persons of various faiths not to make any claims of truth, even if the claims are essential to their faith, if these claims cannot be shared by persons of other faiths.

Relativistic religious pluralism is religious pluralism as religious relativism, which imposes the belief that all religions are equally true in describing the same reality.

Authentic religious pluralism is religious pluralism that respects a person's right to maintain his or her particular religious beliefs, including exclusive truth claims, and grants that person the freedom to express those beliefs in ways that do not harm other human beings. This is not an unlimited right, just as one's right to swing freely one's arms and hands stops at the end of another person's nose.

9.2.1 Prohibitive religious pluralism is religious totalitarianism.

In analyzing the events of 9/11, Thomas Friedman, the foreign affairs columnist for the *New York Times*, wrote an article on November 27, 2001, entitled "The Real War." His position was that the war on terrorism is really a war on "religious totalitarianism." In his words:

> If 9/11 was indeed the onset of World War III, we have to understand what this war is about. We're not fighting to eradicate "terrorism." Ter-

rorism is just a tool. We're fighting to defeat an ideology: religious totalitarianism. . . . The opposite of religious totalitarianism is an ideology
of pluralism—an ideology that embraces religious diversity and the idea
that my faith can be nurtured *without claiming exclusive truth* (emphasis
added).

Friedman is right in his attack on religious totalitarianism. Any
totalitarianism must be avoided—only free societies have any hope of
genuine peace. He is also right about embracing religious diversity. We
should respect the rights of persons to hold differing religious beliefs.
But he works against his aversion to totalitarianism when he adds the
last four words of the quotation: "without claiming exclusive truth."

The problem with prohibiting exclusive truth claims is that such
claims are frequently central to the integrity of a religious faith. If religious pluralism means prescribing a prohibition against exclusive truth
claims, such a prescription will prohibit a person from following his or
her faith. The three monotheistic faiths of Judaism, Christianity, and
Islam all have exclusive truth claims as essential, integral parts of their
religious systems. To remove these claims would destroy the essence of
these faiths. For example, to prohibit a Muslim from making the claim
that the Qur'an is the final recited revelation of God is to prohibit him
from believing a central tenet of Islam. That truth claim is exclusive,
and it is central to the internal integrity of his Islamic faith.

The prohibition against exclusive truth claims works against Friedman's laudable efforts to embrace religious diversity and avoid totalitarianism because in practice such a prescriptive prohibition is religious
totalitarianism itself. In other words, his prescription for an ideology of
pluralism that does not allow the various religions to make conflicting
truth claims is actually a prescription for an ideology (a belief) that
denies freedom of religion.

Such a pluralism is an example of what Michel Foucault described as
"policing"—that is to say, a repressive enforcement of a predetermined
concept of what something or someone should be. (This policing, by
the way, causes the sad state of repression that exists in most of our
universities today. Contemporary college students in the United States
may be the most politically silenced generation in American history.)
To abolish the truth claims of all faiths, except for the faith that one
has in the ideology of pluralism, is tyrannical. A central question about
any claim is: Is it true?

Claims to absolute truth are always suspect in our culture, as well they should be. But that does not mean that there are no absolute truths. If someone believes that they know an absolute truth, they should have the freedom to express it, provided they do so in a humane manner. To a growing number in our culture, religious truth claims are completely subjective. In other words, these truth claims can be "true for you" but not true in the sense that they agree with a reality that requires them to also be "true for me." This subjectivity raises disturbing questions, such as: What about those who believed in the virtue of burning widows alive at Hindu funerals?

Should such a belief go uncontested? Is it as valid as a belief that one should love one's neighbor? Isn't there some standard of judgment that allows us to say that something is wrong? Without an objective standard for right or wrong the most we can say about September 11 is that we do not like what happened. It is then only a matter of taste and not a matter of truth.

Of course many philosophers have tried to take the position that there are no absolute truths but never without inconsistencies and contradictions. For example, Jean-Paul Sartre maintained that there was no objective right or wrong. But he could not live consistently with that proposition and felt compelled to sign the Algerian Manifesto, which was a protest of France's occupation of Algeria. In doing so he made a statement that the French were wrong. He could not in practice live his philosophy that there is no standard of right or wrong.

Instead of muzzling persons of faith, we should allow them to make religious truth claims. These claims can then be examined, analyzed, weighed, and considered by all interested persons. No one should be afraid of truth. Each of us should be allowed to examine all of the evidence for religious truth claims in an atmosphere that encourages their expression.

9.2.2 Relativistic religious pluralism is also a form of religious totalitarianism.

Turning to the second meaning of religious pluralism—relativistic religious pluralism—we face a pluralism that requires that we view all religions as equally true in describing ultimate reality. Relativistic religious pluralism grows out of the fact of religious and cultural diversity and develops from a quite legitimate concern about how best to deal with this diversity in a rights-oriented society. We want to minimize our differences for the sake of harmony.

The position that all religions can be equally true is a very attractive concept. For the sake of harmony it presents a line of least resistance, but I do not think we can logically maintain that all religions are describing a path to the same ultimate reality, making consistently compatible truth claims.

We do not have to hold that other religions do not contain elements of truth. All major religions may have elements of truth. What cannot survive logical analysis is the proposition that two essential and irreconcilable truth claims can both be true.

To illustrate this point, let us briefly examine two examples of essential and irreconcilable differences between Christianity and Islam, which if they were minimized would destroy the central essence of these two faiths.

With respect to the Christian claim of God becoming man in Jesus of Nazareth, Muslims regard such a claim as blasphemous, for they think that Christians honor a human being as an equal of God.

In describing the crucifixion of Jesus, the New Testament is emphatic: Jesus died on a cross. The Qur'an is equally emphatic: he did not. Muslims believe that when the crowd came upon Jesus with the intention of crucifying him, God would not allow his chosen messenger to suffer a disgraceful death so he took him up to heaven and then placed his likeness on someone else, who, by mistake, was crucified.

The historical question is crucial: both the New Testament and the Qur'an cannot be right. If one is correct on this historical issue, the other is incorrect. We are not here arguing which one is true, but the simple fact that both cannot be true. We have to admit to genuine and irreducible differences of essential beliefs at this point.

The solution is not simply for Christians to drop the claim of the incarnation and their belief in the historical crucifixion of Jesus and for the Muslims to drop the belief that Mohammed recited the Qur'an as God's final revelation. To eliminate these truth claims would destroy the Christian and Islamic faiths. The religions are not putty to be molded by relativistic ideologues. We have to respect their internal integrity. From what authority or higher perspective do relativists claim a superior knowledge?

We need to ask the question whether real dialogue can take place between Muslims and Christians without facing up to such clear and overt differences. Tolerance is much more likely to result from showing respect to other religions than from forcing them into an artificial framework that suppresses their central tenets. This kind of relativistic religious pluralism is an attempt by those in positions of intellectual power to mold religious beliefs according to their will. It is a form of totalitarianism.

9.2.3 Authentic Religious Pluralism Requires a Dialogue in Mutual Respect Centering on the Effect of One's Faith on One's Life.

Any discussion among persons of different faiths should be conducted on the basis of mutual respect. This respect can be expressed in dialogue, which is to be understood as an attempt on everyone's part to gain a better understanding of the other. Such a dialogue cannot be conducted on the presupposition that each faith is saying the same thing. Dialogue implies respect and intellectual honesty; it does not presuppose agreement.

In considering how to engage persons of other faiths with authentic religious pluralism, we can learn from Sir Norman Anderson, a lawyer with Christian commitments, who was also an expert on Islamic law. In reflecting on his early encounters with persons of other faiths, he noted how he often found himself drawn into an argument with a Muslim friend or pupil about the relative excellencies of Jesus or Mohammed. He found that the trouble with any such argument was that both parties easily became heated and said things that irritated the other. Anderson concluded that any spirit of rivalry militated against spiritual understanding.

He decided to avoid arguments and enter into a dialogue by making a proposal on the order of the following: "Instead of arguing the merits of our position, may I ask you instead to tell me, as fully and frankly as you can, what your knowledge of God, as this is ministered to you through the Qur'an, really means to you. I will listen with interest and respect to understand the nature of that knowledge and its practical implications, trying to stand in your shoes. And then perhaps you will permit me to tell you my understanding of God in the Christian faith."

By substituting dialogue for argument and centering on the effect of one's faith on one's life, Anderson was able to engage his Muslim friends with respect and concern. His is a good example of authentic religious pluralism.

Our cultures are becoming more marked by diversity. We need to explore ways that allow us to be deeply committed to our faith and also appropriately tolerant and accepting of diversity. Of course, one of the best examples we can look to is Mother Teresa in her work with the poorest of the poor in India. I know that you have heard so many stories about her; she had doubts (doubting is a part of faith) but persisted with her faith in caring for the poor. I want to relate one more story that describes her calling in engaging persons of the Hindu faith. Many years ago a *New York Times* reporter was given the assignment of writing an extensive article on Mother Teresa for the paper's Sunday magazine. He was not looking forward to his visit to Calcutta and decided to write an article that questioned her motivation. Watching her hold and care for persons of the Hindu faith in their last days, he was impressed with her work and the care given by the Sisters of Charity in the home for the dying. Then it occurred to him that perhaps the love shown to the dying was not so much love but an effort to convert the Hindus to Christianity, to see the conversion as a mark, a victory, on their behalf for God. So he asked Mother Teresa, as she held a very sick man, "I suppose with all the wonderful work that you do for these people that you now believe that you have the right to convert them?" "Oh no," she responded, "My task is to love them."

APPENDIX A

The Following Passages May Be Hymnic, Creedal, or, in a Few Instances, Old Testament Quotations

MATTHEW 28:19

"Go therefore, and make disciples of all nations, baptizing them in the name of the Father and of the Son and of the Holy Spirit."

MARK 8:29

He asked them, "But who do you say that I am?" Peter answered him, "You are the Messiah."

LUKE 1:46–55

And Mary said,
"My soul magnifies the Lord,
and my spirit rejoices in God
      my Savior,
for he has looked with favor on

the lowliness of his servant.
Surely, from now on all
generations will call
me blessed;
for the Mighty One has done
great things for me,
and holy is his name.
His mercy is for those who fear
him
from generation to generation.
He has shown strength with
his arm;
he has scattered the proud in the
thoughts of their hearts.
He has brought down the
powerful from their
thrones,
and lifted up the lowly;
he has filled the hungry with
good things,
and sent the rich away empty.
He has helped his servant Israel,
in remembrance of his mercy,
according to the promise he made
to our ancestors,
to Abraham and to his
descendants forever."

LUKE 1:68–79

"Blessed be the Lord God of
Israel
for he has looked favorably on
his people and redeemed
them.
He has raised up a mighty savior
for us.
in the house of his servant
David,

as he spoke through the mouth of
     his holy prophets from of old,
that we would be saved from
     our enemies and from the
     hand of all who hate us.
Thus he has shown the mercy
     promised to our ancestors,
and has remembered his
     holy covenant,
the oath that he swore to our
     ancestor Abraham,
to grant us that we, being
     rescued from the hands of
     our enemies,
might serve him without fear, in
     holiness and righteousness
before him all our days.
And you, child, will be called the
     prophet of the Most High;
for you will go before the Lord
     to prepare his ways,
to give knowledge of salvation to
     his people
by the forgiveness of their sins.
By the tender mercy of our God,
  the dawn from on high will
     break upon us,
to give light to those who sit in
     darkness and in the shadow
     of death,
to guide our feet into the way
     of peace."

LUKE 2:14

"Glory to God in the highest
     heaven,
and on earth peace among those
     whom he favors!"

LUKE: 2:29–32

"Master, now you are dismissing
      your servant in peace,
 according to your word;
for my eyes have seen your
      salvation,
 which you have prepared in the
      presence of all peoples,
a light for revelation to the
      Gentiles
 and for glory to your people
      Israel."

JOHN 1:1–16

"In the beginning was the Word, and the Word was with God, and the Word was God. He was in the beginning with God. All things came into being through Him, and without him not one thing came into being. What has come into in him was life, and the life was the light of all people. The light shines in the darkness, and the darkness did not overcome it.

There was a man sent from God, whose name was John. He came as a witness to testify to the light, so that all might believe through him. He himself was not the light, but he came to testify to the light. The true light, which enlightens everyone, was coming into the world.

He was in the world, and the world came into being through him. He came to what was his own, and his own people did not accept him. But to all who received him, who believed in his name, he gave power to become children of God, who were born, not of blood or of the will of the flesh or of the will of man, but of God.

And the Word became flesh and lived among us, and we have seen his glory, the glory as of a father's only son, full of grace and truth. From his fullness we have all received, grace upon grace. The law indeed was given through Moses; grace and truth came through Jesus Christ. No one has ever seen God. It is God the only Son, who is close to the Father's heart, who has made him known."

ACTS 4:24–30 (OR 24–26)

When they heard it, they raised their voices together to God and said, "Sovereign Lord, who made the heaven and the earth, the sea, and everything in them, it is you who said by the Holy Spirit through our ancestor David, your servant:
'Why did the Gentiles rage,
 and the peoples imagine vain
       things?
The kings of the earth took their
       stand,
and the rulers have gathered
       together
against the Lord and against
       his Messiah.'"

ACTS 5:42

"And every day in the temple and at home they did not cease to teach and proclaim Jesus as the Messiah."

ACTS 9:20

" . . . and immediately he began to proclaim Jesus in the synagogues, saying, 'He is the Son of God.'"

ACTS 9:22

"Saul became increasingly more powerful and confounded the Jews who lived in Damascus by proving that Jesus was the Messiah."

ACTS 10:36

"You know the message he sent to the people of Israel, preaching peace by Jesus Christ—he is Lord of all."

ACTS 11:20

"But among them were some men of Cyprus and Cyrene who, on coming to Antioch, spoke to the Hellenists also, proclaiming the Lord Jesus."

ACTS 17:3

" . . . explaining and proving that it was necessary for the Messiah to suffer and to rise from the dead, and saying, 'This is the Messiah, Jesus whom I am proclaiming to you.'"

ACTS 18:5

"When Silas and Timothy arrived from Macedonia, Paul was occupied with proclaiming the word, testifying to the Jews that the Messiah was Jesus."

ACTS 18:28

" . . . for he powerfully refuted the Jews in public, showing by the scriptures that the Messiah is Jesus."

ACTS 22:6

"While I was on my way and approaching Damascus, about noon a great light from heaven suddenly shone about me."

ROMANS 1:3–4

" . . . who was descended from David according to the flesh and was declared to be Son of God with power according to the spirit of holiness by resurrection from the dead, Jesus Christ our Lord . . ."

ROMANS 3:24–26

" . . . they are now justified by his grace as a gift, through the redemption that is in Christ Jesus, whom God put forward as a sacrifice of atonement by his blood, effective through faith. He did this to show his righteousness, because in his divine forbearance he had passed over the sins previously committed; it was to prove at the present time that he himself is righteous and that he justifies the one who has faith in Jesus."

ROMANS 10:9–10

" . . . because if you confess with your lips that *Jesus is Lord* and believe in your heart that *God raised him from the dead*, you will be saved. For one believes with the heart and so is justified, and one confesses with the mouth and so is saved."

ROMANS 11:33–36

O the depth of the riches and wisdom and knowledge of God! How unsearchable are his judgments and how inscrutable his ways!
"For who has known the mind of
the Lord?
Or who has been his
counselor?
Or who has given a gift to him,
to receive a gift in return?
For from him and through him and to him are all things. To him be the glory forever. Amen."

FIRST CORINTHIANS 5:4

" . . . in the name of the Lord Jesus on the man who has done such a thing. When you are assembled, and my spirit is present with the power of our Lord Jesus."

FIRST CORINTHIANS 8:6

" . . . yet for us there is one God, the Father, from whom are all things and for whom we exist, and one Lord, Jesus Christ, through whom are all things and through whom we exist."

FIRST CORINTHIANS 11:26

"For as often as you eat this bread and drink the cup, you proclaim the Lord's death until he comes."

FIRST CORINTHIANS 12:3

"Therefore I want you to understand that no one speaking by the Spirit of God ever says 'Let Jesus be cursed!' and no one can say 'Jesus is Lord' except by the Holy Spirit."

FIRST CORINTHIANS 13:1–4

"If I speak in the tongues of mortals and of angels, but do not have love, I am a noisy gong or a clanging cymbal. And if I have prophetic powers, and understand all mysteries and all knowledge, and if I have all faith, so as to remove mountains, but do not have love, I am nothing. If I give away all my possessions, and if I hand over my body so that I may boast, but do not have love, I gain nothing. Love is patient; love is kind; love is not envious or boastful or arrogant."

FIRST CORINTHIANS 15:3–5

"For I handed on to you as of first importance what I in turn had received: that Christ died for our sins in accordance with the scriptures, and that he was buried, and that he was raised on the third day in accordance with the scriptures, and that he appeared to Cephas, then to the twelve."

SECOND CORINTHIANS 1:3–4

"Blessed be the God and Father of our Lord Jesus Christ, the Father of mercies and the God of all consolation, who consoles us in all our affliction, so that we may be able to console those who are in any affliction with the consolation with which we ourselves are consoled by God."

SECOND CORINTHIANS 5:18–21

"All this is from God, who reconciled us to himself through Christ, and has given us the ministry of reconciliation; that is, in Christ God was reconciling the world to himself, not counting their trespasses against them, and entrusting the message of reconciliation to us. So we are ambassadors for Christ, since God is making his appeal through us; we entreat you on behalf of Christ, be reconciled to God. For our sake he made him to be sin who knew no sin, so that in him we might become the righteousness of God."

SECOND CORINTHIANS 11:12–15

"And what I do I will also continue to do, in order to deny an opportunity to those who want an opportunity to be recognized as our equals in what they boast about. For such boasters are false apostles, deceitful workers, disguising themselves as apostles of Christ. And no wonder! Even Satan disguises himself as an angel of light. So it is not strange if his ministers also disguise themselves as ministers of righteousness. Their end will match their deeds."

SECOND CORINTHIANS 13:13

"The grace of the Lord Jesus Christ, the love of God, and the communion of the Holy Spirit be with all of you."

EPHESIANS 1:3–14

"Blessed be the God and Father of our Lord Jesus Christ, who has blessed us in Christ with every spiritual blessing in the heavenly places, just as he chose us in Christ before the foundation of the world to be holy and blameless before him in love. He destined us for adoption as his children through Jesus Christ, according to the good pleasure of his will, to the praise of his glorious grace that he freely bestowed on us in the Beloved. In him we have redemption through his blood, the forgiveness of our trespasses, according to the riches of his grace that he lavished on us. With all wisdom and insight he has made known to us the mystery of his will, according to his good pleasure that he set forth in Christ, as a plan for the fullness of time, to gather up all things on earth. In Christ we have also obtained an inheritance, having been destined according to the purpose of him who accomplishes all things according to his counsel and will, so that we, who were the first to set our hope on Christ, might live for the praise of his glory. In him you also, when you had heard the word of truth, the gospel of your salvation, and had believed in him, were marked with the seal of the promised Holy Spirit; this is the pledge of our inheritance toward redemption as God's own people, to the praise of his glory."

EPHESIANS 2:12–22

" . . . remember that you were at that time without Christ, being aliens from the commonwealth of Israel, and strangers to the covenants of promise, having no hope and without God in the world. But now in Christ Jesus you who once were far off have been brought near by the blood of Christ. For he is our peace; in his flesh he has made both groups into one and has broken down the dividing wall, that is, the hostility between us. He has abolished the law with its commandments and ordinances, that he might create in himself one new humanity in place of the two, thus making peace, and might reconcile both groups to God in one body through the cross, thus putting to death that hostility through it. So he came and proclaimed peace to you who were far off and peace to those who were near; for through him both of us have access in one Spirit to the Father. So then you are no longer strangers and aliens, but you are citizens with the saints and also members of the household of God. . . ."

EPHESIANS 4:9–10

"(When it says, 'He ascended,' what does it mean but that he had also descended into the lower parts of the earth? He who descended is the same one who ascended far above all the heavens, so that he might fill all things.)"

EPHESIANS 5:14

" . . . for everything that becomes visible is light. Therefore it says,
'Sleeper, awake!
        Rise from the dead,
and Christ will shine on you.'"

PHILIPPIANS 2:(5)6–11

"Let the same mind be in you that was in Christ Jesus,
  who, though he was in the form
        of God,
  did not regard equality with
        God
  as something to be exploited,
  but emptied himself,
          taking the form of a slave,
          being born in human likeness,
          And being found in human form,
          he humbled himself
          and became obedient to the
                  point of death—
          even death on a cross.
Therefore God also highly
        exalted him
  and gave him the name
  that is above every name,
  so that at the name of Jesus
  every knee should bend,
  in heaven and on earth and
          under the earth,

and every tongue should confess
that Jesus Christ is Lord,
to the glory of God the Father."

COLOSSIANS 1:15-20

"He is the image of the invisible God, the firstborn of all creation; for in him all things in heaven and on earth were created, things visible and invisible, whether thrones or dominions or rulers or powers—all things have been created through him and for him. He himself is before all things, and in him all things hold together. He is the head of the body, the church; he is the beginning, the firstborn from the dead, so that he might come to have first place in everything. For in him all the fullness of God was pleased to dwell, and through him God was pleased to reconcile to himself all things, whether on earth or in heaven, by making peace through the blood of his cross."

COLOSSIANS 2:8-15

"See to it that no one takes you captive through philosophy and empty deceit, according to human tradition, according to the elemental spirits of the universe, and not according to Christ. For in him the whole fullness of deity dwells bodily, and you have come to fullness in him, who is the head of every ruler and authority. In him also you were circumcised with a spiritual circumcision, by putting off the body of the flesh in the circumcision of Christ; when you were buried with him in baptism, you were also raised with him through faith in the power of God, who raised him from the dead. And when you were dead in trespasses and the uncircumcision of your flesh, God made you alive together with him, when he forgave us all our trespasses, erasing the record that stood against us with its legal demands. He set this aside, nailing it to the cross. He disarmed the rulers and authorities and made a public example of them, triumphing over them in it."

FIRST TIMOTHY 1:15

"The saying is sure and worthy of full acceptance, that Christ Jesus came into the world to save sinners—of whom I am the foremost."

FIRST TIMOTHY 1:17

"To the King of the ages, immortal, invisible, the only God, be honor and glory forever and ever. Amen."

FIRST TIMOTHY 3:16

"Without any doubt, the mystery of our religion is great:
He was revealed in flesh,
vindicated in spirit,
          seen by angels,
proclaimed among Gentiles,
believed in throughout the
          world,
          taken up in glory."

FIRST TIMOTHY 6:12

"Fight the good fight of the faith; take hold of eternal life, to which you were called and for which you made the good confession in the presence of many witnesses."

FIRST TIMOTHY 6:15-16

" . . . which he will bring about at the right time—he who is the blessed and only Sovereign, the King of kings and Lord of lords. It is he alone who has immortality and dwells in unapproachable light, who no one has ever seen or can see; to him be honor and eternal dominion."

SECOND TIMOTHY 1:8-10

"Do not be ashamed, then, of the testimony about our Lord or of me his prisoner, but join with me in suffering for the gospel, relying on the power of God, who saved us and called us with a holy calling, not according to our works but according to his own purpose and grace. This grace was given to us in Christ Jesus before the ages began, but it has now been revealed through the appearing of our Savior Christ Jesus, who abolished death and brought life and immortality to light through the gospel."

SECOND TIMOTHY 2:11–13

"The saying is sure;
 If we have died with him, we will
         also live with him;
 if we endure, we will also reign
         with him;
 if we deny him, he will also
         deny us;
 if we are faithless, he remains
         faithful—
 for he cannot deny himself."

TITUS 3:4–7

"But when the goodness and loving kindness of God our Savior appeared, he saved us, not because of any works of righteousness that we had done, but according to his mercy, through the water of rebirth and renewal by the Holy Spirit. This Spirit he poured out on us richly through Jesus Christ our Savior, so that, having been justified by his grace, we might become heirs according to the hope of eternal life."

HEBREWS 1:3

"He is the reflection of God's glory and the exact imprint of God's very being, and he sustains all things by his powerful word. When he had made purification for sins, he sat down at the right hand of the Majesty on high. . . ."

JAMES 2:19

"You believe that God is one; you do well. Even the demons believe—and shudder."

JAMES 4:12

"There is one lawgiver and judge who is able to save and to destroy. So who, then, are you to judge your neighbor?"

FIRST PETER 1:3-9

"Blessed be the God and Father of our Lord Jesus Christ! By his great mercy he has given us a new birth into a living hope through the resurrection of Jesus Christ from the dead, and into an inheritance that is imperishable, undefiled, and unfading, kept in heaven for you, who are being protected by the power of God through faith for a salvation ready to be revealed in the last time. In this you rejoice, even if now for a little while you have had to suffer various trials, so that the genuineness of your faith—being more precious than gold that, though perishable, is tested by fire—may be found to result in praise and glory and honor when Jesus Christ is revealed. Although you have not seen him, you love him, and even though you do not see him now, you believe in him and rejoice with an indescribable and glorious joy, for you are receiving the outcome of your faith, the salvation of your souls."

FIRST PETER 1:18-21

"You know that you were ransomed from the futile ways inherited from your ancestors, not with perishable things like silver or gold, but with the precious blood of Christ, like that of a lamb without defect or blemish. He was destined before the foundation of the world, but was revealed at the end of the ages for your sake. Through him you have come to trust in God, who raised him from the dead and gave him glory, so that your faith and hope are set on God."

FIRST PETER 2:4–8

Come to him, a living stone, though rejected by mortals yet chosen and precious in God's sight, and like living stones, let yourselves be built into a spiritual house, to be a holy priesthood, to offer spiritual sacrifices acceptable to God through Jesus Christ. For it stands in scripture:
"See, I am laying in Zion a stone,
 a cornerstone chosen and
        precious;
 and whoever believes in him will
        not be put to shame."
To you then who believe, he is precious; but for those who do not believe,
"The stone that the builders
        rejected
 has become the very head of
        the corner,"
and
"A stone that makes them
        stumble,
 and a rock that makes them
        fall."
They stumble because they disobey the word, as they were destined to do.

FIRST PETER 2:21–25

For to this you have been called, because Christ also suffered for you, leaving you an example, so that you should follow in his steps.
"He committed no sin,
 and no deceit was found in
        his mouth."
When he was abused, he did not return abuse; when he suffered, he did not threaten; but he entrusted himself to the one who judges justly. He himself bore our sins in his body on the cross, so that, free from sins, we might live for righteousness; by his wounds you have been healed. For you were going astray like sheep, but now you have returned to the shepherd and guardian of your souls.

FIRST PETER 3:18–22

"For Christ also suffered for sins once and for all, the righteous for the unrighteous, in order to bring you to God. He was put to death in the flesh, but made alive in the spirit, in which also he went and made a proclamation to the spirits in prison, who in former times did not obey, when God waited patiently in the days of Noah, during the building of the ark, in which a few, that is, eight persons, were saved through water. And baptism, which this prefigured, now saves you—not as a removal of dirt from the body, but as an appeal to God for a good conscience, through the resurrection of Jesus Christ, who has gone into heaven and is at the right hand of God, with angels, authorities, and powers made subject to him."

FIRST JOHN 2:2

" . . . and he is the atoning sacrifice for our sins, and not for ours only but also for the sins of the whole world."

FIRST JOHN 2:22

"Who is the liar but the one who denies that Jesus is the Christ?"

FIRST JOHN 4:2

"By this you know the Spirit of God: every spirit that confesses that Jesus Christ has come in the flesh is from God, and every spirit that does not confess Jesus is not from God."

FIRST JOHN 4:10

"In this is love, not that we loved God but that he loved us and sent his Son to be the atoning sacrifice for our sins."

FIRST JOHN 4:15

"God abides in those who confess that Jesus is the Son of God, and they abide in God."

FIRST JOHN 5:1

"Everyone who believes that Jesus is the Christ has been born of God, and everyone who loves the parent loves the child."

FIRST JOHN 5:5

"Who is it that conquers the world but the one who believes that Jesus is the Son of God?"

JUDE 24–25

"Now to him who is able to keep you from falling, and to make you stand without blemish in the presence of his glory with rejoicing, to the only God our Savior, through Jesus Christ our Lord, be glory, majesty, power, and authority, before all time and now and forever. Amen."

REVELATION 1:4–8

John to the seven churches that are in Asia: Grace to you and peace from him who is and who was and who is to come, and from the seven spirits who are before his throne, and from Jesus Christ, the faithful witness, the firstborn of the dead, and the ruler of the kings of the earth. To him who loves us and freed us from our sins by his blood, and made us to be a kingdom, priests serving his God and Father, to him be glory and dominion forever and ever. Amen.
 Look! He is coming with the
        clouds
 every eye will see him,
 even those who pierced him;

and on his account all the tribes
of the earth will wail.
So it is to be. Amen.
"I am the Alpha and the Omega," says the Lord God, who is and who
was and who is to come, the Almighty.

REVELATION 5:9–10

They sing a new song:
"You are worthy to take the scroll
and to open its seals,
for you were slaughtered and by
your blood you ransomed
for God
saints from every tribe and
language and people
and nation;
you have made them to be a
kingdom and priests
serving our God,
and they will reign on earth."

REVELATION 5:12

. . . singing with full voice,
"Worthy is the Lamb that was
slaughtered
to receive power and wealth and
wisdom and might
and honor and glory and
blessing!"

REVELATION 5:13

Then I heard every creature in heaven and on earth and under the
earth and in the sea, and all that is in them, singing,

"To the one seated on the throne
 and to the Lamb
be blessing and honor and glory
 and might
forever and ever!"

REVELATION 7:10

They cried out in a loud voice, saying,
 "Salvation belongs to our God
 who is seated on the
 throne, and to the Lamb!"

REVELATION 7:12

singing,
 "Amen! Blessing and glory
 and wisdom
and thanksgiving and honor
and power and might
be to our God forever and ever!
 Amen."

REVELATION 11:15

Then the seventh angel blew his trumpet, and there were loud voices
in heaven, saying,
 "The kingdom of the world has
 become the kingdom of
 our Lord
and of his Messiah.
and he will reign forever and ever."

REVELATION 11:17–18

singing,
 "We give you thanks, Lord

God Almighty
who are and who were,
for you have taken your
    great power
and begun to reign."

REVELATION 12:10–12

Then I heard a loud voice in heaven, proclaiming,
"Now have come the salvation
    and the power
and the kingdom of our God
and the authority of his
    Messiah,
for the accuser of our comrades
    has been thrown down,
who accuses them day and night
    before our God.
But they have conquered him by
    the blood of the Lamb
and by the word of their
    testimony,
for they did not cling to life even
    in the face of death.
Rejoice then, you heavens
and those who dwell in them!
But woe to the earth and the sea,
for the devil has come down
    to you
with great wrath,
because he knows that his time
    is short!"

REVELATION 14:3

. . . and they sing a new song before the throne and before the four
living creatures and before the elders. No one could learn that song

except the one hundred forty-four thousand who have been redeemed
from the earth.

REVELATION 15:3–4

And they sing the song of Moses, the servant of God, and the song of
the Lamb:
"Great and amazing are your
     deeds,
Lord God the Almighty!
Just and true are your ways,
King of the nations!
Lord, who will not fear
and glorify your name?
For you alone are holy.
All nations will come
and worship before you,
for your judgments have been
     revealed."

REVELATION 16:5

And I heard the angel of the waters say,
"You are just, O Holy One, who
     are and were,
for you have judged these
     things;
because they shed the blood of
     saints and prophets,
you have given them blood to
     drink.
It is what they deserve!"
And I heard the altar respond,
"Yes, O Lord God, the Almighty,
your judgments are true and
     just!"

REVELATION 19:1–3

After this I heard what seemed to be the loud voice of a great multitude
in heaven, saying,
"Hallelujah!
Salvation and glory and power
      to our God,
for his judgments are true
      and just;
he has judged the great whore
who corrupted the earth with
      her fornication,
and he has avenged on her the
      blood of his servants."
Once more they said,
"Hallelujah!
The smoke goes up from her
      forever and ever."

REVELATION 19:6–8

Then I heard what seemed to be the voice of a great multitude, like
the sound of many waters and like the sound of mighty thunderpeals,
crying out,
"Hallelujah!
For the Lord our God
the Almighty reigns.
Let us rejoice and exult
and give him the glory,
for the marriage of the Lamb
      has come,
and his bride has made
      herself ready;
to her it has been granted to
      be clothed
with fine linen, bright and
      pure"—
for the fine linen is the righteous deeds of the saints.

REVELATION 22:17

The Spirit and the bride say,
      "Come."
And let everyone who hears say,
      "Come."
And let everyone who is thirsty
      come.
Let anyone who wishes take the
      water of life as a gift.

APPENDIX B

Bart Ehrman's Recently Published *Jesus Interrupted*
Is Contradicted by the Conclusions of Bruce M. Metzger

As this book begins the production process, Bart Ehrman's *Jesus Interrupted* became available. I reviewed this new book and offer a few comments in this appendix as it relates to my case for the divinity of Jesus and the reliability of the texts that proclaim that divinity.

Ehrman's work rests on the foundation of a questionable presupposition that the issue of the possibility of God's action in the world is outside the scope of historical exploration. As with Rudolf Bultmann's presupposition against supernatural events, such a foundation precludes an objective examination of evidence and, with respect to the divinity of Jesus, also ignores the earliest evidence for the rationale behind the beginning of the Christian faith.

This rationale was a certain belief in the resurrection of Jesus. Bruce M. Metzger held that the evidence for the resurrection of Jesus was overwhelming. The earliest texts and the earliest preliterary worship patterns of the primitive church demonstrate that the disciples were completely convinced that, after his crucifixion and burial, Jesus rose from the dead. This belief began the Christian church. The disciples of the man from Nazareth were downcast, frightened, and scattered in hiding, but something radically transformed them into a community that proclaimed the resurrection in a dangerous (for them) environment in Jerusalem.

This resurrection was at the heart of the most primitive Christian community and became for the disciples the signature of God on Jesus. This is corroborated by the evidence from the earliest worship patterns of the church (see my chapter 2, supra). One cannot rationally dismiss the evidence by means of an a priori (prior to examination) presupposition. One's openness to the possibility of resurrection depends upon one's assumptions and presuppositions concerning the possibility of God's existence. In *A Case for the Existence of God* I set forth a rational argument for the constant activity of God in preserving the cosmos and our own existence so that every breath we draw requires God's sustaining activity. When one considers the necessity of God's constant preserving and sustaining activity for the mere existence of a physical world, the concept of divine activity in the world is not strange at all. (Nor is it so strange as to be completely inconceivable, given the creative nature of contemporary quantum mechanics and the new discoveries in biology (see my chapter 6, supra).

In his new book Ehrman claims that "the idea that Jesus was divine was a later Christian invention, one found, among our gospels, only in John."[1] I do not know what he means by the term "later Christian invention," but, as described in my chapter 2, our earliest evidence shows that Jesus was worshipped as divine immediately after his crucifixion. Ehrman's claim also appears to ignore: (1) the substantial evidence for the "I am" statements in the Synoptic gospels and (2) the first-century Jewish concept of blasphemy (see Mark 14) that indicate that Jesus's words were interpreted as referring to himself as divine (see my chapter 3, *supra*). Moreover, he fails to acknowledge the evidence from Matthew and Luke that signal a transcendent perspective of Jesus's nature (see section 3.2, supra). Respected New Testament scholar Larry Hurtado has devoted over twenty-five years of his life to an examination of the earliest worship patterns of the Christian faith and concluded that devotion to Jesus erupted like a volcano almost simultaneously with the time of his crucifixion. Does Ehrman not know the literature behind Hurtado's exhaustive studies?

Ehrman overlooks the preliterary liturgical formulae and the corroborative evidence for the gospels in the letters of the New Testament that are earlier than the gospel accounts. At page 177 he states that our first reference to Jesus's empty tomb is in the gospel of Mark, gives an unsubstantiated late date for the composition of that gospel, and ignores the fact that our earliest reference to the empty tomb is the implication of the preexisting oral creed in First Cor. 15:3–8 incorporated by Paul writing within two decades of the crucifixion:

> For I handed on to you [*paradidomi*] as of first importance what I in turn had received [*paralambano*] that Christ died for our sins in accordance with the scriptures, and that he was buried, and that he was raised on the third day. . . .

This creed does not use the words "empty tomb," but definitely implies it. As N. T. Wright notes, adding the words "empty tomb" to the creed would be extraneous and tantamount to explaining that I walked down the street "on my feet."

The passage also refers to Jesus's death as an atonement for sin. Ehrman tries to remove this in discussing the gospel of Luke at pp. 187–188 in his book, but the far earlier evidence of this oral preliterary creed (in First Cor. 15) held that Jesus's death was an atoning death. This concept was not added to the Christian faith by a scribe altering Luke's gospel (as Ehrman indicates).

A complete analysis of Ehrman's book would require a separate book. I assume that such a book will be forthcoming from several New Testament scholars. For my purposes I merely want to note that, contrary to the fundamentalist strawman that he attacks with missionary zeal throughout this new book, a more balanced and thoughtful approach to the reliability of the New Testament appears in the writings of Bruce M. Metzger.

Metzger held that the authors of the canonical gospel accounts had not produced a photographic reproduction of Jesus's activities and deeds, but interpretative portraits of him. Contrary to some more extreme form critics, Metzger agreed with Joachim Jeremias that the original meaning of Jesus' sayings had not been deformed by these authors. He pointed to many circumstances that prevented the invention of words or deeds that could distort the original gospel. He cited the presence of original eyewitnesses who would have served to correct any wholesale deformation of Jesus' words and deeds. He agreed with Birger Gerhaardsson's scholarship to the effect that the passing on and receiving of Jesus's teaching also guaranteed a "high degree of fidelity" in the transmission of Jesus' sayings and activities.

After decades of research as a leader in textual criticism, Metzger concluded that "a consideration of the actual state of the evidence will lead one to the conclusion that there was no large-scale introduction of extraneous materials into the Gospels." He was certain that the early Church did not invent a large part of the contents of the canonical gospels. One reason for his certainty was the complete absence of parables in Acts or in any of the New Testament letters. If the gospel accounts were the creation of the early church, one would expect the authors of the letters of the early church to put words into the mouth of Jesus. But Metzger concluded that this never happened. On the contrary, the followers of Jesus retained passages or sayings that became increasingly embarrassing to the young church. The early followers of Jesus could have ignored or changed these sayings, but they faithfully maintained them despite pressure to modify or remove them from the gospel tradition.

Unlike Ehrman's rigid interpretation of shades of differences in the gospels. Metzger had the grace to see that each gospel account made a special contribution to a composite, common and unified portrait of Jesus. Metzger concluded that we have a balanced and coherent representation of the words and deeds of Jesus. As Metzger wrote:

"It is obvious that despite the many similarities among the three Synoptic Gospels, each evangelist has produced a distinctive presentation of the common Gospel message. The most obvious reason that accounts for their variety is that each writer had access to a somewhat different body of oral traditions regarding Jesus' words and works. Moreover, since each evangelist had in mind a special reading public, he would naturally choose to emphasize those details which, in his view, were most suited to communicate the message of the gospel to that reading public. The natural consequence is that each evangelist as a literary artist has drawn his own distinctive portrait of Jesus Christ. A unified outlook pervades the component parts of each Gospel and is apparent in the connective tissues by which each writer has linked together the various parts of his narrative.

". . . The four accounts agree in essentials because they are not imaginative compositions but go back to a historical person who had made a profound impression upon his followers. . . . What the evangelists have preserved for us is not a photographic reproduction of all the words and all the deeds of Jesus, but something more like four interpretative portraits. Each of these portraits presents distinctive highlights of Jesus' person and work, and, taken together, the four provide a varied and balanced account of what Jesus said and did."[2]

The evidence for the divinity of Jesus is not affected by Ehrman's new book. I do not disagree with everything he writes; my disagreement with him (and I assume Metzger's disagreement if he were alive) is that Ehrman takes critical points here and there, which all New Testament scholars know, and then exaggerates their significance by creating a false dichotomy: either the New Testament contains no errors whatsoever or one cannot trust any of it. An overwhelming number of scholars find this rigid, fundamentalist based dichotomy to be a strawman far removed from a balanced perspective on the reliability of the gospel tradition and the canonical gospel accounts. As I have discussed in chapters 3 through 6, the vast consensus of scholarly opinion joins Metzger in his assurance of the essential fidelity of the New Testament and the absence of a large scale introduction of extraneous material into the gospel accounts.

The absurdity of the fundamentalist dichotomy that Ehrman presents is derived from a rigid, constricted view of divine inspiration. If one were to push the reasoning in this false dichotomy, as New Testament scholar Robert Gundry well notes, one would also have to require an errorless inspired translation of the New Testament and this would mean a divinely inspired translation in every language. Languages are always changing with new words meaning new things and old words changing meaning so, to follow Ehrman's logic, a newly inspired New Testament for all human languages would have to be inspired constantly anew, on a moment by moment basis, forever. Moreover, to satisfy his rigid view of divine inspiration, the interpretation of all of these texts would have to be inerrantly inspired, copied, translated, and updated.[3] This view confines the action of an infinite divine being into a small, legalistic box based on a false dichotomy.

NOTES

CHAPTER 1

1. All quotes from the Bible are from the New Revised Standard Version unless otherwise indicated.

2. Dubay 1999, 133–134.

3. Green 2002, 58.

4. Barnett 2005, 8.

5. Longenecker 2005, 69.

6. Stauffer 1955, 237.

7. Stauffer 1955, 236.

8. Neufeld 1963, 8.

9. A list of some preexisting hymns and creeds is included in appendix A.

10. Neufeld 1963, 1.

11. Richard Longenecker has written an excellent overview of the scholarly work done in the last century on the primitive liturgical formulae. (See his discussion in *New Wine into Fresh Wineskins*.) Longenecker 1999.

12. Neufeld 1963, 20.

13. See discussion in Neufeld 1963, 14.

14. Neufeld 1963, 16–19.

15. Neufeld 1963, 20.

16. The "word of faith" that is contained in the primitive confession "Jesus is Lord" is a *homologia* that was essential to the gospel proclaimed by the primitive church and the confession to which the earliest Christian community adhered. Neufeld 1963, 24. See also Rom. 10:8ff.

17. Mk. 8:29; cf. Mt. 14:33; Jn. 1:49. Neufeld 1963, 141.

18. "Paul inherited the early church's conviction that in the resurrection and ascension, God had made Jesus the Lord, now seated at the right hand of God. By the manner in which Paul uses *kyrios* of Jesus Christ, he indicates an earlier history of such usage in the primitive church, where *kyrios* was uttered in invocations (1 Cor. 16.22), in confession (Rom. 10.9), and in the proclamation (Acts 2.34–36)." Neufeld 1963, 56.

19. Stauffer 1955, 255.

20. Longenecker 1999, 2. One must distinguish between substantive evidence and questionable speculation. Bart Ehrman, Elaine Pagels, and others promoting a speculation about diversity or a pro-gnostic position are inevitably speculating from *later* developments or compositions in the second century, not evidence that can be reliably traced to the first two decades of the Christian faith.

21. As Stauffer writes:

Astonishingly early in the history of primitive Christianity there appeared an authoritative teaching tradition in which dogmatic formulae of the most varied stamp and importance had their fixed place. For a long time "tradition' has been thought of as a malevolent invention of Catholicism, but we know today that the principle of "tradition" is older than Christianity itself. Thus we read in Jub.7.38 of a pre-Mosaic legal tradition stretching back past Enoch and Methuselah and Lamech right down to Noah and his sons and grandsons. In Ab.1.1 this principle of tradition is applied to the law given on Sinai: "Moses *received* the Torah on Sinai and *delivered* it to Joshua, and Joshua to the elders, the elders to the prophets, and the prophets to the men of the Great Synagogue. . . ." Later apocalyptic joined these two lines of tradition: In Hen.48.10 the chain of tradition runs from God via Metatron, Moses, Joshua, the Elders, the Prophets, the men of the Great Synagogue, Ezra, Hillel, Abbahu, Zera down to "the men of faith." . . . In the same sense, indeed with the selfsame formulae and words (*received* and *delivered*), Paul introduces the account of the Last Supper in I Cor. 11.23. Even before Paul the individual points of doctrine had been arranged within the tradition according to their meaning and significance. According to I Cor. 15.3 the Christological formulae concerning the death and resurrection of Christ belonged to the most important part (cf. I Cor. 3.11). The tradition is the stream which carries dogmatic propositions down the centuries. But it is at the same time the guarantee which authenticates their normative importance.

(1 Tim. 3:15f; 2 Tim. 2:2). Stauffer 1955, 237–238 (emphasis added).

22. Stauffer 1955, 244.

23. Longenecker 1999, 10–11.
24. Longenecker 2005, 70–71.
25. Hengel 1983, 93.
26. Hengel 1983, 93.
27. Jeremias 2002, 98.

CHAPTER 2

1. Moule 1977, 4.
2. Moule 1977, 99.
3. Moule 1977, 149.
4. I encourage any serious person attempting to understand the patterns of devotion to Jesus in earliest Christianity to read Hurtado's book *Lord Jesus Christ*. Although this 746-page analysis will require some time, it is a definitive and magisterial opus with unsurpassed scholarship. It represents a meticulous and compelling examination of the available evidence and is far more rigorous and less speculative than the scholarship of several authors whose bizarre interpretations of Jesus lack Hurtado's thorough and precise research.
5. Hurtado 2003, 7.
6. *Kyrios* could refer to a person with a superior social position or with power or authority. For example, in Paul's direction to slaves to obey their masters with respect contained in Ephesians 6:5, the Greek word for "masters" is *kyrios*. This Greek word was used to address someone politely and indicate esteem (just as we would say "sir" in English or "monsieur" in French), but this word could also mean God. Cullman 1963, 196.
7. I will use the New Jerusalem Bible for the Old Testament passages in these verses because of its literal translation of the Hebrew term for God (*Yahweh*).
8. Bruce 1986, 203.
9. *Kyrios Iēsous* means "Lord Jesus or Jesus is Lord."
10. Quoted as Joel 2:32 in the New Jerusalem Bible.
11. Hurtado 2003, 112.
12. Bauckham 2008, 190.
13. Neufeld 1963, 67.
14. Greek, Hebrew, and Aramaic were the three most common languages in Israel during the first century. Although Aramaic was one of the major languages of ancient Palestine, only isolated communities in the Middle East still speak a dialect of this language. For example, some communities in Syria, Turkey, Azerbaijan, Iran, and Iraq currently use a dialect of Aramaic.
15. Cullman 1963, 208–209.
16. Cullman 1963, 208–209.

17. Bruce 1986, 196.
18. Bruce 1986, 196.
19. Bruce 1986, 197.
20. Cullman 1963, 210.
21. First Cor. 15:3–8.
22. See Gal. 1:18 and Ladd 1975, 105.
23. Jeremias 1966, 101.
24. Baukham 2006, 264–265.
25. Dunn 2003, 142–143 (parentheses added).
26. Pannenberg 1977, 90.
27. Richard Bauckham also verifies the careful transmission of evidence from these eyewitnesses to Paul and other teachers in the earliest Christian community:

> Thus Paul provides ample evidence of the formal transmission of traditions within the early Christian movement, and good evidence more precisely for *the formal transmission of traditions of the words and deeds of Jesus.* Paul himself learned such traditions from Peter by a formal process of learning, not merely to the communities he founded as a whole, but also, with special attention, to persons designated as teachers within each community. Finally, we should remember that Paul did not work alone in his missionary work but with colleagues, some of whom had been prominent members of the Jerusalem church: Barnabas, Mark, and Silvanus (= Silas in Acts). They would have had considerably more opportunity to become thoroughly familiar with the Jesus traditions of the Jerusalem church, and it may be that they took part of the responsibility for transmitting the Jesus traditions to the churches in whose founding they participated with Paul.

Bauckham 2006, 271.
28. Hurtado 2003, 168–169.
29. Rom. 16:7.
30. Hurtado 2003, 120–129.
31. Hurtado 2003, 133. Despite the speculative claims of twenty-first-century gnostic scholars who do not regard Jesus's death as redemptive, there is no first-century evidence contradicting this view of the redemptive nature of his suffering and crucifixion.
32. Jeremias 1966, 203.
33. The New King James Version. The eucharist liturgy provided the source for many of the dogmatic formulae used in the primitive church: "But first and foremost it was in the framework of the eucharistic liturgy that confessional formulae very quickly became important. The Creed has doxological significance and a liturgical form. The liturgy in turn has dogmatic content and is studded with various confessional forms (1 Cor. 16:22; Rev. 22:20). Many confessions were hymn-like, and many hymns were creed-like." Col. 3:16; Eph. 5:19. See discussion in Stauffer 1955, 237.

34. Jeremias 1966, 101–102.
35. Jeremias 1966, 103.
36. Jeremias 1966, 101.
37. Jeremias 1966, 104–105.
38. The New King James Version.
39. Moule 1982, 34.
40. Moule 1982, 35.
41. Hurtado 2003, 505.
42. Proctor et al. 2000, 235.
43. Stauffer described the hymn's structure as follows:

This formula is also given in two strophes, the first telling of the significance of Christ for cosmic history, and the second of his meaning in the history of salvation. Paul includes the beginning of all things: "Who is the image of the invisible God, the first born of all creation." That is how the first verse begins—with a relative clause in the present tense, whose titles refer to the persons of Christ. Then the verse proceeds with a causal clause, which refers in the past tense to the works of Christ in creation. The second strophe takes the theological summary of history further. It, too, begins with a relative clause in the present tense, and contains some titles which apply to the person of Christ. Then it also continues with a causal clause in the past tense which tells of the work of Christ in salvation, which he effected by his incarnation, death and resurrection (cf. Col. 2:9ff). The hymnodic formula concludes with a reference to the end of all things.

Stauffer 1955, 247.
44. Longenecker 1999, 16.
45. Persons promoting the concept of vast diversity have no comparable evidence for this very early period. They inevitably cite second-century distortions of the traditional, orthodox view or speculate with strained interpretations of New Testament texts. See discussion in chapter 7, infra.
46. See Hurtado 2003, 506.
47. Hurtado 2003, 135–136.
48. Bauckham points out that in this passage Paul is clearly rearranging all of the words of the Shema (*Yahweh, our God, Yahweh, is one*) so that he is not adding a second diety:

The only possible way to understand Paul as maintaining monotheism is to understand him to be including Jesus in the unique identity of the one God affirmed in the Shema. But this is, in any case, clear from the fact that the term 'Lord', applied there to Jesus as the 'one Lord,' is taken from the Shema itself. Paul is not adding to the one God of the Shema a 'Lord' the Shema does not mention. He is identifying Jesus as the 'Lord' (YHWH) whom the Shema affirms to be one. Thus, in Paul's quite unprecedented reformulation of the Shema, the unique identity of the one God *consists of* the one God, the Father, *and* the one Lord, his Messiah (who is implicitly regarded as the Son of the Father). Contrary to what many exegetes who have not sufficiently understood the way in which the unique identity of God was understood in Second Temple Judaism seem to suppose, by including Jesus in this unique identity Paul is precisely *not* repudiating Jewish monotheism, whereas were he merely associating Jesus with the unique God he certainly *would* be repudiating monotheism.

Bauckham 2008, 213.

49. Neufeld notes that the preexistence of Jesus is also taken for granted in Second Cor. 8:9: "For you know the generous act of our Lord Jesus Christ, that though he was rich, yet for your sake he became poor, so that by his poverty, you might become rich." See discussion in Hurtado 2003, 124, and discussion concerning a corresponding concept of preexistence in the gospel of John in chapter 3.

50. Hurtado 2003, 125–126.

51. The vast majority of New Testament scholars consider this Philippians passage to be a non-Pauline hymn. See Martin 1997. For an alternative view, see Fee 1995.

52. Philippians 2:6–11.

53. Isaiah 45:23.

54. Bruce 1986, 202.

55. Cullman 1963, 217–218.

56. Bruce 1986, 203.

57. Quoted in Martin 1997, 25.

58. Jeremias, however, concluded that the hymn was set in three strophes, rather than six, with four lines to each strophe and that the hymn included *parallelismus membrorum*.

59. Martin 1997, 27.

60. Martin 1997, 27–28.

61. Martin 1997, 27–28.

62. It is significant to remember that the passage under consideration is a creedal formulation from no later than the first half of the first century; it is not a passage derived from a second-century document such as the gnostic texts found in the Nag Hammadi library. The dates of those texts are more than a hundred years after the use of this hymn in Palestinian worship services. Regardless of the historic origin of this early narrative of the Christian faith, one must not lose sight of the significant role given to humility in its content. Just as Paul was not in favor of any triumphalist pride, so as contemporary readers of this passage, we need to remember that the point of the narrative is about Jesus as an example for us of humble self-sacrifice on behalf of others. Humble love for others is the emphasis, not arrogant triumphalism. Gordon D. Fee captures this significance in this passage:

Here is the closest thing to Christology that one finds in Paul; and here we see again why the "scandal of the cross" was so central to his understanding of everything Christian. For in "pouring himself out" and "humbling himself to death on the cross," Christ Jesus has revealed the character of God himself. Here is the epitome of God-likeness: the pre-existent Christ was not a "grasping, selfish" being, but one whose love for others found its consummate expression in "pouring himself out," in taking on the role of a slave, in humbling himself to the point of death on behalf of those so loved. No wonder Paul cannot abide triumphalism—in any of its forms. It goes against everything that God is and that God is about. To be sure, there is final vindication in eschatological, not present. Discipleship in the present calls for servanthood, a self-sacrifice for the sake of others.

Fee 1995, 197.

63. See for example, the verses and references in Rom. 5:6; 14:9, 15; First Cor. 5–7; 8:11; 15:20; Gal. 2:21; 3:13, where Paul often uses preexisting formulae containing this term from earlier Christian communities. Also see Hurtado 2003, 100–101.

64. Hurtado 2003, 101.

65. Bruce Metzger, certainly one of the most highly regarded New Testament scholars in the last century, considered Jesus' claim to be the unique Son of God also pervasive throughout all four canonical gospels:

From what has been said it will be seen that an exalted view of Jesus' person is pervasive throughout all four Gospels. His words and attitudes reported in the earliest literary strata of the Synoptic Gospels are not different in kind (though many are different in language) from his testimony reported in the Fourth Gospel. After making the most rigorous examination of the sources, one must conclude that Jesus of Nazareth, in his bearing as well as in his words, made claim to be the unique Son of God. It was because of this lofty claim that Jesus was condemned to death by those who regarded him guilty of blasphemy (Mark 14:61–64). Of all of Jesus' teaching, therefore, none can be said to be more surely grounded in history, for without this element there is nothing in his life that can satisfactorily account for the inveterate acrimony and hostility that pursued him to the death. The attitude of orthodox Jewish piety is summed up in the taunt that was flung at him as he hung on the cross, "If you are the Son of God, come down from the cross" (Matt. 27:40; compare verses 41–44).

Metzger 2003, 182.

66 First Thess. 3:11–13.
67. First Cor. 16:23–24.
68. Hurtado 2003, 139.
69. Acts 7:59–60.
70. First Cor. 1:2–3.
71. Hurtado 2003, 86.

72. Richard Bauckham argues that Second Temple Judaism understood the identity of the God of Israel as including two main features: the creative and sovereign activities of God. He explains his rationale and its relationship to the inclusion of Jesus in the identity of God:

> The point of isolating these two features was that it was on God as the Creator of all things and as the sovereign Ruler of all things that Jewish understanding of the uniqueness of the one God focused. These are the two features of the divine identity which serve most clearly to distinguish God from all other reality and to identify God as the unique One, who alone relates to all other things as their Creator and Sovereign. These features, therefore, also served to make unequivocally clear the New Testament writers inclusion of Jesus in the unique divine identity. . . . (O)nce we understand Jewish monotheism properly, we can see that the New Testament writers are already . . . expressing a fully divine Christology (Jesus as creator and sovereign ruler) by including Jesus in the unique identity of God as defined by Second Temple Judaism. . . . (I)t is an expression of a fully divine Christology. It is, as I have called it, a Christology of divine identity. The developmental model, according to which the New Testament sets a christological direction only completed in the fourth century, is therefore seriously flawed.

Bauckham 2008, 52, 58 (parenthesis added).
73. Hurtado 2003, 84.
74. See discussion in Barnett 2005, 76–78.
75. Hurtado 2003, 175.
76. Acts 2:38.
77. Acts 9:14.
78. Hurtado 2003, 175.
79. For example, see Second Tim 2:19 referring to Num. 16:5; Acts 2:21 referring to Joel 2:32; First Peter 2:3 referring to Ps. 34:8.
80. The earliest Jewish Christians worshipped Jesus within the context of Jewish monotheism by regarding him as part of the unique identity of *Yahweh*. Jesus was exalted to the divine throne as one in whom God's unique sovereignty would be acknowledged by everyone. In this sovereign exaltation Jesus rules over all creation and is integral to the identity of the one unique God:

> God's rule over all things defines who God is: it cannot be delegated as a mere function to a creature. Thus, the earliest Christology was already *in nuce* the highest Christology. . . . If Jesus was integral to the identity of God, he must have been so eternally; and so the great passages of protological Christology, such as the Johannine Prologue, Colossians 1 and Hebrews 1, include Jesus also in the unique creative activity of God and in the uniquely divine eternity. This was the early Christians' Jewish way of preserving monotheism against the ditheism that any

kind of adoptionist Christology was bound to involve. . . . Jesus cannot function as God without being God.

Bauckham 2008, 235.

81. Hebrews 1:8–9.
82. Longenecker 1970, 137.
83. Second Peter 1:1.
84. Longenecker 1970, 137–138.
85. Longenecker 1970, 138n62.
86. Rev. 1:17–18.
87. Isa. 4:6.
88. See Jos. 3:10; Ps. 42:2; 84:2.
89. Rev. 22:12–13.
90. Hurtado 2003, 50.
91. Revelation 5:11–14.
92. Johnston 1998 and Hurtado 2005.
93. Hurtado 2003, 72.
94. Rom. 1:3–4.
95. Acts 4:27.
96. Acts 2:22.
97. Acts 10:36–38.
98. Acts 10:42.
99. Rom. 4:25. Redemption from sin is an orthodox concept, not a gnostic concept. In gnosticism the crucifixion as an act of atonement is not relevant to salvation.
100. "The important thing here is that all these writings including the Gospels grew out of worship, the focal point of the earliest church, and were written to be used in worship. They have come down to us only because they were read in worship." Hengel 1983, xiii.

CHAPTER 3

1. Hurtado has written in *How on Earth Did Jesus Become a God?*:

In GJohn, the Jewish accusation of blasphemy is directed against Jesus in a scene of dialogue and debate between Jesus and "the Jews," and is connected with Jesus' claim to be "Son of God" (10:36), which the Jewish leaders construe as Jesus making an outrageous claim to divinity ("You though a man, make yourself a god/ God," 10:33). In 19:7 "the Jews" claim that Jesus is guilty of a capital violation of the Torah in making himself "Son of God." In the Synoptics, the blasphemy charge appears in two scenes: (1) the forgiveness/healing of the paralytic (Mark 2:7; Matt.

9:3; Luke 5:21), and (2) Jesus' arraignment before the Jewish authorities in the passion account (Mark 14:64; Matt. 26:65). In the first of these Synoptics scenes, the scribes' rationale is that Jesus takes unto himself an exclusive prerogative of God (explicit in Mark 2:7; Luke 5:21). This is very close to the reason for the blasphemy charge in GJohn. . . . In short both Synoptic and Johannine accounts of the accusations of blasphemy hurled against Jesus link the charge to offensive Christological claims that form a key component of the devotional pattern of the Christians whose experience is reflected in those accounts.

Hurtado 2005, 154–55.
2. Mark 4:41.
3. Exodus 3:13–14.
4. Matt. 14:27.
5. Matt. 28:19–20, emphasis added.
6. Mark 14:61–64.
7. Hurtado 2005, 162–163.
8. Metzger was Bart Ehrman's teacher and mentor at Princeton Theological Seminary. See discussion in chapter 4 on Ehrman and Metzger's different conclusions concerning the significance of textual critical studies.
9. Metzger 2003, 179–180.
10. Evans and Wright 2009, 19.
11. Matt. 4:9–10.
12. Hurtado 2003, 345.
13. Mark 14:62–64; Matt. 26:63–64; Luke 22:70; John 3:16.
14. Matt. 16:16. Hurtado 2003, 339.
15. Matt. 11:27.
16. Matt. 28:18–19.
17. Mark 13:32.
18. Luke 13:32.
19. John 8:58–39.
20. Hurtado 2003, 370–373.
21. John 11:25.
22. John 1:1–3, 10, 14.
23. John 14:9.
24. See also John 5:22–23.
25. Mark 9:37.
26. Mark 9:41.
27. Matt. 7:22.
28. Luke 10:17.
29. First Cor. 2:10.
30. Hurtado 2005, 2122.
31. The basic text for the house of David is 2 Samuel 7 where, through the prophet Nathan, God promises David a perpetual royal dynasty. This promise

or covenant between God and David appears to be threatened at the time of the composition of Psalm 89, and yet the psalmist re-asserts the covenant: "You said, 'David, my servant, is my chosen one, and this is the agreement I make with him: David, one of your descendants will always be king.'" (Psalm 89:3-4)

32. Emphasis added.

33. Heb. 1:5, 8, 13 (emphasis added).

34. Ps. 45:6-7.

35. Hurtado (2003), p. 392.

36. Ibid. p. 573.

37. Private correspondence with Craig A. Evans.

38. Ratzinger, J. (Pope Benedict XVI) (2007), p. 103.

39. Cf. Jn 7:40-41.

40. See *Ancient Christian Commentary on Scripture*, OT Vol. III at 304 (Inter-Varsity Press 2001).

41. Ratzinger, J. (Pope Benedict XVI) (2007), 5–6 (emphasis added).

42. Ibid., 7, 120, 116–17, 119–20 (emphasis added).

43. Ibid, 116–17. (My talented and brilliant law partner Hurd Baruch made this argument of Pope Benedict XVI available to me. I am deeply grateful for this and all of Hurd's keen insights.)

CHAPTER 4

1. For example, we have only one copy of Tacitus's history of the early emperors of Rome, and that copy dates from about the twelfth century. We have only about ten copies of Caesar's *Gallic War* with the earliest copy dating to around AD 900. The earliest of the eight manuscripts of the history of Thucydides is also from around AD 900.

2. Bruce 1960, 19.

3. Quoted in Bruce 1960, 21.

4. Ehrman 2005, 9.

5. See chapter 3.

6. Evans 2006, 31.

7. Metzger 2003, 327, emphasis added. New Testament scholar Ben Witherington, who also studied textual criticism under Metzger, agrees with Metzger's conclusion and writes:

(Ehrman's) conclusions far outstrip his evidence for them. Textual variants in manuscripts of New Testament books are many and varied to be sure, but it is simply a myth to take the variants Ehrman deals with in his books as evidence that some essential Christian belief was cooked up after the fact and retrojected into the text of New Testament documents by overzealous and less than scrupulous scribes. There is no hard evidence in any of the variants he treats either in *The Orthodox Corruption of Scripture* or his more recent *Misquoting Jesus* that in any way demonstrates that ideas like the virginal conception, crucifixion, bodily resurrection of Jesus, or even the Trinity were ideas later added to copies of New Testament documents to create them more "orthodox." This is simply false. What is the case is that we have evidence of such ideas being amplified or clarified by overzealous scribes in a text like 1 John 5:7b. That is the most sober historical judgment will allow in regard to such variants. There is a reason that both Ehrman's mentor in text criticism and mine, Bruce Metzger, has said that there is nothing in these variants that really challenges any essential Christian belief: they don't. I would add that other experts in text criticism, such as Gordon Fee, have been equally emphatic about the flawed nature of Ehrman's analysis of the significance of such textual variants.

Witherington 2006, 7.
    8. Evans 2006, 29.
    9. See discussion in chapter 5.
  10. Metzger 2003, 177.
  11. Metzger 2003, 150–151.
  12. Metzger 2003, 51.
  13. Tournier 1958, 197.
  14. This is the sentiment of theologian-martyr Dietrich Bonhoeffer as he wrote: "One simply cannot read the Bible like other books. We must be prepared really to question it. Only in this way is it revealed to us. Only if we await the final answer from it does it give that Word to us. The reason for this is that in the Bible God speaks to us. And we cannot simply reflect upon God from ourselves; rather, we must ask God. Only when we seek God does God answer." Bonhoeffer 1995, 172.
  15. www.bible-researcher.com/rieu.html.
  16. Rieu 1952, xxxiii.
  17. Bonhoeffer 1995, 54.
  18. Bruce 1960, 12.
  19. Bruce 1960, 13.
  20. Blomberg 1987, 27.
  21. Quoted in Wilkens et al. 1995, 31–32.
  22. Van Voorst 2000, 81.
  23. Van Voorst 2000, 82.
  24. Boyd 1995, 253.
  25. Robinson 1976, 13–14.
  26. Cambridge New Testament scholar, C. F. D. Moule, also believed that the explanation offered for the absence of reference to the Jewish War and the destruction of Jerusalem and its Temple is insufficient. As noted, early Christianity had strong ties to the city of Jerusalem. After all Jerusalem was

the location where the initial mother congregation began the church. See his discussion in Moule 1982, 173–176.

27. Maier 1994, 373.
28. Quoted in Robinson 1976, 14.
29. Boyd 1995, 254.
30. Robinson 1976, 16.
31. Robinson 1976, 17.
32. Quoted in Robinson 1976, 18.
33. Bainton 1960, 19.
34. Quoted in Van Voorst 2000, 83.
35. As France wrote:

What *is* important for our purpose is the way Josephus records this title of Jesus in passing, without comment or explanation. The term *Christos* occurs nowhere else in Josephus, except in the passage we are shortly to study. . . . This bare mention of James, the brother of Jesus, with no account of his significance in the Christian movement, and no attempt either to deny the charge of law-breaking or to enhance his image in any way, does not look like a Christian interpolation. Still less does the phrase "the so-called Messiah" (*ho legomenos Christos*), which is hardly the way a Christian would refer to his Lord. And the authenticity of the passage is further supported by the fact that Origen, writing in the first half of the third century, expresses his surprise that Josephus, who did not accept Jesus as the Messia, none-theless testified to the innocence of James. . . . (Origin) . . . *Antiquities* XX 200 is, therefore, generally accepted to be what Josephus wrote. It tells little about Jesus by itself, but the mere fact that it presupposes an earlier explanation of the phrase *ho legomenos Christos* makes it very difficult to eliminate the earlier and longer ac-count of Jesus as a Christian interpolation.

France 1986, 26–27.

36. Van Voorst 2000, 83–84.
37. New Testament scholar Craig Blomberg agrees and emphasizes how the internal evidence in Luke gives a strong indication for a dating of the Synoptic gospels prior to AD 62:

Early external evidence does not enable us to date Luke, but internal evidence does give a hint. Despite a variety of other suggestions, the most plausible reason for the abrupt ending of Acts is that Luke was still writing at the time of the events he describes in Acts 28—Paul's two-year house arrest in Rome. No other explanation convincingly accounts for why Acts 19–28 devotes ten whole chapters to the events leading up to and including Paul's arrest and trials, only to leave us completely in the dark about the outcome of his appeal to Caesar. But if Luke did not know that outcome because Caesar had not yet tried Paul's case, then his omission is under-standable. If, then, Luke wrote Acts while Paul was still awaiting the result of his appeal to Rome, we must date that book to no later than A.D. 62. Then Luke's Gospel, as the first of his two-part work (cf. Luke 1:1–4 and Acts 1:1–2), must be

dated to the same year or even earlier. The internal evidence of the literary relationship among Matthew, Mark, and Luke has also suggested to most scholars that
Mark wrote before the other two Synoptics. *All of this adds up to a strong case that
all three Gospels were composed within about thirty years of Christ's death (probably
A.D. 30) and well within the period of time when people could check up on the accuracy
of the facts they contain.*

Blomberg writing in Wilkins and Moreland 1995, 29.

38. Robinson 1976, 92.

39. Quoted in Robinson 1976, 105.

40. Boyd 1995, 254–255.

41. In chapter 2, I discuss how the ancient creeds, hymns, and liturgical
formulae incorporated into the New Testament writings show a well-developed
high Christology, worshipping Jesus as divine at the very beginning of the
Christian church. The presupposition that the church needed time to develop
the theology disclosed in the gospel narratives cannot be made a priori. As
Robinson argues:

> The objection will doubtless still be raised that all this allows too little time for the
> development in the theology and practice of the church presupposed by the gospels
> and Acts. But this judgment is precariously subjective. It is impossible to say *a priori*
> how long is required for any development, or for the processes, communal and re-
> dactional, to which scholarly study has rightly drawn attention. . . . There is nothing,
> I believe in the theology of the gospels or Acts or in the organization of the church
> there depicted that requires a longer span, which was already enough, if we are right,
> for the creation of the whole Pauline corpus, including the Pastoral Epistles. But if
> the production of the synoptic gospels and Acts does in fact cover the years 30 to
> 60+ which the latter records (the gradual committal to writing occupying perhaps the
> period 40 to 60+), then this in turn provides a valuable yardstick by which to assess
> the chronology of the documents that remain for us still to consider.

Robinson 1976, 116–117.

42. Matt. 9:9–13.

43. Eusebius, *H.E.* iii, 39, as quoted in Bruce 1960, 38.

44. Bruce 1960, 39.

45. Wilkins and Moreland 1995, 25.

46. See Acts 2:14–41; 3:12–26; 4:8–12; 5:29–32.

47. *Adumbr.*, First Peter 5:13 quoted in Robinson 1976, 109.

48. See Acts 16:10–17; 20:5–15; 21:1–18; 27:1–28:16.

49. Col. 4:14.

50. Philemon 23 and 24.

51. Irenaeus, "Against All Heresies," 3.1.38–41.

52. Luke 1:1–4.

53. John 5:2.

54. John 9:7.
55. John 4:5.
56. John 9:13.
57. Writing in Wilkins and Moreland, 40–41.
58. Writing in Wilkins and Moreland, 40–41.
59. Metzger 2003, 117–118.
60. Blomberg writing in Craig 1994, 221.

CHAPTER 5

1. Bruce Metzger is impressed with the reliability of the New Testament and with the essential fidelity of the gospel tradition as described in the work of Birger Gerhardsson:

Noteworthy among scholarly examination of ancient Jewish and early Christian methods of transmission of tradition is Birger Gerhardsson's landmark study *Memory and Manuscript: Oral Tradition and Written Transmission in Rabbinic Judaism and Early Christianity*. Here he departs from the form-critical approach and directs biblical investigation to the prehistory of the written Gospels. Gerhardsson's viewpoint is that the primary setting for early Christian transmission of the Jesus tradition is tradition itself. Gerhardsson's subsequent publications, especially *The Origins of the Gospel Traditions*, present a Scandinavian alternative to continental form-criticism in biblical studies. Acknowledging the creative character of early Christian interpretation, Gerhardsson declares that "it is one thing to take these charges in the transmittal material in all seriousness, and quite another thing to presume that the early church freely constructed the Jesus traditions, placing the words of early Christian prophets and teachers in Jesus' mouth, and so on."

Metzger 2003, 103–106.

2. McGrath 1997, 59. One also has to take into consideration the use of tachygraphy and the use of notebooks in the first century. Tachygraphy was a kind of speed writing or shorthand that was frequently used in the school systems for the making of notes as an aid to memorization of a text. These can be thought of as memoranda that were part of the educational system. The disciples of Jesus may have used this form of writing as they heard Jesus's longer discourse, such as the Sermon on the Mount.

3. As Richard Bauckham writes: "Memorization was universal in the ancient world. Learning meant, to a significant degree, memorizing." Bauckham 2006, 280. In the 1980s a British actor, Alec McCowan, memorized and recited the gospel of Mark, memoritor, on Broadway and at the Kennedy Center. Wib Walling and Hurd Baruch remember his incredible performance. He had a chair, a table, and a glass of water and nothing else; he took an intermission

break and went right on until he finished the whole gospel. Hurd called it "spellbinding" and it taught him that theories about ancient bards memorizing Homeric verse were plausible.

4. Gerhardsson 1998, xxvi.

5. Boyd 1995, 121.

6. Gerhardsson 1998, xii.

7. Gerhardsson 2005, 9 (emphases added).

8. Blomberg 1987, 29

9. Gerhardsson 2001, 28.

10. Gerhardsson 1998, 329.

11. Metzger 2003, 103–106.

12. See Gal. 1:14 and discussion on Paul's allusion to his training and zealousness toward the Torah tradition in Gerhardsson 2001, 14.

13. Gerhardsson 2001, 14–15.

14. As discussed above in describing the terms *paradidonai* (delivering or handing over tradition) and *paralambanein* (receiving tradition) set forth in the preexisting creeds in First Cor. 11:23 and First Cor. 15:3 (see chapter 2 above), Paul is giving technical terms for the transmission of tradition in a careful manner. This technical language also appears in Gal. 1:9; Phil. 4:9; First Thess. 2:13, 4:1; and Second Thess. 3:6. One should not underestimate the care and precision involved in this transmission process.

15. Gerhardsson 2001, 15.

16. Bauckham 2006, 265.

17. Gerhardsson 2001, 38.

18. Riesner writing in Wansbrough 1991, 188.

19. See John 18:20; Mark 1:21; Mark 6:2; Matthew 4:23; Matthew 9:35; Luke 4:15, 31; and Luke 13:10.

20. Riesner writing in Wansbrough 1991, 189.

21. Riesner writing in Wansbrough 1991, 191.

22. See Dunn 2003, 224.

23. See Matt. 10:24–25; Luke 6:40; Matt. 10:42; Luke 14:26f; and Riesner writing in Wansbrough 1991, 197.

24. Riesner writing in Wansborough (ed.) 1991, 198.

25. See Luke 1:4 and Riesner writing in Wansbrough 1991, 197–198.

26. Gerhardsson 2001, 45 (parentheses added).

27. Gerhardsson 2001, 42.

28. Riesner writing in Wansbrough 1991, 202.

29. Bruce 1960, 39–40.

30. Bauckham 2006, 282.

31. Riesner writing in Wansbrough 1991, 204–205.

32. Jeremias 1971, 23.

33. Jeremias 1971, 4.

34. Jeremias 1971, 20.
35. Matt. 11:5-6.
36. The New King James Version.
37. Jeremias 1971, 22.
38. Jeremias 1971, 27.
39. Jeremias 1971, 27.
40. Jeremias 1971, 27.
41. Robinson 1977, 23.
42. Dunn 2003, 225.
43. Jeremias 1971, 8.
44. Dunn 2003, 225.
45. Jeremias 2002, 9-10.
46. Dunn 2003, 226.
47. Dunn 2003, 254.
48. Gerhardsson 2001, xxiv.
49. See discussion in Riesner writing in Wansbrough 1991, 207-209.
50. Riesner writing in Wansbrough 1991, 207-209.
51. Riesner writing in Wansbrough 1991, 209.
52. Gerhardsson 2001, xii.
53.

The Gospels preserve more than one saying attributed to Jesus, which as the years went by, became more and more embarrassing to the church. For example, the difficult sayings of Jesus to his disciples, "Truly I tell you, you will not have gone through all the towns of Israel before the Son of Man comes" (Matt. 10:23), and "Truly I tell you, there are some standing here who will not taste death until they see that the kingdom of God has come with power" (Mark 9:1), both of which seem to predict the imminent end of the age, were retained despite the embarrassment that must have been felt increasingly as time passed without their being fulfilled in the way that many thought they must be fulfilled. The early church could have allowed such sayings to fall into oblivion, yet these and others have been faithfully preserved despite strong pressures to modify or forget them.

Metzger 2003, 103-106.
54. Gerhardsson 1968, 42-43.
55. Metzger 2003, 104-5.
56. Bauckham 2006, 306.
57. Gerhardsson 2001, 75.
58. Gerhardsson 2001, 50.
59. Dunn 2003, 206-207.
60.

But Bailey does not distinguish these "minor" eyewitnesses, of whom there were certainly very many (including the five hundred to whom 1 Cor. 15:6 refers), from those who were eyewitnesses "from the beginning," those disciples of Jesus who could bear comprehensive witness to the whole course of Jesus' ministry and beyond. Moreover, his picture of Christian groups in the villages of Palestine takes no account of the special authority of the mother church in Jerusalem, which was special no doubt in part because of the leadership of Peter and the Twelve eyewitnesses "from the beginning." Such eyewitnesses would surely have played a more important role as authoritative guarantors of the tradition than Bailey's model seems to allow.

Bauckham 2006, 262.

61. Dunn 2003, 211–212.

62. One must ask why Matthew and Luke in copying Mark's account would depart so freely from a written document:

Once again it is quite possible to argue for a purely literary connection—Matthew and Luke drawing upon and editing Mark's (for them) original. The problem with the purely literary hypothesis is that most of the differences are so inconsequential. Why, for example, as literary editors would it be necessary for them to vary the description of the danger of the boat being swamped (each uses different verbs) and to vary the account of Jesus sleeping and the references to the disciples' fear and lack of faith? Is it not more plausible to deduce that Matthew and Luke knew their own (oral) versions of the story and drew on them primarily or as well? Alternatively, it could be that they followed Mark in oral mode, as we might say; that is, they did not slavishly copy Mark (as they did elsewhere), but having taken the point of Mark's story they retold it as a story-teller would, retaining the constant points which gave the story its identity, and building around the core to bring out their own distinctive emphases.

Dunn 2003, 218.

63. Bauckham 2006, 281–282.

64. Jeremias 1971, 38–41.

65. Jeremias 1971, 39.

66. Jeremias 1971, 39.

67. For further discussion of Luke's "block" technique, see Jeremias 1971, 39–41.

CHAPTER 6

1. Wright 2003, 10.

2. The affirmation of the "signature" of God present in the resurrection of Jesus is confirmed by the confession of Thomas in John 20:28: "My Lord and My God!" The gospel of John is most likely a first-century text. (Rylands fragment of it is dated to 125 AD so it cannot be mid-second century.) I have already noted that the high Christology of John is the same Christology as the earliest liturgical formulae in our possession. Baruch points out that Jesus did

not demur to Thomas's confession. All the apostles present would have left the room knowing that Jesus was accepting the title of "God." They surely spoke about that incident with Thomas in their proclamation of the resurrection.

3. O'Collins 1978, 142.

4. O'Collins reflects upon the importance of the presuppositions one holds and cautions against ruling out any possibility of a resurrection prior to an examination of the evidence for a resurrection:

> Belief in Christ's resurrection presupposes faith in a God who can and does intervene in human history and who, in particular, had already been specially present, active and revealed in the history of Israel. . . . Those who follow a Deist line (Bultmann and many of his pupils) by systematically excluding such divine interventions will rule out in advance any evidence not only for Jesus' personal and bodily resurrection from the dead but also its background, the special (revelatory and redemptive) presence of God in Israel's history.

O'Collins 1987, 136 (first parentheses added).

5. Crowley and Lodge 2006, 64.

6. Lapide 1983, 150–51.

7. As Wright notes: "The fact that dead people do not ordinarily rise is itself part of early Christian belief, not an objection to it. The early Christians insisted that what had happened to Jesus was precisely something new; was, indeed, the start of a whole new mode of existence, a new creation. The fact that Jesus' resurrection was, and remains, without analogy, is not an objection to the early Christian claim. It is part of the claim itself." Wright 2003, 10.

8. Wright 2003, 712.

9. Walker 1999, 63.

10. Wright 2003, 273.

11. This is the meaning of Paul's phrase in First Corinthians 15 where he speaks about a "spiritual body":

> So it is with the resurrection of the dead. What is sown is perishable, what is raised is imperishable. It is sown in dishonor, it is raised in glory. It is sown in weakness, it is raised in power. It is sown a physical body, it is raised a spiritual body. Thus it is written, "The first man, Adam, became a living being"; the last Adam became a life-giving *spirit*. But it is not the spiritual that is first, but the physical, and then the spiritual. The first man was from the earth, a man of dust; the second man is from heaven. As was the man of dust, so are those who are of the dust; and as is the man of heaven, so are those who are of heaven. Just as we have borne the image of the man of dust, we will also bear the image of the man of heaven. What I am saying, brothers and sisters, is this: flesh and blood cannot inherit the kingdom of God, nor does the perishable inherit the imperishable.

First Cor. 15:42–50.

12. Stephen T. Davis explains the meaning of Paul's phrase:

Thus we should not be misled by Paul's use of the term "spiritual body." He is not using this term to signify a body "formed out of spirit" or made of "spiritual matter," whatever that might mean, but rather a body that has been glorified or transformed by God and is now fully dominated by the power of the Holy Spirit. The word *soma* itself carries heavy connotations of physicality in Paul, but, more importantly, the word pneumatikou does not mean "nonbodily." A "spiritual body" is a person taught, led and animated by the Holy Spirit (see 1 Cor. 2:15, 14:37; Gal. 6:1). It is clear to me that Paul's view of the resurrection is a physical view. And the crucial conclusion that can then be drawn is that physical understandings of resurrection are not (as is often charged) late additions to New Testament tradition.

Davis 1993, 56–57.

13. See First Cor. 2:14: "Those who are unspiritual do not receive the gifts of God's Spirit [*pneumatikos*] for they are foolishness to them, and they are unable to understand them because they are spiritually discerned."

14. George Ladd clarifies the meaning of a "spiritual body":

Paul sums up his argument by saying, "It is sown a physical body, it is raised a spiritual body" (v.44). These words are subject to misinterpretation and taken to mean that the resurrection will be in "spiritual," i.e., non-corporeal bodies. This cannot be Paul's meaning. The translation is *psychikon*, from *psyche* which means life or soul. The physical—i.e., mortal—body is not made of *psyche*; it is a body animated by *psyche*. In the same way, the resurrection body will not be made of *pneuma*—spirit. It is true that some Greek philosophers did not consider *pneuma* to be non-material as we do; they thought of *pneuma* as a very fine, invisible, celestial substance capable of interpenetrating all other forms of being. However, this idea is not found in Paul. *Pneuma* to him is God's pneuma—the Holy Spirit. The resurrection body will be one which is completely animated and empowered by the Spirit of God. . . . Thus the *pneumatikon sōma* is a body transformed by the life-giving Spirit of God adapted for existence in the new redeemed order of the Age to Come. The word describing Adam is literally "a living soul" (*psyche*). Adam's existence was altogether on the level of *psyche*—natural, human life. As such, Adam—and all the children of Adam—have "natural" (*psychika*) bodies. Christ in his resurrection entered into a new realm of existence—a new order, which is nothing less than the invisible world of God—the Age to Come. As such, Paul calls him a "life-giving Spirit." He has entered the spiritual realm, taking his resurrected, glorified body with him.

Ladd 1975, 116–117.

15. Professor John Barclay of the University of Glasgow writes that the concept that "flesh and blood cannot inherit the kingdom of God" does not mean that the resurrection involves a noncorporeal entity:

v. 50 makes clear that the present physical body ("flesh and blood") is quite unfit for "the kingdom of God," though whether entry into that kingdom involves the *transformation* of the present body or the granting of an essentially *new* body is left undefined in this chapter and is not consistently dealt with elsewhere (cf. Rom. 8:11; Phil. 3:21; 2 Cor. 5:1–11). vv. 45–49 develop the contrast between the *psychikon sōma* by reference to their two prototypes: Adam, the first man, made from the dust, who became a living (but mortal) *psyche* (Gen. 2:7) and Christ, the final Adam, whose origin is heaven, and who is a life-giving (and immortal) *pneuma*. Our present bodies are as perishable as Adam's ("we bear the image of the Christ" [v. 49]).

Barton and Muddiman, 1132

16. Lapide 1983, 16. (Lapide was convinced that Jesus rose physically from the dead, but did not accept him as messiah.)

17. Lapide 1983, 46 (emphasis added).

18. Ladd 1975, 44.

19. Cullman 1958, 19–20.

20. The breadth of the first-century perspectives is summarized by N. T. Wright:

> Resurrection belongs, then, within the revolutionary worldview of second-Temple Judaism. What part does it play within the Jewish hope for life after death? There was within Judaism a considerable spectrum of belief and speculation about what happened to dead people in general, and to dead Jews in particular. At one end were the Sadducees, who seem to have denied any doctrine of post-mortem existence (Mark 12:18; Josephus, War 2:165). At the other were the Pharisees, who affirmed a future embodied existence, and who seem to have at least begun to develop theories about how people continued to exist in the time between physical death and physical resurrection. And there are further options. Some writings speak of souls in disembodied bliss, some speculate about souls as angelic or astral beings, and so forth. We cannot, then, simply assert that Greeks believed in immortality and Jews in resurrection. Things were never that simple.

Wright 1998, 3.

21. O'Collins 1987, 138.

22. Ulrich Wilckens, former professor of New Testament at the University of Hamburg, emphasized the importance of trust in the foundation of the context of the Jewish hope for resurrection:

> Old Testament piety knows no "Nature" existing *per se*, knows no eternal indestructible universe, knows no eternal return of everything that happens in accord with some inviolably functioning laws of nature. The "reality" of the world in which people live is established by the mighty will of God, and God's will constantly is at work, governing freely and immediately, a will with which one cannot reckon, but a will on which one must put one's trust. Therefore, fundamentally, trust or faith is the sensible attitude most attuned to reality. The world is deeply wonderful, not only at

its periphery, but above all at its daily centre. For man owes himself and his world to the constancy and loyalty of God, to the unchanging continual steadfastness of God's creative goodness, which grants us life and existence. Resurrection of the dead [at the end of history] is therefore, for Judaism, not at all something so absolutely unheard of, nor something so completely suspect as being unreal, as many of us nowadays feel or think. Admittedly, resurrection of the dead for the Jews too falls into the category of something not to be experienced every day; it belongs to the area of things hoped for from God. But such extraordinary hope is only a consequence arising out of ordinary everyday hope. A person who in everyday life has trust, a belief independent of reality, will have trust in his faith also above and beyond all the frontiers of everything he has hitherto met in his experience. It is against this background of Judaism's beliefs about God that the discussion in primitive Christianity about the resurrection of Jesus by the mighty act of God is to be understood.

Wilckens 1977, 17 (parentheses added).

23. As the Psalmist wrote: "You show me the path of life. In your presence there is fullness of joy; in your right hand pleasures forevermore." Ps. 16:10.

24. One can see the development of the Jewish resurrection perspective in Psalm 16:10, where the writer refers to the soul (*nephesh*) departing to Sheol. Death does not mean the end of one's existence. In Proverbs 9:18 persons are described as existing as "shades" [*rephaim*] after death: "But they do not know that the dead are there, that her guests are in the depths of Sheol." *Rephaim*, for example, is mentioned in Isaiah, where life after death is described in chapter 14:9 as follows:

"Sheol beneath is stirred up to meet you when you come;
it rouses the shades (*rephaim*) to greet you,
all who were leaders of the earth;
it raises from their thrones;
all who were kings of the nations."

The concept of persons existing as shades or spirits after death is not synonymous with their earthly life, but only a shadow of their being. Jewish thought began to realize that one's friendship and relationship with a loving God could not be discontinued upon death; Judaism began to hope in immortality, trusting that communion with God could not be severed by death. God was omnipresent, even in Sheol: " . . . if I make my bed in Sheol, you are there." God was clearly more powerful than death, and one's friendship and communion with God could not be abolished by one's physical death. One's existence from beginning through the future depended entirely upon God whose presence is available to his people forever. See Ladd 1975, 45. Ps. 139:8.

25. Wright explains:

This widespread belief in the future resurrection naturally generated a belief in an intermediate state. There were different ways of expressing this: it could even sometimes look fleetingly like a Hellenistic, perhaps Platonic, theory of a continuing soul, without (as has often been suggested) strain or contradiction. "Resurrection" entails some kind of belief in continuing postmortem existence; this need not mean a belief that all humans have an immortal soul in the Platonic sense, since the belief in YHWH as creator which is necessary for belief in the resurrection is also a sufficient explanation for the dead being held in some kind of continuing existence, by divine power rather than in virtue of something inalienable in their own being.

Wright 2003, 203.

26. Wright 2003, 203.

27. In describing the aspects of temporary disembodiment, Stephen T. Davis comments on these distinctions:

The state of being without a body is an abnormal state of the human person. This points to one of the clear differences between temporary disembodiment and immortality of the soul, for the second doctrine (at least in versions of it influenced by Plato) entails that disembodiment is the true or proper or ideal state of the human person. On the theory we are considering, however, the claim is that a disembodied soul lacks many of the properties and abilities that are normal for and proper to human persons. Disembodied existence is a kind of minimal existence. Temporary disembodiment then, entails that human souls can animate both normal earthly bodies and glorified resurrection bodies. Continuity between the two bodies is provided by the presence of both the same soul and the same matter in both bodies. "Nor does the earthly material out of which men's mortal bodies are created ever perish," says Augustine; "but though it may crumble into dust and ashes, or be dissolved into vapors and exhalations, though it may be transformed into the substance of other bodies or be dispersed into the elements, though it should become food for beasts or men, and be changed into their flesh, it returns in a moment of time to that human soul which animated it at the first and which cause it to become man, and to live and grow." The matter of our present bodies may be arranged differently in the resurrection, he says, but the matter will be restored.

Davis 1997, 94.

28. Wright 2003, 203, 205.

29. Ezekiel 37:1–14.

30. Pannenberg 1994, 348.

31. As N. T. Wright emphasizes:

But nobody imagined that any individuals had already been raised, or would be raised in advance of the great last day. There are no traditions about prophets being raised to new bodily life, the closest we come to that is Elijah, who had gone bodily to heaven and would return to herald the new age. There are no traditions about a Messiah being raised to life: most Jews of this period hoped for resurrection, many Jews of this period hoped for a Messiah, but nobody put those two hopes together until the early Christians did.

Wright 2003, 205.

32. O'Collins confirms that no one in Judaism connected the concept of messiah with the concept of resurrection. The proclamation of the original church was original and a completely new concept, contrary to all expectations. As O'Collins writes: "Contemporary Judaism had no concept of a dying and rising Messiah, nor any notion of one person enjoying a final, glorious resurrection from the dead even though the end of the world had not yet occurred. The Easter faith of the disciples was something new; it cannot be traced to Jewish or pagan sources. Nor does it seem explicable in terms of the impact that the life and teachings of Jesus had on his followers, since Jesus' death on the cross tended strongly to negate that impact." Quoted in Davis 1997, 184.

33. John Polkinghorne describes the significance of the change in their attitude:

It is absolutely clear that something happened between Good Friday and Pentecost. The demoralization of the disciples, caused by the arrest and execution of their Master, is undeniable. Equally undeniable is the fact that within a short space of time, those same disciples were defying the authorities who had previously seemed so threatening, and that they were proclaiming the one who had died disgraced and forsaken, as being both Lord and Christ (God's chosen and anointed one). So great a transformation calls for a commensurate cause.

Polkinghorne 1994, p. 109.

34. Lapide 1983, 125–126.

35. Wright 2003, 209.

36. Evans and Wright 2009, 82–84.

37. Quoted in Lapide 1983, 33–34.

38. Lapide 1983, 34.

39. Wright makes this emphasis: "Early Christianity was a 'resurrection' movement through and through, and that, indeed, it stated much more precisely what exactly 'resurrection' involved (it meant going through death and out into a new kind of bodily existence beyond, and it was happening in two stages, with Jesus first and everyone else later); second, that though the literal 'resurrection' of which the early Christians spoke remained firmly in the future, it coloured and gave shape to present Christian living as well." Wright 2003, 210.

40. Ladd 1975, 40.

41. Wright 2003, 211.

42. Wright 1997, 50.

43. As Peter Walker writes:

To question the empty tomb is natural enough. Yet, surprisingly, it does not seem (from what evidence we have) to have been a question asked by skeptics in first-century Jerusalem. The only rumor of an alternative explanation is the charge made that the disciples must have "stolen the body" (Matthew 28:11–15). In other words, the emptiness of the tomb was conceded even by those who would have loved to scotch this rumor. The only point of dispute was how this empty tomb was to be explained. There were many in Jerusalem who would have loved to prove the story false by producing the body or, if there was any confusion about the tomb, by showing the correct tomb. But they did not—because they *could* not.

Walker 1999, 57.

44. As John Stott writes:

We have already seen that within a few weeks of Jesus' death the Christians were boldly proclaiming his resurrection. The news spread rapidly. The new Nazarene movement threatened to undermine the bulwarks of Judaism and to disturb the peace of Jerusalem. The Jews feared conversions; the Romans riots. The authorities had before them one obvious course of action. They could produce the remains of the body. . . . Instead, they were silent and resorted to violence. They arrested the apostles, threatened them, flogged them, imprisoned them, vilified them, plotted against them, and killed them. But all this was unnecessary if they had in their own possession the dead body of Jesus. The church was founded on the resurrection. Disprove the resurrection, and the church would have collapsed. But they could not; the body was not in their possession. The authorities' silence is as eloquent a proof of the resurrection as the apostles' witness.

Stott 1958, 51.

45. William Starr speech, Mount Princeton, August 1960.

46. As John Stott writes:

Are we then to believe that they were proclaiming what they knew to be a deliberate lie? If they had themselves taken the body of Jesus, to preach his resurrection was to spread a known, planned falsehood. They not only preached it; they suffered for it. They were prepared to go to prison, to the flogging post and to death for a fairy-tale. This simply does not ring true. It is so unlikely as to be virtually impossible. If anything is clear from the Gospels and the Acts, it is that the apostles were sincere. They may have been deceived, if you like, but they were not deceivers. Hypocrites and martyrs are not made of the same stuff.

Stott 1958, 50.

47. Walker 1999, 59.

48. George Ladd describes the Old Testament basis for the disqualification of women as legal witnesses:

A woman had no right to bear witness, because it was concluded from Genesis 18:15 that she was a liar. Only in a few very exceptional cases was her witness permissible. In view of this fact, it is surely remarkable that the testimony of women both to the empty tomb and to the resurrection play so large a place in the Gospels. If the faith of the community had entered significantly into the substance of the

bNOTES

resurrection stories, *we would have expected the primary witnesses to have been apostles* instead of women. The only intelligible reason for the primacy of the testimony of the women is that it is historically sound. There is therefore good critical reason for believing that the appearances took place both in Galilee and Jerusalem.

Ladd 1975, 90.

49. George O'Collins comments on the central place of women in the accounts of the empty tomb:

Furthermore, the central place of women in the empty tomb stories speaks for their historical reliability. . . . If these stories had simply been legends created by early Christians, they would have attributed the discovery of the empty tomb to male disciples rather than women. In first century Palestine women were, for all intents and purposes, disqualified as valid witnesses. The natural thing for someone making up a legend about the empty tomb would have been to have ascribed the discovery to men, not women. Legend-makers do not normally invent positively unhelpful material.

O'Collins 1987, 126.

50. See Acts.

51. John Stott agrees:

Are we then seriously to believe that Jesus was all the time only in a swoon? That after the rigors and pains of trial, mockery, flogging and crucifixion he could survive thirty-six hours in a stone sepulcher with neither warmth nor food nor medical care? That he could then rally sufficiently to perform the superhuman feat of shifting a boulder, which secured the mouth of the tomb, and this without disturbing the Roman guard? That then, weak and sickly and hungry, he could appear to the disciples in such a way as to give them the impression that he had vanquished death? That he could go on to claim that he had died and risen, could send them into all the world and promise to be with them unto the end of time? That he could live somewhere in hiding for forty days, making occasional surprise appearances, and then finally disappear without explanation? Such credulity is more incredible than Thomas' unbelief.

Stott 1958, 50.

52. Pannenberg 1977, 91.

53. Wright 2003, 317.

54. Wright 2003, 319.

55. Wright 2003, 613. These widely accepted facts mean that, despite the frequently noted discrepancies in the accounts of the resurrection of Jesus, the most significant aspects of the canonical accounts contain a remarkable unity. As Stephan T. Davis confirms:

All of them affirm that Jesus was dead, that he was buried in a tomb near Jerusalem supplied by a man named Joseph of Arimathea, that early on the day after the

Sabbath certain women in the company of Jesus (among them Mary Magdalene) went to the tomb, that they found the tomb mysteriously empty, that they met an angel or angels, that the women were either told or else discovered that Jesus had been raised from the dead, and that Jesus subsequently appeared a number of times to certain of the women and certain of the disciples. There seems to be no resurrection texts that question any of these items. Furthermore, even the discrepancies themselves testify in a left-handed way to the accuracy of the essential story: if the resurrection of Jesus were a story invented by the later Christian church, or by certain members of it, no discrepancies would have been allowed. The biblical accounts do not bear the earmarks of a lie or conspiracy.

Davis 1993, 181.

56. Ladd 1975, 93–94. Stephen T. Davis is also persuaded that a belief in the resurrection is a rational, plausible belief based on widely accepted facts among all scholars. Davis sets forth six areas of agreement among an overwhelming majority of New Testament scholars and historians:

Virtually all scholars who write about the resurrection of Jesus, whether they believe it happened (in some sense or other) or not, agree that (a) while early first-century Jews expected a Messiah, the idea of a dying and rising Messiah was new to them; (b) Jesus of Nazareth died and was buried; (c) the disciples of Jesus were consequently discouraged and dejected; (d) soon after the burial of Jesus, his tomb was claimed to be empty, and some of the disciples had experiences that they took to be encounters with the risen Jesus; (e) these experiences caused them to believe that Jesus had been raised from the dead; and (f) they started a movement that grew and thrived and that was based on the idea that Jesus had been raised from the dead.

Davis 1993, 180.

57. Wright 2003, 709.

CHAPTER 7

1. Bentley Layton, of the Yale University history faculty and a professor of religious studies (ancient Christianity), has given a clear description of the meaning of gnōsis:

Gnostic scripture describes the salvation of the individual by the Greek word gnōsis, and the self-given name of the "gnostic" sect refers to their ability to attain gnōsis. The meaning of gnōsis is easy to grasp. Unlike its odd derivative gnōstikos, the word gnōsis was an ordinary part of Greek, both in daily life and in religion (including Judaism and Christianity). The basic translation of gnōsis is "knowledge" or "(act of) knowing." But the ancient Greek language could easily differentiate between two kinds of knowledge (a distinction that French, for example, also makes with ease). One kind is propositional knowing—the knowledge *that* something is the case ("I know that Athens is in Greece"). Greek has several words for this kind of knowing—for example, *eidenai* (French *savoir*). The other kind of knowing is personal acquaintance with an object, often a person ("I know Athens well"; "I have known Susan for many years"). In Greek the word for this is *gignōskein* (French *connaître*, and in English one can call this kind of knowledge "acquaintance") The corresponding Greek noun is *gnōsis*. If, for example, two people have been introduced to one another, each one can claim to have *gnōsis* or acquaintance of the other. If one is introduced to god, one has *gnōsis* of god. The ancient gnostics described salvation as a kind of *gnōsis* or acquaintance, and the ultimate object of that acquaintance was nothing less than god.

Layton 1987, 9.

2. King defines gnosticism rather narrowly with a single origin: "There was and is no such thing as gnosticism, if we mean by that some kind of ancient religious entity with a single origin and a distinct set of characteristics. Gnosticism is, rather, a term invented in the early modern period to aid in defining the boundaries of normative Christianity," King 2003, 1–2. Bart Ehrman, however, considers the term gnosticism appropriate in discussing this broad spectrum of doctrines with some identifiable central themes: "There were a large number of gnostic religions, and they differed from one another in lots of ways, large and small. So great was their variety that some scholars have insisted that we shouldn't use the term gnosticism any more. . . . My own view is that this is going too far, it is perfectly legitimate to talk about gnosticism." Ehrman writing in Kasser et al. 2006, 83.

3. Pétrement 1984, 1–2. Darrell Bock also joins Pétrement, Ehrman, and many other scholars in noting the existence of a common core for a gnostic worldview:

> This claim so focuses on the varieties among these texts that it obscures the fact that these texts reflect a set of religious ideas within the same family of concerns. While King asks what single characteristic counts to make a work gnostic and argues, probably correctly, that there is no single, "magical" trait that guarantees a gnostic presence, most working in the area argue that the issue is not which one thing counts, but what does the whole work reflect? Does a given work use several of the possible traits of evidence for a "gnostic" view? Most scholars argue that gnostic works share a common general outlook at the world that we can describe and define.

Bock 2006, 18.

4. Ehrman writing in Kasser et al. 2006, 86.

5. Quoted in McManners 1990, 26. Bart Ehrman confirms Chadwick's understanding of the elitism common in gnostic myths. In describing the gnostic concept of salvation by means of escaping the evil physical world and the

prison of one's body, he stresses the elite status given to the select few who are fortunate to have a bit of divine spark within them: "I should stress that not everyone has the means to escape. That is because not everyone has a spark of the divine within them: Only some of us do. The other people are the creations of the inferior god of this world. They, like other creatures here (dogs, turtles, mosquitoes, and so on), will die and that will be the end of their story." Ehrman writing in Kasser et al. 2006, 86–87.

6. As Ehrman notes, "Some gnostics taught that Christ was an aeon from the realm above—that he was not a man of flesh and blood, born into this world of the creator, but that he came from above only in the *appearance* of human flesh. Other gnostics taught that Jesus was a real man, but that he did not have a typical spark of the divine within. His soul was a special divine being who came from above to be temporarily housed with the man Jesus, to use him as a conduit through which to reveal the necessary truths to his close followers." Ehrman writing in Kasser et al. 2006, 87–88.

7. Genesis 3:4.

8. Houston 2006, 31–32.

9. Layton 1987, 12–13.

10. Layton 1987, 5.

11. See discussion on Barbēlo in Kasser et al. 2006, 140–141.

12. Layton 1987, 16.

13. Layton 1987, 16.

14. Layton 1987, 12–17.

15. This city of about thirty thousand persons was also known as Per-medjed or Pemje. The ruins are located near the current Muslim town of Behmesa, about 180 miles south of Alexandria on a branch of the Nile River. Oxyrhynchus is the name of a sharp-nosed fish (pike) that was worshipped by the early Greek settlers of this city.

16. Layton 1987, 46.

17. Layton 1987, 18.

18. See modified Layton's diagram in chapter 7, supra.

19. See discussion of characteristics of gnostic teaching in Cross and Livingston 2005, 687.

20. See discussion from Nicholas Perrin's writings, infra.

21. See Meier 1991, 123, for the story of the discovery of the Nag Hammadi Library. For more detail of its intriguing aspects, see also Pagels 1979, xiii–xvii; and Ehrman 2003, 51–53.

22. Ehrman writing in Kasser et al. 2006, xvi–xvii.

23. Layton 1987, 378.

24. Meier 1991, 125–126.

25. All sayings are quotations from Robinson 1990.

26. As Meier writes:

It is clear that the overarching intention of the redactor of the Gospel of Thomas is a gnostic one and that the Synoptic-like sayings are meant to be (re-)interpreted according to their "genuine," secret, gnostic meaning. Since a gnostic world view of this sort was not employed to "reinterpret" Christianity in such a thorough-going way before sometime in the 2d century A.D., there can be no question of the Gospel of Thomas as a whole, as it stands in the Coptic text, being a reliable reflection of the historical Jesus or of the earliest sources of 1st-century Christianity. Indeed, it is symptomatic that the earliest of the Oxyrhynchus papyri, the first witnesses (in Greek) to the Gospel of Thomas, is usually dated ca. A.D. 200; it is somewhere in the 2d century that the composition we know as the Gospel of Thomas took shape as one expression of 2d-century gnostic Christianity.

Meier 1991, 127.

27. Ehrman also ascribes a second-century date to the gospel of Thomas.

28. Ehrman 2003, 58.

29. Ehrman 2003, p. 59.

30. Ehrman writes: "Let me stress that I do not think the gospel of Thomas attempts to describe such a Gnostic view for its readers or to explicate its mythological undergirding. I think that *it presupposes* some such viewpoint and that if readers read the text with these presuppositions in mind, they can make sense of almost all the difficult sayings of the book." Ehrman 2003, p. 60 (emphasis added).

31. Layton 1987, 376 (parentheses added). "HPrl" refers to the Hymn of the Pearl, a Hellenistic gnostic writing with the following non-Christian allegorical meaning: "The first principle of the spiritual realm providentially causes the individual soul to descend past the heavenly bodies into incarnate life in a material body, in order to be educated (get salvation). The soul becomes unconscious and inert because of matter. But it disengages itself in response to the savior or message of philosophy (wisdom). It becomes acquainted with itself and its career and is metaphysically reunited with itself (i.e., becomes integral) and with the first principle gaining true repose." Layton 1987, 367. HPrl was probably composed in the second century in Edessa, but the date and place of composition cannot be ascertained with certainty.

32. Perrin writes that "the words 'Didymus' and 'Thomas' both mean 'twin,' in Greek and Aramaic/Syriac, respectively." Perrin 2007, 77.

33. Layton 1987, 367.

34. Evans 2006, 66-67.

35. Wright 2006, 95–97 (emphasis added).

36. F. F. Bruce provides the following history of the composition and use of the *Diatessaron*:

We are on firmer ground when we come to Justin's disciple Tatian. After Justin's martyrdom (AD 165), Tatian went back to his native Assyria, and there introduced what was to be for centuries a very influential edition of the gospels, his *Diatessaron*. This word is a musical term, meaning "harmony of four"; it indicates clearly what this edition was. It was a continuous gospel narrative, produced by unstitching the units of the four individual gospels and restitching them together in what was taken to be their chronological order. The gospel of John provided the framework into which material from the gospels of Matthew, Mark and Luke fitted. The *Diatessaron* began with John 1:1–5, after which, instead of John 1:6 ("There was a man sent from God, whose name was John"), it reproduced Luke's account of the birth of John (Luke 1:5–80). But John's order was not followed slavishly: the cleansing of the temple, for example, was located in Holy Week, where the synoptic account places it (Mark 11:15–17 and parallels), and not at the beginning of Jesus' ministry, where it appears in John 2:13–22.

Bruce 1988, 127–128.

37. Pagels 2003, 29 (emphasis added).

38. Perrin 2002, 25.

39. Perrin 2002, 17. Several scholars have argued that the lack of a pattern to the order or sequence of the sayings in the gospel of Thomas is evidence of independence from the Synoptic patterns. But, as I shall relate, Perrin's analysis provides evidence for a contrary argument, because in Syriac the text takes on a tightly woven, unified pattern, indicating a highly structured and carefully arranged sequential order.

40. I will describe Perrin's basic argument, but anyone interested in understanding a definitive reason why the gospel of Thomas depended on the *Diatessaron* (which in turn depended on the canonical gospels) should read Perrin's *Thomas and Tatian*, together with his recent book, *Thomas: The Other Gospel*. He defines "catchwords" as words "which can be semantically, etymologically, or phonologically associated with another word found in an adjacent logion (saying)." Perrin 2002, 50.

41. Perrin 2002, 17.

42. Perrin 2002, 49.

43. See Perrin 2002, 192–193, on the use of paronomasia in the *Odes of Solomon*, another Syriac text of the second-century.

44. Perrin 2002, 193.

45. Perrin 2002, 189.

46. N. T. Wright summarizes Perrin's evidence for a late second-century date for the gospel of Thomas:

As quite a strong index of where things stand, we note the language of the book "Thomas" as we have it is written in Coptic, an Egyptian language of the time. It is simply a collection of sayings attributed to Jesus, and, in the Coptic version, they are in no particular order. But if we translate the Coptic back into the Syriac, the likely original language of the collection, we discover that in Syriac the sayings of Jesus have been collected into a careful pattern, with connecting words linking the different sayings each to the next. And the Syriac in question, and the method of this linking of sayings, is closely cognate with the language and style of writers known to us from the late second century church, not least Tatian. The strong probability is that the collection we call "Thomas" was put together nearly 200 years after the time of Jesus and not earlier.

Wright 2005.

47. Evans 2006, 72.

48. Evans 2006, 73–74.

49. Evans 2006, 76–77.

50. Metzger 2003, 122.

51. Metzger 2003, 12–13 (emphasis added).

52. Wright, 1998.

53. John P. Meier shares Wright's conviction that the redactor of the gospel of Thomas, unlike the authors of the canonical gospels, is unconcerned with historical accuracy:

> In other words, *Thomas'* view of salvation is ahistorical, atemporal, amaterial, and so he regularly removes from the Four Gospels anything that contradicts his view. Sevrin, for instance, demonstrates convincingly how Thomas pulls together three diverse parables in sayings 63, 64, and 65 (the parables of the rich man who dies suddenly, of the great supper, and of the murderous tenants of the vineyard) to develop his own *gnostic* polemic against "capitalism," while rigorously censoring out of the parables any allegory, any reference to salvation history, and any eschatological perspective. The result is a dehistoricized, timeless message of self-salvation through self-knowledge and ascetic detachment from this material world. At times, Thomas will introduce amplifications into the tradition, but they always serve his theological program.

Meier 1991, 134.

54. Meier 1991, 140.

55. Pagels and King 2007, xiii, xiv, emphasis added. Bart Ehrman also dates the gospel of Judas's composition to the middle of the second century. See Ehrman writing in Kasser et al. 2006, 91.

56. General editor of *The Nag Hammadi Library* and founding director emeritus of the Institute for Antiquity and Christianity at Claremont Graduate University.

57. Robinson 2006, 1.

58. Robinson 2006, 1.

59. In his commentary on the gospel of Judas, Bart Ehrman sets forth these central points of the gnostic myth:

> This world is not the creation of the one true God. The god who made this world—
> the God of the Old Testament—is a secondary, inferior deity. He is not the God

above all who is to be worshiped. Rather, he is to be avoided, by learning the truth about the ultimate divine realm, this evil material world, our entrapment here, and how we can escape. . . . I should stress that not everyone has the means to escape. That is because not everyone has a spark of the divine within them: Only some of us do. The other people are the creations of the inferior god of this world. They, like other creatures here (dogs, turtles, mosquitoes, and so on), will die and that will be the end of their story. But some of us are trapped divinities. And we need to learn how to return to our heavenly home.

Ehrman writing in Kasser et al. 2006, 86–87.

60. Ehrman writing in Kasser et al. 2006, 23n22.
61. Ehrman writing in Kasser et al. 2006, 115.
62. Ehrman writing in Kasser et al. 2006, 29n59.
63. Ehrman writing in Kasser et al. 2006, 110.
64. Ehrman writing in Kasser et al. 2006, 111.
65.

This understanding of the creator god (Yahweh) as an inferior deity is most clearly stated in the myth that Jesus expounds privately to Judas. . . . Even before the creator god came into being, there were enormous numbers of other divine beings: seventy-two aeons, each with a "luminary" and each with five firmaments of the heavens (for a total of 360 firmaments), along with countless angels worshiping each one. Moreover, this world belongs to the realm of "perdition" or, as the word could also be translated, "corruption." It is not the good creation of the one true God. Only after the other divine entities come into existence does the God of the Old Testament—named El—come into being, followed by his helpers, the blood-stained rebel Yaldabaoth and the fool Saklas. These latter two created the world, and then humans. When the disciples worship "their God," it is the rebel and fool they worship, the makers of this bloody, senseless material existence. They do not worship the true God, the one who is above all else, who is all-knowing, all-powerful, entirely spirit, and completely removed from this transient world of pain and suffering created by a rebel and a fool.

Ehrman writing in Kasser et al. 2006, 105–106.

66. Wright 2006, 80–82.
67. See Porter and Heath 2007, 106.
68. Jenkins 2001, 72.
69. Wright 2006, 111.
70. Bock 2006, 84–85. Bock continues with a description of the core of the early faith:

This orthodoxy can also be stated in terms of what was to be excluded and included: (1) God was not to be divided in such a way that He was not the Creator. God was a Creator of all things, and that initial creation was good. (2) A division between Jesus and the Christ in terms of His basic person and work was not acceptable. Orthodoxy was that Jesus as Son of God was sent from God, came truly in the flesh, and truly suffered. (3) Redemption only on a spiritual plane was not the true faith. Salvation included a physical dimension of resurrection and extended into the material creation. (4) Jesus did not come only to point the way to faith, to be a prophet, merely a teacher of religious wisdom, or to be a mere example of religious faith. Rather, His work provided the means to salvation. Jesus was far more than a prophet, which is why He was worshipped and affirmed as sharing glory with God as His Son.

Bock 2006, 207–208.
   71. Bock 2006, 190 (parentheses added).
   72. Meier 1991, 156–157.
   73. Evans 2006, 9.
   74. Evans 2006, 189, 193–203.
   75. Evans 2006, 2.

CHAPTER 8

   1. Ward 2004, 9.
   2. Ward 2004, 9.
   3. Ward 2004, 142.
   4. Smart 1989, 62.
   5. Smart 1989, 61.
   6. Polkinghorne 1994, 182.
   7. Beckwith and Koukl 1998, 47.
   8. Beckwith and Koukl 1998, 1–3.
   9. Polkinghorne 1994, 17.
   10. As C. S. Lewis noted: "There is no half-way house, and there is no parallel in other religions. If you had gone to Buddha and asked him, 'Are you the son of Bramah?' He would have said, 'My son, you are still in the vale of illusion.' If you had gone to Socrates and asked, 'Are you Zeus?' he would have laughed at you. If you had gone to Muhammad and asked, 'Are you Allah?' he would first have rent his clothes and then cut off your head." As quoted in Green 2002, 43.
   11. The claims of the Christian faith are unique and should be evaluated on the evidence available from history, science, and philosophy: "When we come to consider Christian claims about Jesus, we find that they are not just claims about whether some general teaching is more or less true. They are also claims about Jesus himself, claims that he really was in some sense the founder of the kingdom of God on earth. . . . It is in that point that the human nature of Jesus is said by orthodox Christians to be different from all other human natures. . . . He is God in human form, with a true human nature, that 'the Word be-

came flesh and dwelt among us . . . and we beheld his glory' (John 1:14)." Ward 2002, 142–143, 163.

12. Ward 2002, 164.

13. Ward writes:

> But we have to face the fact that there will always be such disagreements. Giving up belief in the incarnation will not magically make disagreements about religious doctrines disappear. Orthodox Jews do not believe that Jesus was of greater authority than Moses, and regard the cavalier attitude towards Torah that his followers display as wholly retrograde. Orthodox Muslims generally deny that Jesus died on the cross, and regard the teaching of the Sermon on the Mount as unrealistic and probably harmful. We are not going to eliminate disagreement by denying the incarnation. Some people are very unhappy about the existence of disagreements between religions, and try to devise forms of belief that would eliminate them in some way. Every such proposal . . . simply produces more disagreement! The only way one could do it would be to drop all beliefs that religions disagree about, or reformulate them in ways that could be agreed, but that is impossible. Suppose a Christian believes in a personal creator and a Buddhist does not. One might suggest dropping the idea of God—but that would hardly satisfy the Christian. Or one might suggest getting the Buddhist to accept some rather vague idea of God, such as "Pure Mind." But Theravada Buddhists have long ago rejected such Mahayana Buddhist ideas, so there is not much hope of progress towards agreement there. . . . As soon as one tries to spell out what the goal is, how it is to be attained, and who is in the best position to know such things anyway, new disagreements will be generated. The empirical evidence of this is the large number of new religious movements in the modern world, many of them claiming that "all religions are true," which nevertheless form new religions, sometimes persecuted by older religions, and which all have distinct particular beliefs.

Ward 2002, 165–166.

14. Ward 2002, 167.

APPENDIX B

1. Ehrman (2009), 249.
2. Metzger (2003), 106, 116, 117.
3. Gundry (2006).

SELECTED BIBLIOGRAPHY

Allport, G. W. 1950. *The Individual and His Religion*. New York: MacMillan Company.

Anderson, J. N. D. 1974. *A Lawyer among the Theologians*. Grand Rapids, MI: Wm. B. Eerdmans Publishing Co.

——. 1984. *Christianity and World Religions*. Downers Grove, IL: InterVarsity Press.

Bainton, R. H. 1960. *Early Christianity*. New York: D. Van Nostrand Company. Inc.

Barnett, P. 1999. *Jesus and the Rise of Early Christianity: A History of New Testament Times*. Downers Grove, IL: InterVarsity Press.

——. 2003. *Is the New Testament Reliable?* Second Edition. Downers Grove, IL: InterVarsity Press.

——. 2005. *The Birth of Christianity: The First Twenty Years*. Grand Rapids, MI: Wm. B. Eerdmans Publishing Co.

Barton, J., and J. Muddiman (eds.) 2001. *The Oxford Bible Commentary*. Oxford: Oxford University Press.

Bauckham, R. 1998. *God Crucified*. Grand Rapids, MI: Wm. B. Eerdmans Publishing Co.

——. 2006. *Jesus and the Eyewitnesses: The Gospel as Eyewitness Testimony*. Grand Rapids, MI: Wm. B. Eerdmans Publishing Co.

——. 2008. *Jesus and the God of Israel.* Grand Rapids, MI: Eerdmans Publishing Co.

Beckwith, F., and G. Koukl. 1998. *Relativism: Feet Planted Firmly in Mid-Air.* Grand Rapids, MI: Baker Books.

Berger, K. 2003. *Identity and Experience in the New Testament.* Minneapolis, MI: Fortress Press.

Blomberg, C. 1987. *The Historical Reliability of the Gospels.* Downers Grove, IL: InterVarsity Press.

Bock, D. L. 2006. *The Missing Gospels.* Nashville, TN: Thomas Nelson Publishers.

Bonhoeffer, D. 1995. *A Testament to Freedom.* New York: HarperOne.

Boyd, G. A. 1995. *Cynic Sage or Son of God?* Grand Rapids, MI: Baker Book House.

Brown, R. E. 1994. *An Introduction to New Testament Christology.* Mahwah, NJ: Paulist Press.

Bruce, F. F. 1960. *The New Testament Documents: Are They Reliable?* Downers Grove, IL: InterVarsity Press.

——. 1969. *New Testament History.* New York: Anchor Books/Doubleday & Company, Inc.

——. 1986. *Jesus: Lord and Savior.* Downers Grove, IL: InterVarsity Press.

——. 1988. *The Canon of Scripture.* Downers Grove, IL: InterVarsity Press.

Burney, C. F. 1925. *The Poetry of Our Lord.* Oxford: Clarendon.

——. 2004. *The Aramaic Origin of the Fourth Gospel.* Eugene, OR: Wipf & Stock Publishers.

Burroughs, D. 2006. *Misquotes in Misquoting Jesus: Why You Can Still Believe.* Ann Arbor, MI: Nimble Books, LLC.

Carmignac, J. 1987. *The Birth of the Synoptics.* Chicago: Franciscan Herald Press.

Craig, W. L. 1981. *Knowing the Truth about the Resurrection.* Ann Arbor, MI: Servant Books.

——. 1994. *Reasonable Faith.* Wheaton, IL: Crossway Books.

Cross, F. L., and E. A. Livingston, eds. 2005. *The Oxford Dictionary of the Christian Church.* Oxford: Oxford University Press.

Crossan, John Dominic. 1999. *The Birth of Christianity.* New York: HarperCollins.

Crowley, C., and H. S. Lodge. 2006. *Younger Next Year.* New York: Workman Publishing Company.

Cullman, O. 1958. *Immortality of the Soul or Resurrection of the Dead?* London: Epworth Press.

——. 1963. *The Christology of the New Testament.* Norwich, UK: SCM Press Ltd./ Westminster Press.

——. 1995. *Prayer in the New Testament.* Trans. J. Bowden. Minneapolis, MN: Fortress Press.

Davis, S. T. 1993. *Risen Indeed*. Grand Rapids, MI: Wm. B. Eerdmans Publishing Co.

———. 1997. *God, Reason and Theistic Proofs*. Edinburgh, UK: Edinburgh University Press.

Davis, S. T., D. Kendall, and G. O'Collins, eds. 2002. *The Incarnation*. Oxford: Oxford University Press.

D'Costa, G., ed. 1996. *Resurrection Reconsidered*. Oxford, UK: OneWorld Publications.

Dubay, T. 1999. *The Evidential Power of Beauty*. Ft. Collins, CO: Ignatius Press.

Dunn, J. D. G. 1975. *Jesus and the Spirit*. Norwich, UK: SCM Press, Ltd./Wm. B. Eerdmans Publishing Co.

———. 1997. *Unity and Diversity in the New Testament*. Norwich, UK: SCM Press, Ltd.

———. 2003. *Jesus Remembered*. Grand Rapids, MI: Wm. B. Eerdmans Publishing Co.

Ehrman, B. D. 2003. *Lost Christianities*. Oxford: Oxford University Press.

———. 2005. *Misquoting Jesus*. New York: Harper Collins.

———. 2006. *The Lost Gospel of Judas Iscariot*. Oxford: Oxford University Press.

———. 2009. *Jesus Interrupted*. New York: HarperCollins.

Ellul, J. 1977. *Hope in Time of Abandonment*. New York: Seabury Press.

Evans, C. A. 2006. *Fabricating Jesus: How Modern Scholars Distort the Gospels*. Downers Grove, IL: InterVarsity Press.

Evans, C. A., and N. T. Wright. 2009. *Jesus: The Final Days*. Louisville, KY: Westminster John Knox Press.

Evans, C. S. 1982. *Philosophy of Religion: Thinking about Faith*. Downers Grove, IL: InterVarsity Press.

———. 1986. *Why Believe? Reason and Mystery as Pointers to God*. Grand Rapids, MI: Wm. B. Eerdmans Publishing Co./InterVarsity Press.

———. 1998. *Faith Beyond Reason*. Grand Rapids, MI: Wm. D. Eerdmans Publishing Co.

Fee, G. D. 1995. *Paul's Letter to the Philippians*. Grand Rapids, MI: Wm. B. Eerdmans Publishing Co.

Finnegan, Ruth. 1977. *Oral Poetry: Its Nature, Significance and Social Context*. Cambrdige, UK: Cambridge University Press.

France, R. T. 1975. *I Came to Set the Earth on Fire: A Portrait of Jesus*. Grand Rapids, MI: InterVarsity Press.

———. 1986. *The Evidence for Jesus*. London: Hodder and Stoughton, Ltd.

———. 1998. *Jesus and the Old Testament*. Vancouver, BC: Regent College Publishing.

Gerhardsson, B. 1968. *Tradition and Transmission in Earliest Christianity*. New York: Harper & Row.

——. 1998. *Memory and Manuscript: Oral Transmission and Written Transmission in Rabbinic Judaism and Early Christianity.* Grand Rapids, MI: Wm. B. Eerdmans Publishing Co.

——. 2001. *The Reliability of the Gospel Tradition.* Peabody, MA: Hendrickson Publishers, Inc.

——. 2005. "The Secret of the Transmission of the Unwritten Jesus Tradition" http://journals. Cambridge, UK: Cambridge University Press.

——. 2008. *Jesus and the God of Israel.* Grand Rapids, MI: Eerdmans Publishing Co.

Green, M. 2002. *"But Don't All Religions Lead to God?"* Grand Rapids, MI: Baker Books.

——. 2005. *The Books the Church Suppressed.* Raleigh, NC: Monarch Books.

Groothius, D. 2002. *Jesus in an Age of Controversy.* Eugene, OR: Wipf & Stock Publishers.

Guinness, O. 2001. *Long Journey Home.* New York: WaterBrook Press/Doubleday.

Hanson, A. T., and F. P. C. Hanson. 1981. *Reasonable Belief.* Oxford: Oxford University Press.

Hengel, M. 1979. *Acts and the History of Earliest Christianity.* Eugene, OR: Wipf & Stock Publishers.

——. 1983. *Between Jesus and Paul: Studies in the Earliest History of Christianity.* Eugene, OR: Wipf & Stock Publishers.

Houston, J. M., ed. 1989. *The Mind on Fire.* London: Hodder and Stoughton, Ltd.

——. 2006. *Joyful Exiles.* Downers Grove, IL: InterVarsity Press.

Hurtado, L. W. 1998. *One God, One Lord.* Oxford: T & T Clark.

——. 2000. *At the Origins of Christian Worship.* Grand Rapids, MI: Wm. B. Eerdmans Publishing Co.

——. 2003. *Lord Jesus Christ: Devotion to Jesus in Earliest Christianity.* Grand Rapids, MI: Wm. B. Eerdmans Publishing Co.

——. 2005. *How on Earth Did Jesus Become a God?* Grand Rapids, MI: Wm. B. Eerdmans Publishing Co.

Jaki, S. 1978. *The Road of Science and the Ways to God.* Chicago: University of Chicago Press.

Jenkins, P. 2001. *Hidden Gospels.* Oxford: Oxford University Press.

Jeremias, J. 1965. *The Central Message of the New Testament.* London: SCM Press.

——. 1966. *The Eucharistic Words of Jesus.* Minneapolis, MN: Fortress Press.

——. 1967. *The Prayers of Jesus.* London: SCM-Canterbury Press.

——. 1969. *Jerusalem in the Time of Jesus.* Minneapolis, MN: Fortress Press.

——. 1971. *New Testament Theology.* New York: Charles Scribner's Sons.

——. 1972. *The Parables of Jesus.* Upper Saddle River, NJ: Prentice Hall.

——. 2002. *Jesus and the Message of the New Testament*. Minneapolis, MN: Fortress Press.

Johnston, L. T. 1998. *Religious Experience in Earliest Christianity*. Minneapolis, MN: Fortress Press.

Kasser, R., M. Meyer, G. Wurst, and B. D. Ehrman. 2006. *The Gospel of Judas*. Washington, DC: National Geographic.

Kelber, W. H. 1997. *The Oral and the Written Gospel*. Bloomington: Indiana University Press.

King, K. L. 2003. *What Is Gnosticism?* Cambridge, MA: Harvard University Press.

Ladd, G. E. 1975. *I Believe in the Resurrection of Jesus*. Grand Rapids, MI: Wm. B. Eerdmans Publishing Co.

Lapide, P. 1983. *The Resurrection of Jesus*. Peabody, MA: Augsburg Publishing House.

Layton, B. 1987. *The Gnostic Scriptures*. New York: Doubleday.

Lewis, C. S. 1940. *The Problem of Pain*. New York: HarperCollins.

Lohmeyer, E. 1928. *Kyrios Jesus*. Heidelberg, Germany: Akademie der Wissech.

Longenecker, R. N. 1970. *The Christology of Early Jewish Christianity*. Norwich, UK: SCM Press, Ltd./Alec R. Allenson Inc.

——, ed. 1974. *New Dimensions in New Testament Study*. Grand Rapids, MI: Zondervan.

——. 1999. *New Wine into Fresh Wineskins: Contextualizing the Early Christian Confessions*. Peabody, MA: Hendrickson Publishers.

——, ed. 2005. *Contours of Christology in the New Testament*. Grand Rapids, MI: Wm. B. Eerdmans Publishing Co.

Maier, P. L. 1994. *Josephus: The Essential Works*. Grand Rapids, MI: Kregel Publications.

Martin, R. P. 1997. *A Hymn of Christ*. Downers Grove, IL: InterVarsity Press.

McGrath, A. 1997. *An Introduction to Christianity*. Chichester, UK: Blackwell Publishers Ltd.

McLachlen, J. M. 1992. *The Desire to Be God*. New York: Peter Lang Publishing, Inc.

McManners, J., ed. 1990. *The Oxford Illustrated History of Christianity*. Oxford: Oxford University Press.

Meier, J. P. 1991. *A Marginal Jew: Rethinking the Historical Jesus*. Vol. 1: *The Roots of the Problem and the Person*. New York: Doubleday.

Menninger, K. 1973. *Whatever Became of Sin?* New York: Hawthorn Books, Inc.

Metzger, B. M. 1977. *The Early Versions of the New Testament*. Oxford: Oxford University Press.

——. 2003. *The New Testament: Its Background, Growth and Content*. Third Edition. Nashville, TN: Abingdon Press.

Metzger, B. M., and B. D. Ehrman. 2005. *The Text of the New Testament: Its Transmission, Corruption and Restoration.* Fourth Edition. Oxford: Oxford University Press.

Moltmann, J. 1992. *History and the Triune God.* New York: Crossroad Publishing Co.

———. 1995. *The Crucified God.* Minneapolis, MN: Fortress Press.

Moule, C. F. D. 1977. *The Origin of Christology.* Cambridge, UK: Cambridge University Press.

———. 1982. *The Birth of the New Testament.* New York: Harper & Row Publishers.

Neufeld, V. H. 1963. *The Earliest Christian Confession.* Grand Rapids, MI: Wm. B. Eerdmans Publishing Co.

Nielsen, N., N. Hein, F. E. Reynolds, A. L. Miller, S. E. Karff, A. C. Cowan, P. McLean, and T. P. Erdel. 1988. *Religions of the World.* New York: St. Martin's Press.

O'Brien, P. T. 1982. *Word Biblical Commentary: Colossians, Philemon.* Nashville, TN: Thomas Nelson Publishers.

———. 1991. *The Epistle to the Philippians: A Commentary on the Greek Text.* Grand Rapids, MI: Wm. B. Eerdmans Publishing Co.

O'Collins, G. 1978. *What Are They Saying about the Resurrection?* Mahwah, NJ: Paulist Press.

———. 1987. *Jesus Risen.* London: Darton, Longman and Todd.

Overman, D. L. 1997. *A Case against Accident and Self-Organization.* Lanham, MD: Rowman & Littlefield Publishers, Inc.

———. 2008. *A Case for the Existence of God.* Lanham, MD: Rowman & Littlefield Publishers, Inc.

Pagels, E. 1979. *The Gnostic Gospels.* Colchester, UK: Vintage Books.

———. 2003. *Beyond Belief: The Secret Gospel of Thomas.* New York: Random House.

Pagels, E., and K. G. King. 2007. *Reading Judas.* New York: Viking Penguin.

Pagels, H. R. 1983. *The Cosmic Code.* New York: Bantam Books.

Pannenberg, W. 1976. *Theology and the Philosophy of Science.* London: Darton, Longman and Todd.

———. 1977. *Jesus—God and Man.* Philadelphia, PA: Westminster Press.

———. 1994. *Systematic Theology.* Volume 2. Grand Rapids, MI: Wm. B. Eerdmans Publishing Co.

Perkins, P. 1993. *Gnosticism and the New Testament.* Minneapolis, MN: Fortress Press.

Perrin, N. 2002. *Thomas and Tatian: The Relationship between the Gospel of Thomas and the Diatesseron.* Atlanta, GA: Society of Biblical Literature.

———. 2007. *Thomas: The Other Gospel.* Louisville, KY: Westminster John Knox Press.

Pétrement, S. 1984. *A Separate God*. San Francisco: Harper San Francisco.

Polanyi, M. 1958. *Personal Knowledge*. Chicago: University of Chicago Press.

Polkinghorne, J. C. 1986. *One World: The Interaction of Science and Theology*. Princeton, NJ: Princeton University Press.

———. 1994. *The Faith of a Physicist*. Princeton, NJ: Princeton University Press.

———. 2002. *The God of Hope and the End of the World*. New Haven, CT: Yale University Press.

Porter, S. E., and G. L. Heath 2007. *The Lost Gospel of Judas: Separating Fact from Fiction*. Grand Rapids, MI: Wm. B. Eerdmans Publishing Co.

Proctor, W. J., et al. 2000. *Dictionary of New Testament Background*. Downers Grove, IL: InterVarsity Press.

Radice, B., and E. V. Rieu, eds. 1982. *Early Christian Writings*. New York: Penguin Classics.

Riesner, Rainer. 2005. *Jesus als Lehrer*. Philadelphia, PA: Coronet Books.

———. 1998. *Paul's Early Period*. Grand Rapids, MI: Wm. B. Eerdmans Publishing Co.

Rieu, E.V. 1952. *The Four Gospels: A New Translation from the Greek*. New York: Penguin Books Ltd.

Robinson, J. A. T. 1976. *Redating the New Testament*. Eugene, OR: Wipf & Stock Publishers/SCM Press.

———. 1977. *Can We Trust the New Testament?* Grand Rapids, MI: Wm. B. Eerdmans Publishing Co.

Robinson, J. M., ed. 1990. *The Nag Hammadi Library*. Leiden, The Netherlands: HarperCollins/E. J. Brill.

———. 2006. *The Secrets of Judas: The Story of the Misunderstood Disciple and His Lost Gospel*. San Francisco: Harper SanFrancisco.

Rudolph, K. 1987. *Gnosis: The Nature and History of Gnosticism*. New York: HarperCollins.

Smart, N. 1989. *The World's Religions*. Upper Saddle River, NJ: Prentice Hall.

Staudinger, H. 1981. *The Trustworthiness of the Gospels*. Trans. R. T. Hammond. Edinburgh: Handsel Press.

Stauffer, E. 1955. *New Testament Theology*. New York: MacMillan Company.

Stott, J. R. W. 1958. *Basic Christianity*. Grand Rapids, MI: Wm. B. Eerdmans Publishing Co.

Swinburne, R. 2008. *Was Jesus God?* Oxford: Oxford University Press.

Torrance, T. F. 1989. *The Christian Frame of Mind*. Colorado Springs, CO: Helmers & Howard.

Tournier, P. 1958. *Guilt and Grace*. New York: Harper & Row.

Van Voorst, R. E. 2000. *Jesus Outside the New Testament*. Grand Rapids, MI: Wm. B. Eerdmans Publishing Co.

Walker, P. W. 1999. *The Weekend that Changed the World*. Louisville, KY: Westminster John Knox.

Wansbrough, H., ed. 1991. *Jesus and the Oral Gospel Tradition*. Sheffield, UK: JSOT Press.

Ward, K. 1996. *God, Chance and Necessity*. Oxford: OneWorld Publications.

——. 2002. *God: A Guide for the Perplexed*. Oxford: OneWorld Publications.

——. 2004. *The Case for Religion*. Oxford: OneWorld Publications.

Wenham, D. 1995. *Paul: Follower of Jesus or Founder of Christianity?* Grand Rapids, MI: Wm. B. Eerdmans Publishing Co.

Wilckens, U. 1977. *Resurrection*. Louisville, KY: John Knox Press.

Wilkins, M. J., and J. P. Moreland, eds. 1995. *Jesus under Fire*. Grand Rapids, MI: Zondervan Publishing House.

Witherington, Ben, III. 2006. *What Have They Done with Jesus?* New York: Harpers Collins.

Wright, N. T. 1997. *What Paul Really Said*. Grand Rapids, MI: Wm. B. Eerdmans Publishing Co.

——. 2003. *The Resurrection of the Son of God*. Minneapolis, MN: Fortress Press.

——. 2005. *Paul*. Minneapolis, MN: Fortress Press.

——. 2006. *Judas and the Gospel of Jesus*. Grand Rapids, MI: Baker Books.

——. 2006. *Simply Christian*. New York: HarperCollins.

Yamauchi, E. M. 2003. *Pre-Christian Gnosticism: A Survey of the Proposed Evidence*. Second Edition. Eugene, OR: Wipf & Stock Publishers.

Yockey, H. 1992. *Information Theory and Molecular Biology*. Cambridge, UK: Cambridge University Press.

ARTICLES, LECTURES, AND ESSAYS

Bailey, K. E. 1991. "Informal Controlled Oral Tradition and the Synoptic Gospels." *Asia Journal of Theology* 5, 34–54.

Gundry, R. H. 2006. "Post-Mortem: Death by Hardening of the Categories."

Koukl, G. 1998. "The Trouble with the Elephant." www.str.org.

Overman, D., and H. Yockey. 2001. "Information Algorithms and the Unknowable Nature of Life's Origin." *Princeton Theological Review* 8, no. 4.

Wright, N. T. 1998. "Early Traditions and the Origins of Christianity." *Sewanee Theological Review* 41, no. 2.

——. Summer 2005. "The Christian Challenge in the Post Modern World." *Response* 25, no. 2.

INDEX

ABOUT THE AUTHOR

For several decades **Dean L.Overman** was a senior partner of Winston & Strawn, a large international law firm. While practicing in the area of international law, he taught a secured financing course as a member of the faculty of the University of Virginia Law School and also served as a Visiting Scholar at Harvard University. He was a White House Fellow and served as special assistant to Vice President Nelson Rockefeller and as associate director of the White House Domestic Council for President Ford. He is the coauthor of several law books and the author of many law review articles on banking, commercial, corporate, tax and securities laws; the coauthor of a book on quantitative financial valuation; the author of a book on effective writing; the author of *A Case Against Accident and Self-Organization*, for which he was selected as a Templeton Scholar at Oxford University; and the author of *A Case for the Existence of God*, for which he was awarded a Templeton Foundation grant.

He received his J.D. from the University of California at Berkeley (Boalt Hall), his B.A. from Hope College, and did graduate work at the University of Chicago and Princeton Theological Seminary.